British strategy in the Napoleonic War

Christopher D. Hall

British strategy in the Napoleonic War 1803–15

MANCHESTER
UNIVERSITY PRESS

First published by Manchester University Press 1992
Special edition for Sandpiper Books Ltd, 1999

Published by Manchester University Press
Oxford Road, Manchester M13 9NR
http://www.man.ac.uk/mup

British Library Cataloguing-in-Publication Data
A catalogue record for this book is available from the British Library

05 04 03 02 01 00 99 7 6 5 4 3 2

ISBN 0 7190 3606 2

Printed in Great Britain by
Bookcraft (Bath) Ltd, Midsomer Norton

Contents

List of maps

Acknowledgements

This book started life as a thesis and during the course of both incarnations I have got into debts of gratitude with many people and institutions.

Sources have been quoted from with the kind permission of the following individuals: the Earl Bathurst for B.M. Loan 57; the estate of the Earl of Harrowby for the Harrowby Papers; the Earl of Harewood for the Canning Papers; Viscount Melville (and the Keeper of the Records of Scotland) for the Melville muniments; and the Marquess of Normanby for the Mulgrave Papers. The following institutions have also granted me permission to quote from their collections: Buckinghamshire Record Office for the Hobart Papers; the Devon Record Office for the Sidmouth Papers; Durham University Library for the Grey Papers, second Earl; and Nottingham University Library for the Portland Papers. Also allowing me to quote from their numerous collections are the British Museum, Greenwich Maritime Museum and the Public Record Office at Kew. To all these individuals and bodies I extend my grateful thanks and appreciation. I would also like to thank the staff of Cornwall County and Truro City Libraries: they laboured constantly to meet my seemingly endless demands for books and articles and were generally successful, despite the inadequacies of the British library system.

Doing any extended research is intellectually demanding, but such activity from a wheelchair has physical pressures as well. Those places that I visited, some listed above and some not, treated me with a courtesy and willingness to help that I value greatly. Only one institution, Leeds University Library, showed itself unhelpful and indifferent; this served merely to make me appreciate the kindness I received at the other places all the more.

I am also happy to be able to acknowledge my debt of gratitude to Dr Michael Duffy of Exeter University, who gave me crucial support during the thesis stage of things, and to Dr Ian Beckett of the Royal Military Academy, Sandhurst, who was kind enough to read through these chapters prior to publication and to proffer much welcome and valued advice. My thanks also to Nick Gladstone for the maps and the work that he put into them.

Last, but in no sense least, my thanks to my mother. She pushed my wheelchair; she carried heavy volumes of documents back and forth; she sat for hours on end in assorted museums and record offices. She did not complain once. Without her support none of this would have been possible.

C.D.H.

Abbreviations

P.R.O.	Public Record Office
R.O.	Record Office
B.M.	British Museum
FO	Foreign Office
WO	War Office
CO	Colonial Office
ADM	Admiralty

Introduction

This book is concerned with the diverse, and at times conflicting, elements which combined to constitute Britain's military strategy in her struggle with Napoleon in 1803–15. To a great extent that war was just a continuation of the one waged against revolutionary France in 1793–1801 and briefly interrupted by the Peace of Amiens. However, the years after 1803 saw France under the complete control of one of history's greatest military minds, a man who came to dominate virtually all of mainland Europe, with only island Britain able consistently to resist him. Over the years this warfare with Napoleon has spawned a massive literature and, given its moments of high drama, from the initial threat of invasion in 1803 to the culminating battle at Waterloo in 1815, this is hardly surprising. Yet although particular aspects of Britain's war have been closely studied, little has been written about the country's overall strategic policy, taking into account the means available to pursue the war, the factors which influenced decision-making, and the implementation of policy itself in the light of the actual circumstances.

I hope to make clear that, whatever else was involved, fighting the war was a very complex business. It is also too easy, with hindsight and in ignorance, to condemn particular military operations in this or any other period: despite the fact that early nineteenth-century Britain was a wealthy and powerful nation, it will become clear that the politicians whose responsibility it was to formulate policy often did so in circumstances of very limited strategic choice. Because of her imperial responsibilities, because of her essentially commercial nature, because of her relative smallness in comparison with the Napoleonic empire, Britain had to face very particular drawbacks in fighting the war. Some of these elements provided her with strength, but each advantage tended to have a corresponding disadvantage. Island Britain was difficult to invade, but equally that made it difficult for her to attack her enemies; British commerce provided the wealth to fund the conflict but was very vulnerable to dislocation; Britain's colonies helped support her trade and naval power but required extensive resources to preserve them from attack.

It is also rather too easy to be misled into focusing attention for the war's success on the great military figures at the expense of the politicians in London. Men like Nelson, Moore and Wellington commanded events of great impact on the imagination, yet the strategy which lay behind their actions was usually the result of decisions made by less well known ministers. The latter get more than their share of the blame for mistakes of judgement, but little praise or understanding when such things are due. The efforts of men like Pitt, Castlereagh and Liverpool have often been sneered at for what has been seen as inadequacy or incompetence but, once the factors which dictated strategy are better understood, their decisions, if not always correct, can be seen to have been logical and considered. In short, to comprehend a nation's strategy in a war requires that all the divergent elements in that policy be studied rather than any battle or campaign in isolation.

In memory of Peter Brightwell

1

Manpower and money

A whole variety of factors combine to determine the military policy of any nation at war, but first and foremost comes its capacity to provide the manpower for its armed forces. In the protracted struggle with Napoleon it was vital for Britain to make the best possible use of her human resources, particularly bearing in mind the extensive populations of Europe from which the French emperor could, for much of the time, man his armies and navies. To oppose him, taking 1809 as an example, the middle year of the period, Britain's army had 234,177 effective rank-and-file soldiers, a considerable body of men and more so when one adds a further eighth to this figure to allow for the army's officers, NCOs and suchlike. Similarly the Royal Navy was a powerful maritime force, having in commission 108 ships of the line, 150 frigates and 424 sloops; when schooners, cutters and other small warships are added, the whole fleet numbered over a thousand vessels. To man all these some 141,989 seamen and marines were listed in its books. Substantial though both these services were, however, each had a multitude of diverse duties to perform in prosecuting the war.[1]

Parliament was told in 1812 that the British population from which this manpower had to be drawn had numbered just under 11 million in 1801, the figure having risen to just over 12.5 million by 1811. To this should be added the population of Ireland, standing at over 5 million. When it came to recruiting from this mass of people, those raised tended to fall into two categories: those whose enlistment was of a limited nature, aimed at providing home defence, and those who joined the regular forces for unlimited service. It must be stressed at the outset that early nineteenth-century British governments did not enjoy the facility of nationwide conscription. There was no successful precedent for general military recruitment, the closest example of some attempt coming in the previous war with Pitt's effort to man the fleet via the Quota Acts of 1795–96, measures enjoying little success. Britain did not have the sort of bureaucratic and communications infrastructure that would have made mass conscription viable; nor would such a measure have been politically acceptable. No ministry tried to introduce such a scheme at the time and instead reliance was placed on a whole series of varyingly effective hand-to-mouth expedients.[2]

Considering the army first, in purely numerical terms the business of raising men for home defence was not unsuccessful. Addington responded to the growing military tension by calling out the Militia in March and April 1803 before hostilities commenced. This body had some measure of compulsion about it in that it was raised by ballot, though those reluctant to serve could buy their way out via the purchase of a substitute. Militia service was for five years, but it was restricted to Britain, units not being liable for duty outside the country without consent. Nevertheless the Militia was not a popular body. Many men resented having to pay to find substitutes, a penalty compounded by counties that did not meet their recruiting quota having to pay fines. It also drew labourers away from local industries and from agriculture. However, such feelings did not run deep, and there were not the sort of Militia-inspired disorders that had been widespread in 1757 and 1796, events prompted by fears that the government was introducing universal conscription. Similar troubles were experienced in 1759, 1761, 1778 and 1779, loss of life being caused on occasion. One indication of the general willingness to fight Napoleon is that the Militia was not energetically resisted after 1803. Although individual units gave periodic signs of discontent or disorder, these were usually prompted by particular grievances over pay and/or conditions. Certainly the Militia made a substantial contribution to the army's manpower, its total strength between 1804 and 1813 dropping below 70,000 on only one occasion, in 1808, and reaching a peak of over 89,000 in 1805. As a rule it constituted approximately 20 per cent of the army's total force.[3]

Numerically speaking the most striking body raised for home defence was the Volunteers. Seeking to mobilise all sources of recruitment, Addington's ministry invited people to join this body in March 1803. For the individual it offered a way of serving the country without suffering much inconvenience, training being confined to a mere twelve or twenty-four days a year. More attractive still was the fact that service with the Volunteers exempted men from the ballot for the Militia and, via the Billeting Act of August 1803, it also meant an avoidance of the ballot for the Army of the Reserve. With the threat of a *Levée en Masse* Act making Volunteer service compulsory anyway, the inducements to join were considerable. From the government's viewpoint the Volunteers not only provided a body for home service, but they also served a political purpose, allowing many civilians to demonstrate their support of the war while at the same time providing a force that could help maintain internal order. Certainly the call produced a flood of men wishing to serve, J. W. Fortescue estimating that by December 1803 the Volunteers in Britain and Ireland numbered 414,000, their strength remaining at over 300,000 in 1804–06. Not until 1808, when Castlereagh reorganised the Militia into 'Regular' and 'Local' bodies, the latter enjoying more restricted conditions of service prior to any emergency, did Volunteer strength start to diminish. Many Volunteers tended thereafter to see service in the Local Militia, and Volunteer strength, by 1812, had fallen to 68,643.[4]

Standing between the home defence bodies and the regulars came the Army of the Reserve. This force, as already indicated, was raised by ballot and aimed at securing 50,000 men from Britain and Ireland who would serve in defence of the British Isles. Once deductions had been made for deaths, desertions and rejections, the measure brought in some 30,000 men. However, it had a wider effect in that some 19,500 of these men were later induced to join the army proper for unlimited service.[5]

Judging by these bodies alone, the methods of raising manpower were highly successful. Unfortunately, though, recruiting for the regular armed forces, whose service was unlimited and of a more highly trained nature, was much more difficult. With many men being drawn into domestic military units, the net population upon which the regulars could draw was inevitably smaller, nor was army service at all agreeable for the ordinary citizen. Pay was poor compared to many civilian salaries, which tended to rise in wartime anyway: a private soldier in 1806 received 30*s* 4*d* per month, compared to which an 'artisan' could earn 112*s*. The latter sum was earned by common labourers in the royal dockyards, and pay in the civilian variety was higher still; such men could also earn 10*s* a day digging canals. Nor were the conditions of army life attractive. There was no system of transmitting pay to wives and children unable to accompany the soldier abroad, and such deserted dependants were not entitled to parish relief, though, inconsistently, penurious families of militiamen did receive such help. For the soldier himself discipline was invariably harsh and enlistment was usually for life; an attempt in 1806 to itroduce limited service, for only seven years, was difficult to administer. Perhaps the greatest barrier to recruitment, though, was the army's fearsome reputation for loss of life, gained largely in Pitt's abortive Caribbean campaigns in the 1790s, when thousands of men perished through disease.[6]

Given such drawbacks, the army inevitably faced problems in securing regular recruits, and a variety of expedients were resorted to in an effort to meet its needs. One such was the crimps, dubious figures who provided men in return for payment, their methods often being little better than kidnapping. Another means was the practice of raising men for rank, officers receiving promotion if they provided recruits. This tried to make use of the gentry's local influence but enjoyed little success: the last attempt, in 1804, sought to raise 5,000 men, but only 200 were forthcoming. More usually recruitment relied on the offer of bounties, but here the competition from other bodies was intense. In 1803 men joining the regulars could command a bounty of £7 12*s* 6*d*, but at the same time could earn £25 serving as a substitute in the Militia and simultaneously avoid all the miseries of foreign service. Inevitably the professional army suffered in these circumstances, its Commander-in-Chief, the Duke of York, complaining in 1804 that it was 30,000 men short of requirements. He blamed this on the demands of the home defence bodies, they both luring away potential recruits and tempting men to desert in pursuit of higher bounties.[7]

It was fortunate that a more successful means of enlistment lay in the process of encouraging men to volunteer for regular service once their term in the home defence forces was at an end. There were precedents for this from the previous war, over 15,000 militiamen having been so induced in 1799, and York was urging such a step in 1804, though initially the Cabinet was undecided. There was also the group of men brought into the professional ranks via the Army of the Reserve that has already been noticed.[8]

When Pitt returned to office in 1804 steps were taken to improve the Volunteers' organisation but little success was enjoyed in expanding the regulars; his attempt to raise troops for unlimited service came as only a secondary aspect of the Permanent Additional Force Act (June 1804), a measure aimed at home service but with the hope of men joining the regulars. Reminiscent of the Quota Acts, it tried to compel parishes to provide men on pain of being fined at the rate of £20 for each man they were lacking. However, parishes preferred to pay the fines, and some recruits were discouraged by not being allowed to join the regiment of their choice. Hopes that 20,000 men would be raised in two months were disappointed, it taking almost two years to raise 13,000.[9]

From 1807 ministries returned to York's suggestion and implemented a series of substantial transfers from the Militia, a process encouraged by the decreased invasion threat after 1805, with Napoleon increasingly involved in Continental campaigns and Britain's own fixed defences against invasion being much improved. The latter consisted most obviously of the Martello towers, small armed strongpoints built at sensitive coastal points, but also harbours were made more defensible, crucial river crossings were fortified, and in Kent the Royal Military Canal was constructed.[10] These permitted a reduction in home defence forces, while at the same time the idea of regular service was not quite so dreadful a prospect. New recruits still enjoyed the ubiquitous bounties, but the dread of West Indian service had declined with the avoidance of such campaigns by successive ministries – though it should be acknowledged that the losses through disease during Walcheren's occupation in 1809 can have done little to enhance the army's reputation. Nevertheless, from 1808, Peninsular victories brought a measure of prestige to the army, it appearing as more of a fighting force and less of a death sentence as the period progressed. Perhaps most important of all in prompting militiamen to join the regulars was their contentment with the military life and their willingness to extend it once their duty in the Militia was over. Such transfers were made in 1805–06, but then on a much larger scale in 1807 and in the first quarter of 1808. The latter period saw 27,505 militiamen transferring to the regulars, and with most of them being at the end of their period of service the net reduction in the Militia's strength was only 8,000. Although not as successful, this expedient was repeated in later years as well: in 1809–10 25,492 men were transferred, in 1811 some 11,455 and in 1812 a further 9,927.[11]

By dint of all these measures the army's strength showed a more or less steady increase during the period. From a total of 150,593

British and foreign regular soldiers in January 1804 it grew to just under 200,000 by January 1807 and to over 250,000 by January 1813. Only in January 1811 was there a small decrease from the previous year's figure. Despite providing so many recruits from its own ranks, the Militia's strengh also remained remarkably constant.[12]

These statistics suggest that some credit ought to be given to ministers for their handling of the army's manning problems. Despite the steadily mounting annual casualty lists, these never being less than 16,000 each year and reaching a maximum of 24,563 in 1809, the army's strength was not merely maintained but was increased. Strategically speaking, Cabinets were sensible in their attitude to manpower. When the invasion threat was at its height in 1803–05 the rapid expansion of the home defence forces is hard to fault. It reduced the numbers available for unrestricted service, but allowed the government, by the end of 1803, to point to 615,000 men as being available for the nation's defence.[13] Most of these were in the Volunteers, of course, a body whose military training was minimal. However, they were enthusiastic and even the critical Fortescue acknowledges that some of them behaved well in the 1805 invasion scare. Lowther, the Lord Lieutenant of Cumberland and Westmorland, observed that:

> It is really wonderful to see the rapid progress they have made and tho' I have no great reliance on such troops in general, yet I think the Resource this system has afforded at this moment, forms an essential part of our Security.

They provided ministers with a rapid addition to domestic security, while also permitting the use of regular formations outside Britain should that be necessary. Pitt in particular believed that, with the Volunteers in Britain, more first-line troops could be sent to Ireland in an emergency.[14] Once the immediate invasion threat had passed, however, efforts could be turned to acquiring troops for more offensive operations. Despite Elting's view that in manpower terms 'these wars were no great burden on England', in fact, with a general average of around 500,000 men under arms, some 3 per cent to 4 per cent of Britain's population was directly involved in military service on land – these figures do not take account of the navy. In comparison Napoleon, for all his efficiency, maintained an army of 310,000 front-line troops in 1805, this from a population of 24–8 million. To have matched Britain's proportion France would have had to have had somewhere around a million men under arms, a total not met even making allowances for colonial garrisons, the National Guard, and suchlike.[15]

Perhaps the only area where ministers did noticeably fail respecting manpower was in Ireland. Although providing many men for the armed forces, the religious repression inflicted on its Catholic majority curbed any Irish willingness wholeheartedly to support the war. This both lessened Ireland's value as a source of recruits and obliged substantial forces to be tied up in garrisons there to maintain British rule. Furthermore Ireland's uncertain loyalty could also throw doubt on the motives of those Irishmen who were under arms.[16]

Exacerbating the army's manpower shortages was the problem of desertion. This was primarily a domestic problem, for the soldier, unlike the sailor, who could obtain a berth in most ports, found fewer temptations on foreign stations where the prospects of employment and a better life were less certain. At home, however, the army deserter had not only the lure of a friendly environment but, particularly in the early war years, the lucrative temptation of enlisting, receiving the bounty, deserting, and then enlisting again with another unit and repeating the process. Richard Glover views this as 'all too commonly committed', pointing out that a ninth of those called into the Army of the Reserve and a fifth of those enlisted by the Permanent Additional Force Act deserted. Out of 3,481 recruits raised by recruiting parties in the last half of 1803 some 291 fled. For troops outside Britain the statistics seem more favourable, one return noting that during the 1 May 1803–30 April 1804 period there had been 692 desertions on foreign stations. This was at a time when Britain had 50,000 troops serving abroad. Another return, of January 1811, stated that during 1807–09 the army had suffered 17,237 desertions. This was a high figure, but on the other hand, judging from his correspondence, Wellington does not seem to have worried much about this happening in the Peninsula. Those formations which did tend to suffer severely were usually made up of foreigners who had already deserted from enemy units prior to being recruited by the British. During the Peninsular campaign only fifty-two British soldiers were executed for absconding, a further indication that the problem in the field was not a serious one.[17]

Even so, allowing that the army was, overall, comparatively well supplied with recruits, its responsibilities were extensive and of such a nature as severely to restrict strategic options. Thousands of troops, for example, were tied down in colonial garrisons. In August 1804 there were 52,204 soldiers on stations as diverse as New South Wales, Gibraltar and Nova Scotia. By March 1806 the number so employed had risen to 67,033, a figure including those in domestic depots but intended for colonial service: captures had, of course, increased the number of places to be held. The trend was to continue, and by January 1811 there were, excluding Sicily and the Peninsula, 75,760 soldiers serving outside Britain and Ireland.[18] The army had also to provide the defensive backbone of the home defence formations, a duty combined with the need to help maintain law and order. In June 1804 such responsibilities tied down 89,185 regular troops, 30,030 of whom were in Ireland. This figure remained roughly constant up to May 1809, when there were 91,999 regulars in Britain and a further 15,858 in Ireland, the increase being explained by the preparations to attack Walcheren. As late as November 1811 there were still 55,938 regulars at home, 17,375 of whom were in Ireland.[19] Although the limited service formations were a defensive asset, the chief burden of defending the United Kingdom would always fall on the professional soldiers, and large numbers of them were consequently needed to hand.

The correspondence of the leading government figures during 1803–15 constantly indicates just how conscious these men were of the country's manpower limitations. In May 1804 Castlereagh regretted the impossibility of bringing the Indian garrisons up to their establishment of 24,000 men: had the extra 10,000 soldiers been available he doubted if it would have been possible to maintain their numbers thereafter. He again referred to such difficulties in May 1807, stating that the colonial establishments were 10,000 men short and that the home establishment had a deficiency of 47,464.[20] Perhaps the man most concerned was the Duke of York. In the summer of 1808 he protested against a scheme to attack Boulogne on the grounds that there were no more than 10,000 regular troops available, many of whom were old and/or sick. With the scale of her Peninsular commitment Britain had no capacity remaining for secondary operations. In 1811 the duke was still worrying about these problems, believing that no further reductions in the colonial garrisons could be permitted and that the home establishment was 'reduced to the lowest possible scale'.[21]

Such shortages restricted strategy, and on only one occasion were two separate, substantial armies maintained on the Continent simultaneously. This happened during the summer of 1809, there being 35,796 rank and file in the Peninsula and 39,143 rank and file on Walcheren.[22] Maintaining replacements to any Continental army, combined with the demands of home defence, were two barriers to such efforts: significantly the Walcheren army was as close to England as any potential invasion force and so was available in case of need. Maintaining the Peninsular army alone required a massive effort, and even so involved reliance on large numbers of Portuguese troops to boost Wellington's strength. By August 1813 he was leading an army whose British contingent numbered 60,202 rank and file. Outside this the only other armies of significance were in Sicily and in North America, neither numbering more than 17,000.[23] It was indicative of this situation that, when the chance suddenly arose to strike at Napoleon's tottering power in the Low Countries at the end of 1813, the Cabinet could only find 5,500 poor-quality troops for the initial effort.[24] Two years before, the First Lord of the Admiralty had ruled out any possible attack on Flushing because of a lack of resources if for no other reason: 'The Peninsula and Ireland absorb all we have and would do so were it double what it is.'[25]

When moving to consider the manning of the Royal Navy it is apparent that serious problems were equally prevalent. As with the army, the navy too had part of its means tied up in domestic defence, the nautical equivalent of the Militia and Volunteers being the Sea Fencibles. This force had been formed in the 1790s and was revived in 1803, its duties including the manning of Martello towers, the provision of crews for small coastal defence vessels, and the harassing of small enemy vessels likely to be used in any invasion. In 1803 Admiral Keith suggested that the crews might be drawn from men not liable to impressment but with a knowledge of ships, considering that such a force might not exceed 4,510 men. In the event, by the end of that year, they numbered 25,000 and still had over 23,000 members when disbanded in 1810. Their military worth is hard to assess with any accuracy, overall preparedness varying from place to place, and it is also undoubtedly the case that they drew some men away from more valuable service. Having said all that, however, they did provide some extra security at a time of danger, being another body permitting citizens, who would otherwise have done so little, to serve their country and support the war at comparatively little personal inconvenience.[26]

The willingness of men to serve in the Sea Fencibles was not, unfortunately, matched by similar sentiments respecting the navy proper. As with the army, there were many disincentives to naval service. Pay was poor, particularly when compared to the inflated wartime wages earned by civilian mariners, and it was often massively in arrears. Seamen on foreign stations could go for years without being paid, while if transferred to another ship during a commission they were issued with tickets, these being cashed by the navy only after considerable delay or at considerable discount if the seaman turned to private entrepreneurs. A sailor could provide for part of his pay to be turned over to his wife and family, but service afloat was for the duration of the conflict and with no chance of shore leave.[27] Unlike his army counterpart the sailor did, at least, enjoy popular respect as manning the nation's 'wooden walls', but this did little to offset the often miserable conditions of naval service and its constant attendant dangers from the weather.

Under the circumstances the navy looked to several means of recruiting its crews. Some men could be induced to volunteer, encouraged by bounties and, in the case of some successful captains, by the prospect of prize money. The proportion so provided is hard to assess, but somewhere between half and a quarter of the total manpower might come under the 'volunteer' heading. This was particularly so at the start of the war, when signing-on bounties were a greater inducement and the prospects of prize money, with many enemy vessels at sea, were better. Some men were also drawn from those who preferred the nautical life to being incarcerated in jail. These tended to be petty criminals and those imprisoned for debt, for, despite a reputation for accepting the scum of the prisons for its crews, the navy, in fact, was most reluctant to accept hardened criminals.

Most important of all, of course, was the manpower provided by impressment. Although flying in the face of the sort of notions that made nationwide conscription unthinkable, this practice of legalised kidnapping was regarded as the only certain way to man the fleet. The press aimed only at seizing seamen, and then only those who could not produce protections granting them exemption: landmen scooped up by the gangs were released. The system of impressment was highly organised, naval officers and their gangs being stationed at all the major ports of Britain and Ireland. Before war was declared these men were busy imposing a 'hot press' in scores of coastal ports and on merchant vessels in home waters, the necessity of raising men at that moment meaning that even those with protections were not spared. All this, however, was still not sufficient to meet the navy's requirements.

During the war the number of seamen and marines voted by Parliament steadily rose, from 100,000 in 1804 to 145,000 in 1810–13. To put such figures into perspective, in 1760–63, at the height of the Seven Years War, only 70,000 were voted; by the end of the American War of Independence, in 1783, the figure was 110,000; during the 1790s the number was usually 110,000–120,000.

The struggle with Napoleon saw the navy at the zenith of its power in the age of sail, having over a thousand vessels in service in 1808–11 and 1813. Yet its manpower shortage was desperate. Except for 1808–09, the numbers voted were not matched by the numbers borne, the navy invariably being from 3,000 to 16,000 short of its total. Service conditions were partly to blame, but so also were the effects of competition. The merchant marine always offered higher pay and an easier life. Compared to the 25*s* 6*d* per month he was paid in the navy, the ordinary seaman could earn eight to ten guineas per voyage in the coal trade. Even in the Baltic, West Indian and American trades a seaman could earn £4–£6 per month. There was also competition from privateers seeking profits from attacking enemy commerce. In 1793–1815 the Admiralty issued 4,000 letters of marque to privateers and during 1803–06 47,000 men were given protection from impressment because they served in such vessels. Compounding the problem of getting men was that of keeping them, desertion being a constant blight. No precise figures are available, but Admiral Patton estimated at the time that the navy lost over 12,000 deserters in the May 1803 — June 1805 period, Vice-Admiral Nelson venturing the opinion that 42,000 desertions had occurred in 1793–1801. Individual ships' books do nothing to challenge such figures, the *Revenge*, for example, taking on 2,100 men in 1805–11 to maintain her complement of 640.[28]

This manpower shortfall could sometimes have drastic effects. During 1805 Barham, First Lord of the Admiralty, repeatedly bemoaned his lack of crews, many vessels having to lie idle while, he felt, a further 20,000 seamen were needed. In October he complained of 'so many of our most active ships lying inactive in Port for want of men . . .'. The marines were similarly afflicted, St Vincent observing in 1803 that they were 7,000 short of their establishment. Nor did the passage of time help matters. In 1810 it was noted that 481 warships, varying in size from first-rates to sloops, were 11,156 men short of their complement, and by 1813 an acrimonious correspondence was being carried on between Wellington and the then First Lord, Melville, which hinged on this problem. Wellington complained of what he regarded as inadequate naval support for his campaign in northern Spain, Melville responding in glacial terms that, since the start of the American war, he had had to find 19,000 further seamen and that the vessels sent to the Spanish station had, as it was, deprived other commands. He had already lamented to Rear-Admiral Popham the previous year that it was impossible to reinforce the squadron off northern Spain and had instructed the ships already there to remain as long as possible, on what was a very dangerous coast during the winter, so as to support the army's operations.[29]

Individual warships also provided evidence of crew shortages. At the height of the hot press, and before war was even declared, Rear-Admiral Campbell complained that eight out of the ten ships of the line with him in Torbay were short of men, and one, the *Thunderer*, lacked fifty-eight crew members, those she did have being far from ideal. At Trafalgar the *Victory* went into action with a crew of 703, though her theoretical complement was 837. In 1812 the *Victorious* captured the French *Rivoli*, the British vessel lacking eighty-four men, while in 1808 the *San Fiorenzo* frigate fought a notable action off Ceylon with a crew of 186: had she been at full strength it would have numbered 265.[30]

Although Britain retained control of the seas, the margin of success was frequently a narrow one. Mulgrave remarked at one point that meeting all the demands which might suddenly be placed on the navy was an 'impossibility'. At that moment, in 1808, he had only four frigates and nineteen sloops unappropriated, being sure that convoys and the like would soon see them employed.[31] Despite the victory at Trafalgar and in many lesser actions, there was an unending dread of the sort of naval power that Napoleon could accumulate with the huge resources at his disposal. Such fears prompted actual attacks on threatening naval concentrations and caused much thought about other assaults which were not, in the event, implemented. This will be considered in more detail later, but it must be stressed how conscious ministers were of the delicate nature of their naval superiority. As with the army, the navy's duties were global. Squadrons had to be maintained off the primary colonies, large fleets had to be kept in European waters to blockade the main Continental arsenals, and all Britain's trade, troop movements and supply convoys had to be protected, (see appendix 3). With accidents and weather taking a ceaseless toll, and with simple wear and tear putting vessels out of commission for weeks at a time, the Admiralty had to employ its resources with great care. Against this the less numerous, but better built and manned, enemy vessels could lurk in port, increasing their strength and all the while threatening campaigns of raiding and harassment if they could escape the blockading squadrons. As French power expanded neutral fleets also became a danger, liable to fall under Napolean's control, everything combining to curtail the navy's strategic options.

Naturally enough, most recruitment to the services came from British nationals, but both also drew a proportion of their manpower from foreigners. There were 17,039 foreign rank and file serving in the army's formations in January 1804, a figure that had trebled to 52,737 by January 1813 and comprised between a sixth and a seventh of its total strength. The worth of these troops was highly variable, ranging from the excellence of the King's German Legion, a force of several regiments whose members came primarily from the electorate of Hanover, to the Chasseurs Britanniques, a unit composed of enemy deserters who were highly prone to deserting back to Napoleon's armies given half a chance. In the Caribbean the army also recruited black slaves into special regiments for local service, such units not being as vulnerable to disease as their white counterparts and numbering 7,000–8,000 men by 1807–09. Mention may also be made of the Portuguese: although not a part of the British army, they did form a valuable and numerous auxiliary in the Peninsula from 1810. (They will be considered in more detail in chapter four).

Naval figures are much harder to assess precisely, but frequently a marked proportion of any ship's crew would be foreign. At Trafalgar, for example, the *Victory* had seventy-one such seamen aboard, some 8 per cent of her crew; in the same year the *San Domingo* contained sixty-two foreigners – out of a complement of 439. In 1812 the *Warspite* contained eighty-three foreigners, some 17 per cent of her crew, and the *Implacable* had eighty, 14 per cent of her total. This was undoubtedly valuable to a navy always chronically short of men, but it had the unpleasant side effect of including many pressed Americans, a factor helping to sour Anglo-American relations and contribute to the war of 1812.[32]

In one respect, however, both armed forces did enjoy a substantial benefit in the early nineteenth century: the question of health. With the progress made in the previous century, by this period soldiers and sailors tended to be fitter and to live longer than their forefathers. Progress was most evident in the navy. During the 1790s great strides had been made towards the conquest of scurvy via the provision of fresh vegetables and lemon juice. Success had also been enjoyed in the war against smallpox through the first use of injections. Such measures became more prevalent in 1803–15 and together combined to preserve the crews' fighting capacity. Sir Gilbert Blane, one of the foremost physicians of the time, observed that if losses from sickness during 1793–1814 had been at the same level as during 1776–83 the navy would have been shattered. Some 6,694 men would have died annually, a total of 133,380 for the whole period: this figure approximated the navy's entire strength in the years after 1803 and for some years, indeed, exceeded it. In 1779, out of the whole fleet, just under one in three became sick and one in every forty-two died. In 1813, with manpower double that of 1779, just under one in eleven became sick and one in every 143 died. Scurvy and smallpox had been virtually eradicated and the perils of fever and dysentery much reduced; ships' ventilation had been improved and so had the quality of their surgeons. Without all this the vital close blockade of Napoleon's ports could not have been maintained so well, freeing his squadrons to a great extent and much increasing the danger that Britain faced. Nor could escaping enemy squadrons have been pursued so effectively had the British ships been hamstrung by sickness and death.[33]

In the army's case progress was less obvious but nonetheless present. The Medical Board had been founded in the 1790s and with it the overseeing of the provision of drugs, medicines and surgical instruments. There were also quarantine arrangements for troops returning from the Indies and better sanitary provision for those sailing on expeditions. In 1805, for example, Commodore Popham could record that of the troops sailing for the Cape of Good Hope there were only nineteen men in the hospital ship out of a force of eight regiments: this despite their confinement in transports for over four weeks and after enduring two gales. In the previous decade Private John Shipp had sailed to the same destination and remembered cramped conditions, disease and scurvy, with many people dying. Upon its arrival his regiment needed a fortnight to convalesce.[34]

There were some setbacks to these advances, however. The Medical Board was rent by feuds, and the fiasco of its handling of the Walcheren fevers prompted the dismissal of all its members. The treatment of those who survived the Corunna retreat was also inadequate, one surgeon estimating that a thousand lives had been needlessly lost. In theatres of war hospitals were often poorly staffed and insanitary, even convalescents being sent home suffering severely: on one voyage from Portugal in December 1810 sixty-four patients died. Against this grim picture, though, must be set the work of Surgeon General McGrigor, who, from 1811, oversaw medical matters in the Peninsula. There medical standards improved as the war progressed, despite the greater numbers and longer distances involved. Techniques became more professional, adequate supplies were usually on hand, the standards of hospitals were raised and, perhaps most notably, there were no serious complaints from Wellington – a man never slow to acknowledge the shortcomings of other people. McGrigor's biographer estimates that his measures added 4,000–5,000 men to the army's strength in the winter of 1812–13, men who would otherwise have been missing in the following victorious campaign.[35]

Unquestionably, though, the main benefit to the army's health came from the ministers' avoidance of protracted campaigns on pestilential West Indian islands, though Walcheren proved to be a pestilential European alternative. Consequently the army was fitter and, despite long sick lists during the unhealthy summer months in the Peninsula, better able to maintain its fighting strength. Medical advances improved both services' most precious resource: manpower. This in turn spared ministers the spectacle of their strategic plans being ruined by disease.

Alongside the availability of manpower, the question of finance loomed large in the mind of Britain's strategic directors, similarly at times exerting a profound influence on their military alternatives. Certainly the funding of such a vast military effort and for so many years placed great strains on the country's financial capacity. N. J. Silberling estimates that war expenditure and its affiliated services cost £29·78 million in 1804, rising to £42·11 million in 1808, and £70·53 million in 1813. Compared to these figures, government gross revenue in 1804 stood at £40·07 million, was £65·77 million in 1808, and reached £76·69 million in 1813. In other words, the proportion of revenue spent on the war went from over half to almost the whole total sum. This inevitably prompted higher and higher levels of government borrowing, the sums going from £32·86 million in 1804 to £105·3 million in 1813. While expenditure and borrowing grew apace, the money raised from fiscal measures rose more slowly. Throughout the period the particular costs of maintaining the armed forces increased. In 1805 Parliament was told that in the previous twelve months the navy had cost over £11·75 million, the army just under £15·75 million and the Ordnance just over £3·5 million. By 1811 the costs had risen sharply; the navy absorbing over £19·5 million the army over £23.8 million and the Ordnance over £4.5 million.[36]

Economically the war was a mixed blessing. It boosted the progress of the industrial revolution, there being greater production of cotton and iron and more use of steam power. More beneficial, and directly related to the war, was the annihilation of the commerce of Britain's rivals, Britain securing virtually monopolistic powers as the conflict spread beyond France to include Holland, Spain and Denmark, the primary maritime countries of Europe. Only the USA provided a serious commercial challenge, and her trade was swept from the seas after 1812, taking years to recover after the war's conclusion. Matching this was Britain's expansion in the East and West Indies, she becoming the paramount supplier of the colonial goods which Europe craved as, one by one, the other European colonies were conquered. Such success aided strategy, providing a strong financial prop for the conflict, even if trade and colonies tied down considerable military means in their protection.

Against all this, however, was Britain's commercial vulnerability in the face of Napoleon's amazing conquest of most of Europe. The coming of war immediately shattered British trade with France, its value falling from over £2 million in 1802 to a mere £20,000 in 1804. But French military success put Napoleon in a position, from the Berlin Decrees of 1806, where he could try and repeat this blow in an effort to wreck Britain's Continental trade altogether. By 1808 virtually all of mainland Europe, except Sweden, was put into a state of enforced hostility to Britain, her Continental trade, which had been worth £22·5 million in 1802, having fallen to half that. A constant challenge was maintained against this Continental System, but with varying success. Corrupt French officials made fortunes issuing licences for such trade, and some countries, like the Iberian powers, slipped out of the emperor's control. By such means Britain's commerce continued to enter Europe, a fact Napoleon tacitly recognised in 1810 by the Trianon Tariff and the Fontainebleu Decree, measures aimed at creating a massive customs barrier. In future British manufactures were still, theoretically, to be excluded, while colonial goods were permitted, though bearing heavy duties, Napoleon himself taking a share of his subordinates' bribes.

Not only did this cut the value of Britain's trade, but it also caused disruption and uncertainty. Particular sectors would experience boom conditions for a while, then a new French victory or some political/diplomatic change would occur and boom would be followed by bust. For example, the early war years saw extensive trading via Norway and Denmark, this reaching a value of just under £5 million by 1807. Then came the war with the Danes and by 1808 the trade's value had collapsed to a mere £21,000. Holland provides a similar story. A lucrative smuggling trade was carried on with the people of the Netherlands, and by 1807–09 it was worth just under £4·5 million. Thereafter stricter French controls were applied, Napoleon actually removing his brother, Louis, from the Dutch throne in 1810. During 1810–12 the trade slumped to a value of just over £1 million.[37]

With Napoleon having only a limited ability to harm Britain's non-European trade, British commerce could never be completely destroyed by the System. But the restrictions it caused, particularly respecting manufactures, did do harm. They reduced the government's revenue from trade and injured the nation's industrial, commercial and banking system. It was indicative of the pressure felt by the business community that Popham's capture of Buenos Aires in 1806, with the (illusory) prospect of a rich new market, was greeted with joyous relief; very quickly the region was glutted with goods by businessmen desperately seeking a new trade outlet. Such fragility was illustrated yet more clearly by the economic crisis of 1810–12. This first became evident when merchants could not secure payment from their South American customers. By the middle of 1810 five Manchester business houses had gone bankrupt and thereafter such collapses became prolific. Rippling outwards, the crisis caused problems for banking houses, the cotton industry and the hardware trade. With a restricted European market and many businessmen speculating in large quantities of colonial produce, much of it from captured islands, Britain's trade suffered from glut. Uncertainty also weakened the value of sterling, the pound already having dropped nearly 20 per cent on the Hamburg exchange in 1808–10: this further deepened the government's specie problems.[38] In turn, economic dislocation spilled over into social unrest and so made the war harder to pursue. In 1812 military units were tied down preserving internal order and there were peace petitions from such leading industrial and commercial towns as Bolton, Liverpool, Blackburn and Preston. The petitioners felt that the war was inimical to their interests and injurious to Britain's economy, a belief which threatened to terminate the war altogether if it became so widespread and persistent as to undermine the ministers' resolution.[39]

At times ministers despaired of being able to fund the war, and certainly the leaders of the Whig opposition felt that an ultra-cautious strategy ought to be followed in order to preserve the country's means. Lord Grenville suggested at one moment that the Peninsular War should be opposed and a system implemented 'which by husbanding our resources is best calculated to carry us thro' a contest of which the end still appears so remote'. He openly propounded this in Parliament, wanting a strategy 'of husbanding our resources and acting upon a system of home defence'.[40] After Richard Wellesley had left Perceval's Cabinet in 1812 the question of how to use resources proved a major obstacle to any political alliance between his faction and the Whigs. Although Grenville and Grey agreed with him about Catholic Emancipation, their outlook on the war was quite different: 'we cannot in sincerity conceal from Lord Wellesley that in the present state of the Finances we entertain the strongest doubts of the practicability of an increase in any branch of the Public Expenditure'.[41] This extreme financial prudence marked the Whig leaders during their brief tenure of office in 1806–07, most obviously in their attitude to the question of European subsidies (discussed in more detail in chapter six).

Other ministries were equally aware of their financial limitations, but did not allow these to restrict their policy to the same extent. The whole matter was most clearly outlined in a memorandum written by Perceval as Chancellor of the Exchequer in 1809. He pointed out that Parliament had voted supplies totalling £47,587,000 and that, after providing for permanent charges, ordinary revenues and taxation brought in £25.5 million. This left a loan to be raised of £22 million, something demanding revenue to the tune of £1·32 million just to pay interest charges and the Sinking Fund. Perceval came to gloomy conclusions from all this. He doubted whether new taxation could be raised and consequently whether the war could be pursued on its present scale. Peace would see the country saddled with a massive debt and probably still having to maintain a large peacetime establishment. Assuming a gross force of 44,000 men in the Peninsula, Perceval concluded that the minimum annual cost of the war would be £6·68 million. This figure included subsidies that had already been promised, the manning of foreign stations and the cost of the navy. It would be impossible to retain Walcheren, send an army to the Continent or pay substantial further foreign subsidies.

The difficulty therefore of supporting any considerable increase in the Foreign Expenditure of the Country, conspires, with the difficulty of finding new Taxes, to establish the necessity of limiting the Scale of Operations, and of endeavouring as far as possible to confine the War to a War of Defence.

He recommended a massive reduction in military spending, sufficient to reduce the country's borrowing requirement to £12 million – £14 million.[42] Clearly at that moment Perceval's financial worries were moving his strategic thinking towards that of the opposition leaders. In the event his premiership did not witness the implementation of his more stringent ideas, perhaps owing to the influence of men like Liverpool and Richard Wellesley, but then nor was Walcheren held or large new subsidies paid out. Ministers continued to bite the financial bullet, but the scale of their concern is clear.

That Walcheren was attacked at all in 1809 was in part due to financial considerations. When the expedition sailed Castlereagh wrote that the operation:

enables Great Britain to employ a larger proportion of its disposable force against the enemy than it could attempt to do in any other mode, *or in any other direction*; regard being had to the extent of force already employed on foreign service: the present state of the Continent, and the limits necessarily imposed . . . by the state of the exchanges and the scarcity of specie . . .[43]

It was hoped that this army, operating on enemy soil, would ease its monetary difficulties by a strict policy of financial self-interest. Its

Commissary General was instructed either to obtain supplies and local coin at a fixed, low, rate or to procure them by compulsory requisition.[44]

Not surprisingly the most persistent evidence of financial problems came from the Peninsula, the most protracted campaign of the period. Many of the difficulties that were later to haunt Cabinets stemmed from the initial enthusiasm for the campaign displayed by the Portland ministry. Carried away by the sudden opportunity of severely beating the French, the government committed almost all its bullion reserves, worth over £2·5 million, to helping the insurgents. Hoping to avoid the unfavourable discounts on British paper money, only £187,000 was sent in Treasury bills during 1808. In effect ministers gambled the bullion reserves on a quick victory, a gamble that failed. Thereafter procuring specie was very difficult and the campaign's demands had to be met by increasing use of paper money: in 1809–10 over £6·5 million was sent in bills, compared to just over £1.1 million in bullion. From 1808 the Bank of England's hard-currency reserves persistently declined, falling from £6·4 million in that year to £3·4 million in 1810 and to £2·2 million in 1814.[45] Commissaries and those responsible for supporting the Iberian nations financially made constant demands for specie, while those businessmen who accepted Treasury bills could wait years for payment, a circumstance that did nothing for British credit. The net effect was to fuel the price inflation of precious metals, so making specie all the harder to obtain. So the vicious spiral continued: peacetime Portuguese dollars had been worth 4*s* each, by September 1809 the rate had risen to 5*s* 2*d* and by February 1814 they could not be had under 7*s*.[46] All sorts of expedients had to be resorted to keep the campaign funded. Bullion came from India and China and the continued productivity of the Mexican mines was seen as essential. From August 1810 specie was raised in the Peninsula itself and the campaign's later stages even saw the Rothschild banking house supplying bullion via France. Indicative of this activity is one list of the diverse shipments of bullion landed at Lisbon between 19 November 1812 and 15 July 1813: during this brief period there were no fewer than twenty-seven separate deliveries, ranging in value from 50,000 Spanish dollars worth £11,250 to gold coin and dollars worth over £250,000. The total value of all these consignments came to more than £990,000.[47]

For Wellington, campaigning in friendly countries and so unable to indulge in regular requisitions, a flow of money, preferably hard cash, was crucial. Constantly, however, he felt that its shortage would be his undoing. 'I do not know,' he complained in April 1810, 'what we are to do if we cannot get some money.' In what sounded like paranoia, in August 1811 he grumbled, 'I begin to suspect the Government of treachery. Nothing can be so fatal to the cause as to distress us for money, and yet all the measures of the Government appear to have that object in view.' By 1812 the army was 'bankrupt', Wellington's troops not having been paid for five months and his muleteers for thirteen. Nor had matters improved by 1814, the troops' arrears having grown to six months and the army being in debt all over the Peninsula and in France; there was no credit to be had.[48]

Despite Wellington's outbursts, ministers were in fact all too aware of the problem. Castlereagh noted in July 1809 that:

> The scarcity of specie is become the subject of much anxiety . . . there is not more than £100,000 which can be sent from hence, in addition to what you [Sir A. Wellesley] have, till dollars arrive from South America . . .

By December Liverpool believed that economies would have to be found if the war was to be continued (one can sense Perceval's views behind such thoughts) and six months later he frankly admitted that:

> We cannot expect to carry the war on a large scale, without some difficulties, those of a Pecuniary nature are perhaps more trying than any other, but they are at the same time most common, and we are in general such good Paymasters when compared to our Enemies . . .

In 1813 Bathurst refuted Richard Wellesley's claims that the Peninsular War had been pursued with insufficient vigour, pointing out that even a small increase in forces there would cause severe specie problems, out of all proportion to the advantages gained, a state of affairs, he said, which had been caused by the obstacles placed in the way of British trade during the previous two years.[49]

The crux of the problem was that maintaining an army on the Continent cost more than three times as much as keeping the same force in Britain. At home, supplies did not rely on foreigners demanding payment in bullion, and the same fact applied to the troops' pay. The problem was the more marked because it did not apply so much to the navy. There crews went for years on end without being paid while virtual prisoners on board ship: furthermore, as they were paid only at the ports where their vessels were commissioned, i.e. in Britain, the navy was not such a drain on the bullion reserves.[50]

Another demand upon precious finances was the necessity for subsidies for the assorted European allies. Such support was an effort to make up in money what Britain lacked in manpower, and all ministries, except the Talents, continued to feel that such support was strategically vital. This assistance was to be provided on an increasing scale as more and more countries took up arms against Napoleon and sought aid. As one example of the extent of such help, it was intended, had the Third Coalition not collapsed, to pay Britain's allies £7 million during the course of 1806: this at a time when the whole annual cost of the Royal Navy was only just over £15 million.[51]

The conclusion is that ministers must be given great credit for persisting with an active, aggressive strategy in the teeth of such financial obstacles. At times there were excellent reasons that might have prompted a more restricted policy, yet the difficulties were faced and the vast expenditure needed was maintained. It took considerable political nerve. Furthermore, when other nations were prepared to fight, ministers were ready to give them what scale of aid they thought possible, help which invariably turned out to be very costly indeed.

Such was the spectre of financial crisis, though, that ministers did at times attempt a contradictory policy of pursuing war and limiting spending. St Vincent's battle against dockyard corruption and waste in 1803–04 could not have come at a worse moment. In May 1806 Windham planned to curtail the strength of the calvary, of the Guards and of the Waggon Train, measures aimed at saving a comparatively paltry £363,000. Yet such an intention came in the wake of intense efforts to strengthen the army and at a time when Britain was isolated. The Waggon Train was also a target in 1810, when Palmerston, the Secretary at War, sought to cut its strength to save £23,433. In February 1813 the Commissioners of Transports ventured the opinion that their inability to hire tonnage was, in part, due to the limit placed on the rate that they could offer, a restriction that saved £166,00.[52] These were small sums when set against the total costs involved and make little sense when considered in the context of the desperate struggle against Napoleon. Yet they illustrate clearly the ministers' financial concern, all of them seemingly, with the possible exception of Richard Wellesley, being prepared to indulge in penny-pinching. From this evolved the strategy that was followed from 1808: one of hoarding Britain's finances on all matters viewed, correctly or otherwise, as secondary, while directing what resources could be found into those areas where it was felt that dramatic success might be achieved.

Notes

1 J. W. Fortescue, *The County Lieutenancies and the Army, 1803–14*, London, 1909, appendix II, p. 293. Leeds University Library, Brotherton Collection Box VII, Mulgrave Papers, 19/30. C. Lloyd, *The British Seaman*, London, 1970, appendix I, table 3, p. 263.

2 *The Parliamentary Debates from the Year 1803 to the Present Time*, London, 1803–15 (afterwards referred to as *P.D.*), I, p. 186. E. A. Wrigley and R. S. Schofield, *The Population History of England, 1541–1873*, London, 1981, table A/3, p. 534, give the population of England and Wales as 8,664,000 in 1801, rising to 9,886,000 in 1811. C. Emsley, *British Society and the French Wars, 1793–1815*, London, 1979, p. 53.

3 Fortescue, pp. 45–8 and appendix II, p. 293, J. R. Western, *The English Militia in the Eighteenth Century*, London, 1965, pp. 294–9. E. McCawley Renn, 'England faces invasion: the land forces, 1803–05', *Proceedings of the Consortium on Revolutionary Europe, 1750–1850*, 1974, p. 136.

4 Fortescue, pp. 59–70, 198, 260 and appendix III, p. 294. Emsley, pp. 132–3. J. R. Western, 'The Volunteer movement as an anti-revolutionary force, 1793–1801', *English Historical Review*, LXXI, October 1956, pp. 603–14.

5 Emsley, pp. 101–2. Fortescue, p. 73.

6 R. Glover, *Peninsular Preparation. The Reform of the British Army, 1795–1809*, Cambridge, 1963, pp. 162, 186 and 220–1. M. Glover, *Wellington's Army*, London, 1977, pp. 25–9. Emsley, p. 127. T. H. McGuffie, 'Recruiting the ranks of the regular British army during the French wars', *Journal of the Society for Army Historical Research*, XXXIV, 1956, pp. 50–8 and 123–32. R. Morriss, *The Royal Dockyards during the Revolutionary and Napoleonic Wars*, Leicester, 1983, p. 98.

7 J. W. Fortescue, *A History of the British Army*, London, 1899–1930, 5, pp. 223–5. Fortescue, *County Lieutenancies*, pp. 9–10. M. Glover, pp. 26–31. McGuffie, pp. 50–7. Buckinghamshire R.O., Hobart Papers, D/MH/H/War F26.

8 R. Glover, pp. 227–8 and 230–1. Western, *English Militia*, pp. 231–2. Fortescue, *County Lieutenancies*, p. 73. Buckinghamshire R.O., Hobart Papers, D/MH/H/War F26. Northern Ireland R.O., Castlereagh Papers, D3030/1885.

9 Fortescue, *County Lieutenancies*, pp. 129–30 and 154–5. R. Glover, pp. 238–9. Emsley, p. 104.

10 As many as 103 Martello towers were built in 1805–12: see McCawley Renn, pp. 129–33.

11 R. Glover, pp. 229 and 249–50. Fortescue, *County Lieutenancies*, pp. 219, 221–2, 226, 259–60 and 268–9.

12 Fortescue, *County Lieutenancies*, appendix I, p. 291; and appendix II, p. 293.

13 *P.D.*, I, p. 205.

14 Fortescue, *County Lieutenancies*, pp. 79–111 and 149–50. Leeds University Library, Brotherton Collection Box VII, Mulgrave Papers, 13/14. *P.D.*, I, p. 193.

15 J. R. Elting, *Swords around a Throne*, London, 1988, p. 505. France's population from J. Steven Watson, *The Reign of George III, 1760–1815*, Oxford, 1964, pp. 517 n.–18 n. Napoleon's army in 1805 from D. Chandler, *The Campaigns of Napoleon*, London, 1967, pp. 384–5.

16 R. Glover, pp. 225 and n. and 249.

17 R. Glover, pp. 230–1. Fortescue, *County Lieutenancies*, pp. 73–4, B.M. add. Mss 37891, Windham Papers, f. 246. P.R.O. 30/8/243 part 3, Chatham Papers, p. 241. WO 1/946, p. 21. C. T. Atkinson, 'Foreign regiments in the British army, 1793–1802', *Journal of the Society for Army Historical Research*, XXI–XXII, 1942–44, particularly pp. 192–3, 195–7, 273–6 and 243.

18 P.R.O. 30/8/240 part 3, Chatham Papers, pp. 229–41. WO 1/632, pp. 181–3. For 1811 see Second Duke of Wellington (ed.), *Supplementary Despatches, Correspondence and Memoranda of Field Marshal Arthur Duke of Wellington*, London, 1858–72, VII, p. 53 (afterwards referred to as *S.D.W.*).

19 Figures for 1804–09 from Fortescue, *County Lieutenancies*, appendix VII, pp. 303 and 305. For 1811 from B.M. Add. Mss 38378, Liverpool Papers, f. 183.

20 M. Martin (ed.), *The Despatches, Minutes and Correspondence of the Marquess Wellesley during his Administration in India*, London, 1836–37, IV, p. 225. Marquess of Londonderry (ed.), *Memoirs and Correspondence of Viscount Castlereagh*, London, 1848–53, VIII, p. 62 (afterwards referred to as *Castlereagh Correspondence*).

21 A. A. Aspinall (ed.), *The Later Correspondence of George III*, Cambridge, 1962–70, IV, pp. 107–8. B.M. Add. Mss 38375, Liverpool Papers, f. 170v.

22 P.R.O. WO 17/2464 for the Peninsular army's strength on 25 August 1809. *P.D.*, XV, appendix I, pp. iii–v, for the Walcheren figure.

23 P.R.O. WO 17/1517, 1936, 2360 and 2473. See appendix 2.

24 *S.D.W.*, VII, p. 390.

25 Greenwich Maritime Museum, Yorke Papers, YOR/20, letter 21.

26 C. Lloyd (ed.), *The Keith Papers*, III, London, 1955, pp. 134–45. Lloyd, *British Seaman*, pp. 187–8. B. Lavery, *Nelson's Navy*, London, 1989, pp. 274–7. *P.D.*, I, p. 205.

27 Lavery, pp. 130–1.

28 Lloyd, *British Seaman*, pp. 175, 177–209, 241 and appendix I, table 3, pp. 262–3. M. A. Lewis, *A Social History of the Navy, 1793–1815*, London, 1960, pp. 16–116, 133–7 and 39 and n. Lavery, pp. 120–8. J. S. Bromley (ed.), *The Manning of the Royal Navy. Selected Public Pamphlets,*

1693–1873, London, 1974, pp. 153 and 156.

29 Sir J. K. Laughton (ed.), *The Letters and Papers of Charles, Lord Barham*, 1758–1813, III, London, 1910, pp. 82 and 94–6. P.R.O. 30/58/5, Dacre Adams Papers, letter 139. Buckinghamshire R.O., Hobart Papers, D/MH/H/War C113. Leeds University Library, Brotherton Collection Box VII, Mulgrave Papers, 19/33. For Wellington's complaints see J. Gurwood (ed.), *The Dispatches of F.M. the Duke of Wellington, 1799–1818*, London, 1834–39, X, pp. 458–9; XI, pp. 17–19 and 26–8. For Melville's replies see *S.D.W.*, VIII, pp. 144–8 and 223. Also B.M. Loan 57, 108, Melville Papers, ff. 114–18 and 146v.

30 Lloyd, *British Seaman*, p. 110. J. Leyland (ed.), *Papers relating to the Blockade of Brest*, London, 1898, I, pp. 8–10. D. Howarth, *Trafalgar*, London, 1971, pp. 24–5. W. James, *The Naval History of Great Britain*, London, 1837, V, p. 24; VI, p. 66.

31 Leeds R.O., Harewood Collection, Canning Papers, 31, Mulgrave to Canning, 18 July 1808.

32 Army statistics from Fortescue, *County Lieutenancies*, appendix II, p. 293. Atkinson, XXI, pp. 175–81; XX, pp. 2–14, 45–52, 107–15, 134–42, 187–97, 234–50, 265–76 and 313–14. R. N. Buckley, *Slaves in Red Coats. The British West Indian Regiments, 1795–1815*, New Haven, Conn., 1979. For the navy see Lloyd, *British Seaman*, p. 193. D. Pope, *Life in Nelson's Navy*, London, 1981, pp. 108–8; Lavery, pp. 126–8; Bromley, appendix IV, pp. 352–3.

33 C. Lloyd and J. L. S. Coulter, *Medicine and the Navy, 1200–1900*, London, 1961, III, pp. 153–84. C. Lloyd (ed.), *The Health of Seamen*, London, 1965, pp. 136–211.

34 W. G. Perrin (ed.), *The Naval Miscellany*, III, London, 1928, pp. 223–4. G. Avery (ed.), *The Echoing Green*, London, 1974, pp. 43–5.

35 Sir N. Cantlie, *A History of the Army Medical Department*, Edinburgh and London, 1974, I, pp. 283–377. R. L. Blanco, *Wellington's Surgeon-General. Sir James McGrigor*, Durham, N. C., 1974, pp. 90–136.

36 N. J. Silberling, 'The financial and monetary policy of Great Britain during the Napoleonic wars', *Quarterly Journal of Economics*, XXXVIII, 1924, pp. 215 and 217. His statistics differ slightly from those in B. R. Mitchell and P. Deane, *Abstract of British Historical Statistics*, Cambridge, 1962, but the trend of spending more and more gross revenue is the same in both. Armed forces' costs from *P.D.*, V, pp. CCXXV–CCXXVIII; XXII, pp. XV–XVI.

37 F. Crouzet, *L'Économie britannique at le blocus continental, 1806–13*, Paris, 1958, appendix II, p. 883.

38 The best account of the period's economic warfare is E. F. Heckscher, *The Continental System*, Oxford, 1922, particularly pp. 115–213 and 240–7. Also Crouzet, pp. 526–7. For Britain's economic background, A. D. Harvey, *Britain in the early Nineteenth Century*, London, 1978, pp. 323–33.

39 *P.D.*, XXII, pp. 29–30, 94–6, 108–10 and 1067–8. For the naive opponents of the war: J. E. Cookson, *The Friends of Peace*, Cambridge, 1982, particularly pp. 225–40.

40 B.M. Add. Mss 58947, Dropmore Papers, f. 109v. *P.D.*, XV, p. 13.

41 B.M. Add. Mss 37297, Wellesley Papers, ff. 1–3.

42 Nottingham University Library, Portland Papers, PwF 2635.

43 *Castlereagh Correspondence*, VI, p. 300 (Castlereagh's emphasis).

44 D. Gray, *Spencer Perceval, The Evangelical Prime Minister, 1762–1812*, Manchester, 1963, pp. 341–2. *Castlereagh Correspondence*, VI, pp. 287–9 and 304–7.

45 Payments in 1808–10 from *S.D.W.*, VII, p. 35. Bank of England reserves from Silberling, p. 227.

46 M. Glover, pp. 107–8. S. P. G. Ward, *Wellington's Headquarters*, Oxford, 1957, pp. 92–3.

47 Gray, pp. 347–52. G. D. Knight, 'Lord Liverpool and the Peninsular War, 1809–12', University of Florida Ph.D. thesis, 1976, pp. 119 and 133–6. B.M. Add. Mss 57393, Herries Papers, ff. 53–4v (provisional folio order).

48 For these and other complaints, Gurwood, VI, pp. 33, 41, 121, 174 and 347; VIII, pp. 160–2 and 198; IX, p. 319; X, pp. 356 and 425–7.

49 *Castlereagh's Correspondence*, VI, p. 95. For Liverpool's view in 1809: C. D. Yonge, *Life and Administration of Robert Banks Jenkinson, Second Earl of Liverpool*, London, 1868, I, pp. 315–16. For 1810, B.M. Add. Mss 38325, Liverpool Papers, ff. 47–8v. *P.D.*, XXV, p. 72.

50 Gray, p. 342. Lloyd, *British Seaman*, pp. 227–8.

51 The essential source for this is J. Sherwig, *Guineas and Gunpowder, British Foreign Aid in the Wars with France, 1793–1815*, Cambridge, Mass., 1969, pp. 144 ff.

52 For Windham and Palmerston, *P.D.*, VII, pp. 307–9; XV, p. 609, respectively. For the transports, P.R.O. WO 1/813, pp. 177–8.

2

The sinews of war

Manpower and finance, converted into the army and navy, constituted the primary instruments of strategy. It is not the concern of this work to review the tactical minutiae of these military organisations, but suffice it to say that both tended to improve their efficiency and standards as the hard years of warfare passed.[1] That both could be applied effectively, however, meant reliance on an assortment of services that kept them armed, mobile, supplied and informed. All these benefits, or their absence, influenced the implementation of strategy and must now be considered.

Having raised military forces, the next step for any government is to see them armed, and the provision of weapons in the period was to be a tremendous British success, despite early problems. In July 1803 Chatham, the Master General of the Ordnance, told his Cabinet colleagues that, excluding those muskets already issued, there was a reserve of only 115,000 stand of arms. Of these he believed it essential to retain a stock of 90,000–100,000 for any emergency, these being available in the London area but being useless if needed further afield. He felt that it was necessary to have recourse to arms of assorted patterns, to repair as many old weapons and to produce as many new ones as possible, to repurchase arms formerly sold off and to acquire a large supply of muskets from Prussia. Chatham refused to issue further muskets to the growing body of recruits coming forward at that time without specific orders from the Secretary of State. The only, rather dubious, comfort he could offer was that 100,000 pikes would soon be available. The government tried to rectify the shortage by purchases from Europe, but this brought other worries. Of the 293,000 stand of arms that were delivered, many were in poor condition and, coming from different countries, ammunition was a problem. So serious was this question that in November 1803 two ships of the line were ordered to leave their other duties and sail to Trieste, there to collect 100,000 muskets. To ensure sufficient space for the cargo, moreover, the vessels were to take the risk of removing their lower-deck guns on the part of the voyage from Malta to Trieste and back.

The chief sufferers from the arms shortage were the Volunteers, complaints about their deficiency in this respect still reaching ministers as late as 1807. Gradually, however, arms production became more vigorous. In 1804 an Ordnance Board representative was established in Birmingham, the main arms centre, both to boost total production and to test the efficiency of the finished product. Also from 1804 the department started making its own muskets in the Tower of London, a second plant being established in Lewisham in 1808.[2] Phenomenal changes stemmed from all this.

By the time of the Peninsular War Britain's armament production permitted her to become something akin to Europe's arsenal. In July 1809 Canning, for the tenth time in twelve months, badgered Chatham over the importance of arms supplies for the Spaniards. Any shortage of weapons, the Foreign Secretary feared, might be used as an excuse for failure. He also observed, 'We are now in great measure dependent upon them for supplies of money – of silver I mean. Every application that I make for Silver, is met with an application for arms.' This remark reflected both the new link between armaments and bullion and the capacity that Britain had acquired of supplying arms in such numbers as to alleviate specie shortages.[3] An account of 1811 indicates the scale of this capacity: since 1808 Britain had sent the Iberian nations over 336,000 muskets as well as 60 million cartridges, 348 pieces of artillery, over 100,000 swords and over 12,000 pistols. Similarly lavish provision was made to the northern powers fighting Napoleon, particularly in 1813. Between April and June that year 95,000 stand of arms were sent to Russia, Prussia and Sweden, along with arms, accoutrements, clothing and suchlike for a further 3,000 cavalry, 8,000 light infantry and 50,000 line infantry. Russia was also sent 116 pieces of artillery. As the year progressed Austria joined the coalition and the Netherlands revolted, both being sent arms and equipment sufficient for a total of 80,000 troops. Even during the few months of hostilities in 1814 Britain issued 80,000 muskets.[4] All this was a far cry from the shortages experienced in 1803.

In these figures arms other than muskets have been mentioned, and here at least problems were of a much more limited nature: the growth of the steel industry, for instance, making the provision of swords a matter of little concern. Similarly, and perhaps surprisingly, there was never any marked deficiency in the provision of artillery. Although British armies were persistently under-gunned compared to their French opponents, it was more a question of transport difficulties than of any production failure. An Ordnance memorandum in December 1803 sounded a satisfied note when pointing out that its total of 648 artillery pieces throughout the country was an improvement on the situation pertaining in 1801, and had been achieved without any lessening with respect to the needs of Ireland, the foreign settlements or the coastal defence batteries.[5]

The triumph that arms production represented was an important factor in the war effort. Ministers were able to arm their own forces, but were in a position to arm Napoleon's enemies and meet their insistent demands for aid with military supplies in lieu of money. If it was vital for Britain to have armies, navies and allies, it was equally vital for them to be adequately armed.

Lack of armaments was not something that inhibited naval efficiency, but a serious problem came in the shape of support facilities. The outbreak of war saw a rapid mobilisation of naval warships, the number of ships of the line in service going from thirty-two early in 1803 to seventy-two by July that year. By the following March the total stood at eighty-two.[6] Once crews had been secured, however, this process of rapid expansion was comparatively easy, ships being taken from being 'in Ordinary', their peacetime reserve situation, and placed into service. More difficult was the matter of keeping vessels seaworthy once they had been recommissioned. Part of the problem lay in the shortage of royal dockyard capacity, the navy having only four places capable of large-scale work, Plymouth, Portsmouth, Chatham and Sheerness. Work on smaller ships could be managed at Deptford and Woolwich. With vessels constantly requiring repairs as wind and weather took their toll, and, with even limited repair work on a seventy-four-gun ship of the line taking about ten weeks, a substantial number of warships could be out of action at any one time. One expert estimates that in 1801–05 it took, on average, five and a half months simply to begin repairs on a seventy-four-gun warship. At the height of the conflict some 20 per cent of all ships of the line and 16 per cent of all lesser vessels were awaiting work and out of commission.[7]

Initially the navy's strength was in breadth rather than depth, the problem of inadequate dockyards being exacerbated by the struggle between St Vincent, the First Lord of the Admiralty, and the timber merchants who supplied the yards. The former took office determined to reform the navy's civil aspects, an area he regarded as 'rotten to the very core'. In the brief period of post-Amiens peace his retrenchment saw scores of dockyard workers discharged, surplus timber sold off and an effort made to ensure that only good-quality merchandise was purchased in future. This last step infuriated the suppliers, who became unwilling to sell their timber at all, the Navy Board being further hindered during 1802, when St Vincent forbade purchasing from abroad on the grounds of economy. Once warfare resumed the problem became very serious indeed, as the navy's consumption of timber was prodigous. With St Vincent trying to make the cartel supply at peacetime prices, a step they naturally resented, relations between them and the Admiralty became extremely strained. When the Admiralty asked the contractors in September 1803 what timber they had to offer months went by before a reply was even received. For the navy all this meant shortages in particular areas, such as English oak, and a greater use of some sorts of inferior foreign timber, such as fir and Canadian oak, and even unseasoned wood, the latter tending to rot much more rapidly and so cause long-term problems.[8]

Because of the inadequacy of dockyard work prior to their sailing, ships were frequently sent out to their blockade duties in poor condition. Moreover the further such vessels were from home the worse their difficulties became because of their distance from such repair facilities as were available: as late as 1812, for example, there was still no Mediterranean dry dock at Malta. Off Toulon, Nelson observed in July 1804 that five of his ships of the line had either been forced home or would soon be going. One, the *Kent*, was so rotten that her lower-deck guns had to be removed and a transport provided on her voyage to Malta in case she foundered. Off Ferrol four of the blockading squadron's ships of the line were in poor condition in 1804 and off Rochefort Vice-Admiral Collingwood noted that only her copper sheathing saved the *Venerable* from sinking during the first winter of blockade – she did, in fact, sink shortly afterwards.

Worsening matters were the venomous gales that lashed the squadrons during the November–January period of 1803–04.

Not until Melville replaced St Vincent at the Admiralty in May 1804 were the worse excesses of the situation rectified. The change marked a surrender to the timber cartel, they thereafter being free to control supplies and raise prices. However, supplies did now return to the yards and many older vessels could be patched up and rendered suitable for limited duties, mostly with convoys and in the North Sea. In all, some twenty-two ships of the line and five frigates entered service in this fashion: just as important, during May 1804 – October 1805 thirty-nine ships entered the dockyards to be refitted.[9]

This was a relief, but it did not end the problems associated with providing and maintaining shipping. Timber consumption rose steeply with wartime demands, from an eighteenth-century average of 2,000 loads each year to a peak of 74,000 loads in 1812; even the lowest wartime figure, 48,420 loads in 1810, was still huge compared to peacetime levels. Meeting this demand meant a continuing use of inferior timber, it often not being possible to allow the wood sufficient time to mature before use. In consequence vessels constructed during these years rotted quickly. The *Albion* and *Sceptre*, for example, seventy-four-gun ships built in 1802 and 1803 respectively, were unserviceable by 1806. The *Rodney* (74), launched in 1809 had to be rendered inactive by 1812, and the *Dublin* (74), launched in 1812, had to be paid off within a few months.[10]

There was also irony, in this period of its greatest triumph, in the Royal Navy having to look abroad for much of its strength. In 1805 there was a scheme to build ten ships of the line and ten frigates in Russian dockyards, Britain only having to supply the vessels' copper fastenings and ironwork. In the event Anglo-Russian relations were never sufficiently cordial for a long enough period for the plan to come to anything. More successful was the persistent use of captured enemy warships. In the days before the use of high explosives most vessels were captured in battle rather than sunk, those taken from the Spanish and French being particularly prized because of their invariably high standards of construction – in this respect they were usually superior to their British-built counterparts. During 1803–15 some 134 enemy ships of the line and frigates were captured, of which number thirty-three ships of the line and sixty-eight frigates were added to the navy's strength.[11]

Just as vital as keeping Britain's forces armed and maintained was keeping them watered and fed. As far as possible the army tended to satisfy its requirements by local purchase, a list of anticipated stores for the Caribbean garrisons, for example, showing that roughly a seventh of the beef and pork needed would come from local sources. It was also hoped that flour might be bought from British America or the United States, but the uncertainties over this illustrate how political circumstances could alter and possibly disrupt the supply system.[12] Similar use of local purchasing was made on active campaign. In the Peninsula supplies came either from local businessmen who happened to be in the army's vicinity or via long-term contractors like the Sampaio brothers, owners of a business network stretching from the Greek islands and the Barbary Coast to the United States. In fact grain supplies from the latter county formed an important part of the army's provisions during the Peninsular campaign. In 1805 under 20 per cent of the USA's grain exports went to the Peninsula; by 1811 it was taking over 60 per cent, some 835,000 barrels out of 1,385,000. Even in 1812–13, during the Anglo-American war, the totals rose to 938,000 and 972,500 barrels respectively. An abstract of stores in one Portuguese depot in the summer of 1811 shows that items like bread, fresh meat, wood and forage tended to be supplied by local contracts and purchase. Salt beef, rum and oats tended to be shipped direct from Britain.[13]

This still left much of the army's needs being met from home, and such was especially the case with initial expeditions, i.e. those going first to areas where no local contracts had been made or depots formed. The amounts required could beggar the imagination. In October 1805 1,119 tons of shipping were set aside to provide transports to move sufficient supplies for 6,000 men for five months (152 days). The total involved came to 304,000 lb of bread or over 608,000 lb of flour, 598,000 lb of beef or 342,000 lb of pork, and 38,000 gallons of spirits. Even these figures are small compared to what was needed to support an extended and large-scale campaign. In 1808 the troops in the Peninsula were sent over 4·4 million lb of beef, over 2·5 million lb of pork, over 3·3 million lb of flour, over 7·7 million lbs of bread and over 336,000 gallons of spirits.[14]

When it came to moving these provisions from Britain the army's victualling arrangements usually proceeded smoothly. Thus an order from the Victualling Board – the body responsible for naval foodstuffs and associated articles – for large supplies of flour and biscuit for the Peninsula was issued on 13th June 1809: by 29 June the necessary vessels had been loaded. On 13 October 1809 the board was told by the Treasury to supply the Mediterranean troops with over 1·4 million lb of salt meat: by 30 November an abstract noted that four ships had been loaded and were ready to sail. On 16 May 1810 the Treasury was asked to agree to the formation of a depot at Cadiz with ninety days' supply of provisions for 12,000 men and 1,000 horses, together with a reserve magazine of thirty days ration of salt meat, biscuits and spirits. On 20 June five victuallers were duly ordered to be loaded at Plymouth. At one stage at least, in December 1809, Wellington's stores in the Peninsula reached such a level that Liverpool agreed to a Victualling Board suggestion that provisions then afloat at Portsmouth and Plymouth be transferred to the navy's use.[15]

Of course, on occasion the best laid plans could go wrong. This was rare, but one instance comes from the history of the force sent to Corunna in 1808 under Major General Baird. Theoretically all expeditions going abroad had a provision of ten weeks' supplies on board their transports, plus a further three months' on board accompanying victuallers. Baird's command does not appear to have had anything like as much. Arriving at Corunna, his troops were not permitted, at first, to land, running into victualling problems when the army commissary at the port would not feed them until they were ashore, while the commander of their naval escort would not victual them on the grounds that he had no orders for such a step. That the force was so soon embarrassed for supplies may have been due to its rapid dispatch, the usual provisioning arrangements not having functioned effectively.[16]

Supply nightmares for the army really began only with the process of moving materials from the depots to the troops in the field. Two concerns in the Peninsula, where, naturally enough, most problems were encountered, were persistent pilferage from the supply convoys and the provision of food of a reasonable quality. A report from one depot illustrates both points. It refers to 557,000 lb of Indian corn that had been damaged by weevils and which required rapid consumption, to 4,000 lb of salt beef that had gone rotten from being too long in casks, and to 2,000 pints of rum that had been adulterated with water – presumably *en route* to the depot. In January 1812 one commissariat officer grumbled to a subordinate about the losses being experienced while moving provisions by road, mentioning the theft of 1,159 lb of biscuit, 3,185 lb of corn and sixty-four pairs of shoes.[17] Providing food and drink for the troops on campaign was the commissariat's responsibility, and its capacity and success were variable. Partly this was due to the variety of men who worked for the department, some of whom were diligent and efficient, while others were negligent, incompetent and sometimes corrupt: in 1810 two commissaries-general were in Newgate prison for their activities. Wellesley complained in 1808 that the men in his commissariat were incapable of managing a counting house, while four years later Herries, the Commissary-in-Chief, wrote that he was trying to improve the quality of its members: one hopeful had sought a position with the observation that he was 'lernging a letel french', his arithmetic, according to Herries, being on a par with his spelling.[18]

Certainly the commissariat's tasks were formidable and, by their nature, unremitting. As well as food and drink it had also to provide stores coming under the heading of 'Camp Equipage'. These items, such as spades, blankets, power bags, haversacks and the like, were shipped from Britain by the Storekeeper General; thereafter they were placed in storage and issued as required. Similarly articles of clothing, although in theory the regimental colonel's responsibility, were in practice issued by the commissariat. Shoes, for example, were found to wear out very quickly and were replaced either by local purchase or from Britain. A stock of over 42,000 pairs was held at the Lisbon depot in February 1811, a total expanded to over 231,000 pairs by that December. At times, perhaps because of malpractice or simple inefficiency, the Peninsular commissariat was busy purchasing items locally that were either in store there already or which could have been supplied more cheaply from Britain. This caused confusion and waste, as happened over the question of shoes and also over blankets. Wellington complained at one point that he was compelled to buy blankets locally, while Herries countered by noting that over 90,000 had been requested from his department in Britain and all had been sent. He also observed that efficiency was not helped by the fact that he had received no return of the stores in the Peninsula for the period from 31 July 1811 to 15 April 1812. He could, in such circumstances, plead ignorance of any shortages and inability to rectify them.[19]

Nevertheless food remained the most important commissariat responsibility. The average daily consumption in Wellington's army in 1813 included 100,000 lb of biscuit, 200,000 lb of forage corn and

300 cattle. Such amounts could be shipped to Lisbon, and at that time there was sufficient food there to feed the army for seven months. The problems appeared when it came to moving the stores to the army, virtually no formal provision having been made in the military infrastructure for such transfers. There was the Waggon Train, but this was quite inadequate when it came to large-scale duties and was viewed by some politicians as ripe for financial pruning. Indeed, MPs seemed to combine ignorance compounded with ill judged smugness when it came to logistical matters. Both Palmerston and Windham, as observed in chapter one, sought to reduce its already limited capacity, Huskisson called it 'an annoyance on foreign service and useless at home' and Tarleton, one of the Commons' armchair warriors, proferred the amazing 'Let the British Army go where it might, they would always get waggons enough.' Less sanguine were the views of the Duke of York. Fighting against Windham's retrenchment in 1806, he considered that reducing the train from 648 waggons to sixty would seriously impede operations because of food and forage shortages. Without such a body 'movements must be paralysed'. In the Peninsula the train numbered only 136 men in 1811, by the end of the following year still having only eighty-seven horses and eleven waggons – admittedly figures pertaining after a long and gruelling campaign. What waggons it did possess, however, were sprung and were employed in moving the wounded.[20]

Lacking its own transport system, the commissariat was obliged to hire locally. The Peninsular campaign saw a massive reliance on the native muleteers and ox-cart drivers. The latter were used primarily to maintain the forward supply depots, while the muleteers were chiefly responsible for provisioning the fighting formations. By the end of 1811 Wellington had 8,000 mules in service, but this number could not meet all the demands and helped prompt the formation of the Commissariat Car Train during 1811–12, a body eventually comprising 1,300 carts.[21]

S. P. G. Ward expresses the opinion that the army was unfortunate in having to fight its most sustained campaign in the Peninsula, considering it a more poverty-stricken region as compared to the wealthier countries in which it had fought in previous wars. In those conflicts, he believes, the army had been able to acquire plentiful supplies and transport from private contractors, a situation that had enabled Commissary General Watson to conduct the business of the army in Flanders in 1793–95 from his desk in London. Such conclusions are dubious. Previous wars, for one thing, did not always see British forces well provided for. Brunswick's army in western Germany in the Seven Years War, for example, found it hard to procure and to move supplies; Burgogne's troops were on half rations by the time of their surrender at Saratoga in 1777; York's commissariat collapsed during the winter of 1794–95 (presumably Watson's absence did nothing to alleviate this). In fact, given the lack of its own integral transport, the army was blessed in having to campaign in the Peninsula. There the coming of war had dislocated the muleteers' business, throwing many out of work and making them all too ready to hire themselves out for British gold. Such labour spared them conscription into the Spanish armies while simultaneously allowing them to serve against the hated French invaders. Certainly the muleteers had their drawbacks, tending to desert and/or pillage supply convoys when not paid, but any civilian body might well have done the same. Occasionally there were brawls between soldiers and suppliers in the sort of military–civilian clashes prompted by armies the world over, and the Spanish muleteers were always reluctant to serve Portuguese formations for any length of time. For all this, though, they were invaluable to Wellington, serving with commendable loyalty in the light of their perennial arrears of pay: it was noted in July 1812 that the muleteers had not been paid for over a year.

Other factors also benefited supply in the campaign. The long Iberian coastline allowed the British to use an assortment of ports as depots from which to draw supplies, e.g. Lisbon, Cadiz, Corunna, the Biscayan ports from the end of 1813 and the eastern harbours used from 1812. Armies operating in much of Europe would not have had such facilities. Use could also be made of rivers like the Tagus and the Douro for much of the year, barges and country boats relieving pressure on the appalling local roads. In short it is doubtful whether, in terms of overall supply arrangements, the Peninsular armies were any worse off than they would have been elsewhere. Certainly Ward's rosy picture of previous campaigns is suspect. York himself, in his defence of the Waggon Train, referred to logistical difficulties in previous campaigns which had caused 'the greatest inconvenience' and 'most distressing embarrassments'. Interestingly, in one of the few campaigns fought outside the Peninsula and away from convenient coastal depots, Whitelocke's attack on Buenos Aires in 1807 saw the commissariat arrangements break down completely, the British verging on starvation by the time the city was assaulted.[22]

None of this should give the impression that the Peninsula was problem-free for the commissariat, of course. In 1809 the Talavera campaign collapsed because, in part, of supply failures on the Spaniards' part. Thereafter Wellington arranged his own logistics, but at the cost of a much reduced capacity for rapid movement. Mules and ox carts permitted an advance of only about fifteen miles per day; any more than that and the supply network would fail. In 1813, for example, at a time when it took ten weeks for stores ordered from Portugal to reach the troops, the army was obliged to live off the countryside five days before Vitoria.[23]

The fundamental factor was that Britain fought on the soil of friendly nations and could not, unlike the French, seek local requisitions in an effort to make war pay for itself. To keep the natives friendly British armies had to rely on conventional methods of supply, using depots and convoys; in desolate parts of Spain the French had to resort to similar expedients, but it was never so integral a part of their strategy. Compared to Napoleon's sweeping movements, British operations were often ponderous because of these restrictions. In 1805 Lieutenant General Don reported from northern Germany that he hoped to form a supply network for the army assembling there in a 'few weeks': this after the vanguard had already been in the region for eight days.[24] Whatever the drawbacks of such arrangements, though, it is worth remembering that, in the Peninsula at least, the British logistical situation, and with it the efficiency of Wellington's troops, was invariably better than that of the French.

On the question of naval supply an infrastructure of suitable arrangements had gradually been built up as Britain evolved into a major maritime power. However, with the greater scale and complexity of the conflict after 1803, the system became larger, more flexible and more efficient. The necessity for this may immediately be indicated by observing that every seaman was entitled to a weekly diet of 7 lb of biscuit, 6 lb of salt meat, seven gallons of beer, two pints of pease and three pints of oatmeal, plus smaller quantities of butter, cheese and vinegar. When supplies were available, seamen were also issued fresh meat and vegetables.[25] With over 100,000 seamen and marines in the fleet from 1805 the total amounts of provisions that were required can be guessed at. Nor could any question of victualling be taken lightly by authorities eager to keep their naval personnel healthy and their ships effective.

On distant stations it was the practice, as with the army, to try and obtain local supplies as far as possible. Such a policy minimised the need for victualling ships from Britain and for local depots, but the policy had its drawbacks. In August 1805 the Victualling Board petitioned the Admiralty on behalf of one Thomas Pinckerton, a West Indies merchant who had contracted to supply the navy's vessels at Trinidad, Barbados and Antigua for twelve months. Faced by increasing costs, Pinckerton wanted a higher price for the provisions he provided. The board was sympathetic, pointing out that he had accumulated large stocks in anticipation of extensive demands from visting squadrons, only to discover in the event that their needs were small. This left the luckless contractor facing severe financial losses. The board knew the costs involved in maintaining depots on three separate islands and was conscious of the problems of securing future contracts were a man like Pinckerton to be ruined. It was noted that two other businessmen had turned down the contract before he had accepted it. Nor was this an isolated case. Another contractor, by the name of Donaldson, had the responsibility for victualling the Jamaica squadron, and he petitioned for similar relief in November 1805. Despite having previously been granted permission to increase his charges for bread and pease, he claimed to have lost £16,000 in twelve months and was seeking to raise the price of his salt beef and pork. Again the board supported the contractor, confirming that local costs had risen sharply, particularly as supplies of meat from Mexico were unavailable, and providing a testimonial to the effect that Donaldson had been provisioning vessels on the station for twenty-one years. Despite this the Admiralty turned the claim down, at which Donaldson responded by pointing out that he had bought up all the local provisions and that if the navy wanted local supplies they would have to come to him and he would charge what he liked![26]

The alternative to such contracts was to use naval-controlled victuallers and depots. This had to be the case in regions where supplies could not be had or where certain commodities were unavailable, but was just as costly and brought with it all the worries of hiring and moving tonnage. Local suppliers met peacetime needs, when squadrons were smaller and sudden changes in demand due to altered naval dispositions were not as likely, and this practice tended to continue in wartime. Furthermore, however much the navy had tried to manage its own logistics it would still have had to rely on local businessmen for local, i.e. fresh, food. This was even the case when dealing with less than friendly foreigners, Rear-Admiral Cochrane reporting from the blockade of Ferrol in 1804 that he was trying to secure supplies from the locals despite his opinion that they were blatantly dishonest.[27]

With local supplies often doubtful, in some respects at least, there was always a measure of dependence on stores from Britain. In the Mediterranean, despite the provision of water and foodstuffs from the North African states, navy victuallers were constantly needed. Eight such vessels totalling 2,059 tons were on the station during peacetime, but with the wartime expansion of the fleet there the number of victualling ships had risen to twenty-nine totalling 8,384 tons by 1807. Elsewhere at that time there were thirty-two other such ships, of 5,820 tons, in service, most employed in home waters but one being at Buenos Aires and two more at the Cape of Good Hope. The navy's victualling tonnage quadrupled during 1803–07 and was to do so again by 1812, the latter date seeing the employment of 109 vessels of 31,827 tons. To appreciate the scale of the board's responsibilities one need only study a report written in 1803 by two of its members about the stores held at Portsmouth and Plymouth, its main operational centres. Included in over thirty different types of commodity held were almost 2 million lb of biscuit/bread, over 150,000 gallons of beer, over 135,000 lb of beef and just under 30,000 cases of lemon juice. The two port admirals concerned both expressed their approval of the way matters pertaining to supply were being handled.[28]

The crux of this, of course, was the efficiency with which such supplies could be distributed to the squadrons that needed them, and in May 1808 the Admiralty laid down detailed instructions about how matters were to be dealt with respecting the Channel fleet, one of its largest formations and one conveniently situated under its eye. The intention was for all ships to be kept provisioned for five months, a situation allowing the pursuit of any escaping French warships without delays due to preliminary resupplying. To achieve this 2,200 tons of victuallers were to be either with the fleet or at Plymouth, containing food, coal and candles for one month, plus sufficient water for fourteen days. These vessels would operate a shuttle service, sailing from Plymouth once those at sea had exhausted their stocks. Similar arrangements were laid down for the detached squadron blockading l'Orient, though it was later reported that these ships, whose chief responsibility was supplying water, were largely superfluous, as the squadron could obtain a supply from some islands near by. The fleet's commander, Admiral Gambier, was told to make similar arrangements were any other squadrons to be sent on detached duty and also to send his ships back to port whenever possible so as to keep their crews refreshed.[29]

As might be imagined, such a complex logistical organisation did not always function without a hitch. The Portsmouth victualling office provided an example of how and why problems might occur when, in January 1808, it answered a complaint over the time taken to revictual some transports. The officials reported that when the transports arrived, in mid-November the previous year, there had also appeared sixteen ships of the line, plus frigates and sloops, from the Baltic, all of which were nearly out of provisions. Added to them there were already two ships of the line and sundry frigates in the port awaiting provisions for six months' sea service, and, finally, there were twenty-five other transports on their way to Ireland, all demanding supplies of water. Such an influx drained all the available stores of spirits, flour, pease, oatmeal and butter, there being delays while fresh stocks were procured.[30] Such problems were exceptional, but they provide an illustration of how even the day-to-day provision of supplies could run into congestion and delay. One anonymous officer, who claimed many years' experience in the victualling service and whose knowledge tends to confirm this, wrote to Mulgrave to express his fears for the Baltic fleet. He drew attention to the scattered nature of its service, making reprovisioning difficult, and that although the larger ships were fitted out for five months, this was not the case with the smaller vessels. Should supplies from Britain not reach the latter, they were obliged to take provisions from the bigger vessels and impair the efficiency of the whole force. Although Sweden could provide water, she could not supply bread, spirits or wine. With the fleet's 11,000 men consuming prodigious quantities of food each month, the writer was concerned that provisions from Britain were not sent sufficiently early. He backed this up with the startling statement that, two months after its arrival, Gambier's fleet at Copenhagen in 1807, although theoretically victualled for five months, was reduced to a two-thirds allowance of bread through unforseen circumstances.[31]

Such shortages could easily occur in the days of sail and limited means of preserving food. Equally they could be caused by negligence, but, overall, the navy's victualling was handled with considerable success. No great stories of corruption or failure were unearthed by St Vincent's investigations, and in March 1809 an attempt by one opposition MP to attack the board's supposed arrears and inefficiency got nowhere.[32] No major operation was wrecked through victualling failure and the daily grind of blockade was maintained. Given the scale of even routine operations, it was no mean feat.

Britain's most obvious strategic feature is her island nature. This has often enough proved to be her defensive salvation, but equally the sea makes her offensive operations difficult to implement. Any offensive strategy immediately brings with it the dangers and difficulties of overseas movement and possible amphibious landing. During 1803–15 procuring the necessary transport tonnage for any such movements of troops, supplies, ordnance and suchlike was the responsibility of the Transport Board, a body which also theoretically ensured that all hired vessels were of a suitable standard. For troop movements shipping was usually taken up at the rate of one and a half tons per man to be moved, though on long voyages to more distant areas the rate would be increased to two tons or more per man.[33] With compulsory requisition as intolerable as national conscription, such shipping as was required was hired from private shipowners at rates varying according to the length of the hiring and the quality of the vessel concerned. Britain maintained no regular system of service-controlled transports on any scale, converted merchant vessels being relied upon. Only towards the war's conclusion, and then only to a limited extent, did the situation start to change.

The board normally hired for three to six months, though longer or shorter periods were not unknown. The costs were formidable: one estimate for 1806 suggested that securing transports would consume £1·25 million, another for 1810 put that year's figure at £2·41 million and for 1813 it was £1·9 million. The average hiring rate in 1804 for copper-sheathed vessels, ships both faster and better founded, was 19*s* per ton per month; for vessels with unprotected wooden hulls the rate was less, most being raised at 17*s* per ton per month. At that time the board was employing 121 ships of 36,878 tons.[34] As time passed the demand for tonnage grew and with it the costs. In April 1807 an anxious Castlereagh permitted the board to raise the rates to 20*s* and 25*s* per ton for vessels hired for three and six months respectively. Thus stimulated, total hiring went from 115,157 tons in April to 167,734 tons by July.[35] By 1813 a desperate board was suggesting that British-owned, but not British-registered, vessels should be taken up for three months at 20*s* per ton. Bathurst agreed, but it did not end the problem. The end of the year saw the board increasing the rate and, still suffering a shortage, putting forward the notion that neutral vessels might be used, though only for moving stores and only at a moderate rate.[36]

Such reliance on civilian shipping was unsatisfactory in many ways. It was hard to stop owners taking advantage of the nation's needs to make inflated profits in much the same way as the timber cartel. In 1806, for example, the board acknowledged the difficulty: ministers would demand tonnage, but owners were likely to become hostile if, having hired their vessels at one price, they saw their commercial rivals leasing out at a new, increased, rate to meet sudden demand. In 1807 the board specifically blacklisted one broker by the name of Herring who had tried to prevent shipping being taken up at the usual rate by spreading rumours that a higher price would soon be offered. It seemed that Herring, whose honesty was already in question, had tried to secure a degree of monopoly by blocking the raising of tonnage, hoping that he might later provide the board with the tonnage it needed at a higher price and a larger commission for himself.[37]

In 1813 there was a more successful effort to get the rates increased when it was observed in February that, since the rate had been lowered from 25*s* to 21*s* per ton the previous April, shipping had become hard to find. By August the board was 10,000 tons short of requirements and bluntly stated that owners were deliberately withholding vessels to force the price up. Despite the expedient of turning to non-British-registered ships, the board was obliged to capitulate, offering the high price of 30*s* per ton for those who would lease British-registered ships for two months certain. It was the highest price paid during the whole war.[38]

Using more and more shipping for its own purposes also meant that government dislocated the nation's maritime trade and so impared its commercial well-being. C. N. Parkinson estimates the annual average merchant tonnage clearing Britain's ports in

1802–06 at 917,000 tons. Given that many vessels would enter and leave port more than once during a single year, the total tonnage from which a government could draw would have been much less. With the Transport Board regularly employing over 100,000 tons of shipping from 1805, the potential dislocation of the nation's trade was obvious. One especially vulnerable sector was the coal trade, its sturdy colliers being particularly favoured, and in the wake of the Helder expedition in 1799 it was severely disrupted, London's coal prices soaring as a result. The board acknowledged this problem in 1813: ' . . . the enormous quantity [of tonnage] already in service, is said to render Shipping difficult to be obtained for the purposes of Trade, and to have already materially affected the price of coals'. Castlereagh similarly referred to coal price rises in 1809 because of the number of 'North Country' vessels in service, observing freight rate increases for other commodities as well, particularly sugar.[39]

Civilian vessels once in service were often far from ideal. Lieutenant General Moore grumbled about the unwieldy nature of the convoy taking his troops to Sweden in 1808. He noted that it took seven or eight vessels to carry each battalion and that the resulting convoy numbered over 200 ships. He felt that much larger vessels, of at least 1,000 tons, were needed to make his command fully effective: 'what can a convoy of 200 small brigs do, commanded by North Country skippers who will do nothing but what they like themselves . . .?' Simply assembling such convoys was no easy matter. 'Everyone knows,' observed Perceval, 'how much time is consumed in getting Transports out of the River [Thames] to the Ports of departure and how many Expeditions have been delayed for weeks and sometimes months from that cause alone.'[40]

Moore's contempt for the transports' captains also highlights the antipathy between the crews and their military counterparts. Doubtless service snobbery played its part in this, most commonly in the frequently sour relations between naval officers and the merchant skippers in regular convoys. However, there were some legitimate grounds for complaint, Perceval referring to the 'very many delays, and not a few accidents, [that] are occasioned by the desertion, indiscipline, and want of Seamanship – both of Masters and Men in the Transports'. He also noted the grumbles of naval officers who:

> complain of the want of skill or discipline, or perhaps of physical means from inadequate crews in obeying their orders and signals; and indeed I

believe this is the constant complaint on every occasion when a large body of Transports is employed.[41]

In Lisbon Admiral Berkeley, commander of the Portuguese station, raged against the transports' crews, men who were under neither civil nor military command and who, he alleged, had been guilty of a variety of crimes, from robbery to murder. He complained that the only way to control them was via the threat of impressment, and that was illegal.[42] Individual examples tend to support these charges. One shipping firm in 1811 was mulcted of part of its fee because its ship missed a Lisbon convoy: two seamen had deserted and the master had not caught the wind. The firm was not to be paid while it waited for the next convoy and was also to be fined for having a vessel short of its complement. Rifleman Kincaid sailed to Portugal in 1810 and arrived damning the quality of the vessel and her master; the year before a drunken transport captain mistook England for Guernsey.[43]

As with the crews, so the vessels themselves caused concern. Perceval fretted that owners had little incentive to maintain their vessels properly, the scale of the service being such that the Transport Board could not adequately inspect all its ships. Even in 1813 the board would decline to hire if it discovered an unseaworthy vessel, but there were too many of them for this to have much effect. Popham criticised the condition of some of the transports sent to the Cape in 1805, while Berkeley thought some of those at Lisbon in 1810 'might almost occasion a mutiny in the army, if they knew to what rotten and dangerous ships they were consigned'. One decayed and unserviceable transport in the Tagus had just brought out the Brunswick Oels.[44]

The solution was a properly maintained and Admiralty-controlled body of military transports, in short the conversion of warships into transports. Being larger vessels, such ships could carry guns, baggage and ammunition as well as troops, and retaining some of their armaments would lessen the need for naval escorts. Under formal naval control their seaworthiness could be better maintained and their crews would become steadily more experienced in embarkation and disembarkation. Many believed that such increased efficiency would also be accompanied by financial savings. However, there were drawbacks. Some, such as Mulgrave, doubted whether such vessels would be effective, were not convinced that savings would result, and, most important of all, believed that conversions on any scale would deprive the navy of too many warships.[45]

In the event a compromise was reached. By 1808 some nineteen vessels, ranging from sloops to sixty-four-gun ships of the line, were being converted to carry 150–550 soldiers each. In September 1810 nine such ships, former frigates and small ships of the line, were sent to replace civilian vessels in the Tagus. Although few in number, they had the capacity to carry 3,000 men.[46] The navy could not provide the shipping to move large armies, but sufficient could be found to permit the rapid movement of small formations and as such did not harm its overall strength, while also allowing the dismissal of some civilian ships.

Had it been possible to convert more warships to transports it might have been possible to reduce the considerable risks involved when troops had to be landed by amphibious transfer on a hostile shore. The more rowing boats available and manned by experienced seamen the better, though even when large warships with boats to spare were available the landing capacity was still limited. A seventy-four-gun ship of the line had a boat capacity sufficient to move only 230 soldiers at any one time; a frigate enough for around a hundred. At the landing at New Orleans in 1815 only 2,825 troops could be put ashore in one wave, despite the fact that there were twenty-two ships of the line and frigates present.[47] Usually the support was much less. When Major General Fraser's expedition sailed to Egypt in 1807 nineteen out of his thirty-three transports got separated from the convoy, leaving him with few boats to make his landing near Alexandria, and that in rough weather. Only part of his initial group got ashore on the first day, the second having to wait, and no stores or provisions were disembarked at all. Eventually, with only 1,000 troops on hand, Fraser had to bluff his way into Alexandria. Nor was this an isolated incident. An unopposed landing in Denmark in 1807 took a week to complete and setting 9,000 men ashore at Mondego Bay in 1808 took five days. One participant in the latter operation spoke of a terrifying journey in a flat-bottomed boat through 'raging breakers' and of a 'roaring storm of foam'; the landing beach was marked by a chaos of men, animals, equipment and stores. Bad weather hampered the process and drowned four sailors. Another who went through this same landing wrote of one boat overturning and sixty men being drowned.[48]

If transporting men was difficult, moving horses verged on the impossible because of the vast tonnages required. It was stated in 1805 that to send 20,000 infantry across the North Sea to Hanover would require 30,000 tons of shipping: to send a mere 2,000 cavalry, however, would require 16,000 tons, and 1,500 artillery personnel with their appropriate equine establishment would take 10,000 tons. Such demands, coupled with the problems of having animals at sea for any length of time, meant that British expeditions tended to be notoriously short of both cavalry and artillery. Of the 26,000 troops eventually sent to Hanover in 1805 only just over 1,200 were cavalry and there were only three companies of artillery. Of Fraser's 5,813-strong force sent to Egypt in 1807 there were only forty dragoons and 286 artillerymen and staff: yet this meagre provision of horses consumed a tenth of the expedition's tonnage. After years of Peninsular campaigning horses still remained in short supply: in September 1811 Wellington commanded 46,731 British and Portuguese troops, of whom only 4,026 were cavalry and 1,051 artillery.[49]

Such shortages were a serious handicap. Cavalry was essential for reconnaissance, for pursuing a defeated enemy and for countering mounted assaults. Similarly artillery became ever more crucial in the European battles, yet Wellington's guns were usually as limited as his cavalry. This was not because Britain lacked such soldiers, but because they were difficult to transport overseas. In the case of artillery, moreover, with all its limbers, guns, ammunition and the like, it was also cumbersome to move when landed. Wellington estimated that it would take sixty-two days to move his siege train from Lisbon to Almeida; in the event it took even longer and required 384 pairs of oxen and 1,092 country carts.[50] Here again Britain was fortunate in campaigning primarily in the Peninsula. With so much of its terrain broken and rugged, British armies were not, as a rule, exposed to the full force of French cavalry charges and/or artillery fire. The French also found it hard to maintain their horses in the region, with a weakening effect on their own cavalry and artillery arms. Had Britain's armies campaigned in the plains of northern Europe these shortcomings could have had lethal consequences.

By way of a postscript to transport problems some brief mention should be made of the weather. Bearing in mind that sophisticated modern military plans can be hampered or wrecked by adverse weather conditions, how much more was this the case in the age of sail. Out of the navy's total loss of 317 ships in 1803–15, 223 were either wrecked or foundered, the great majority on account of hostile natural elements. Three ships of the line were lost in North Sea gales in December 1811 and 2,000 men perished: at Trafalgar, in comparison, the total British losses, killed and wounded, came to only 1,690. In December 1805 eight transports carrying troops to Germany were wrecked in a storm, 664 men being drowned and many of the 1,552 who were saved being washed up on the wrong side of the Channel and taken prisoner. In March 1810 Cadiz harbour was struck by a gale, a transport with 125 soldiers on board being driven on to the French-controlled shore: five Spanish and Portuguese ships of the line and more than twenty other vessels were also lost.[51]

The weather could impede strategy in less destructive ways as well. Castlereagh complained in November 1805 that adverse winds were delaying troop movements, and similarly in December 1813 Bathurst lamented that troops intended for service in Holland had not been able to sail for a fortnight. He later considered, rather optimistically, that had they been able to sail on time, then Antwerp and Bergen-op-Zoom could have been captured easily.[52] The mere threat of hostile conditions could thwart military intentions, as when Collingwood dashed plans for an attack on Cadiz in 1807 by pointing out the dangers from the weather from October onwards.[53] For expeditions that did reach their destination in one piece and with the minimum of delay, the effects of a sea voyage could still severely impair the troops' effectiveness. Days spent in seasickness and nausea could leave them debilitated and unfit for active duty. At the height of summer one officer on the Copenhagen expedition in 1807 wrote of a 'hard gale', 'adverse wind and high sea' and a 'storm' within the course of his voyage, only to find on arrival that a lack of wind delayed the disembarkation![54]

One final impediment to strategic planning was the question of military intelligence. In general in this crucial area Britain was very poorly served, particularly compared to Napoleon. There was no formal organisation, either independent or attached to the armed forces, designed to acquire and asses information. The chief source of peacetime intelligence came from diplomats abroad, and they continued to be relied upon once hostilities had broken out. Thus in 1805 Thorton, the minister accredited to the Hanse, sent home a series of reports on French military activity in northern Germany, including details of Bernadotte's preparations to march his I Corps out of Hanover and of the supposed military preparations of Prussia.[55] Such reports were obviously valuable as the Cabinet made its plans, but as Napoleon swept from victory to victory the friendly or neutral states from which men like Thornton could operate became fewer and fewer. By 1807 almost all of western Europe had been rendered hostile, and those countries like Portugal where diplomats might still work tended to be on the periphery of events and so of limited usefulness.

Once the diplomats are discounted, Britain's intelligence-gathering was hard placed. There were friendly agents in Europe, but there is little to suggest that their murky activities were encountered with any great success. In 1806 there were complaints that the intelligence gathered by a network of spies run from the Channel Islands by Rear-Admiral D'Auvergne was deficient. Ministers in London were annoyed that reports that France was on the verge of chaos in the wake of defeats in Moravia turned out to be celebrations after the victory of Austerlitz.[56] Only rarely were important military details passed on either by agents or from other potential sources of information, viz. deserters or prisoners from Napoleon's forces, escaped or exchanged British prisoners of war, and smugglers. The ability, for example, of a civilian or a soldier to comment usefully on French naval preparations was limited. Smugglers in particular were looked to for regular items of information, but such professional criminals were even more dubious than other sources and were just as likely to be double agents working for the French as well.[57]

An instance of this weakness on Britain's part came in the shape of a series of papers published in 1810 indicating the chaotic intelligence situation prior to the departure of the Walcheren expedition the previous year. During March–May 1809 a series of reports put the Walcheren garrison at 5,000 men, 4,000 men, 3,000 men and 1,400 men. Another said that there were only 10,000 troops in the whole Cadsand area, with another 10,000 on their way to Walcheren itself. Yet another said that there were only 8,400 soldiers in the whole of Holland![58] After the expedition's failure Chatham confessed that beforehand he had had no precise knowledge of the position of Antwerp's arsenals, had only a vague idea of the city's fortifications and had not been provided with a detailed map of the place. Indicative of the whole unprofessional approach was that Chatham was provided with money to finance secret service activities only a mere twelve days before he sailed. As late as August 1809 he referred to his intelligence being 'so vague and unsatisfactory, that any opinion I can venture to give [on future operations] must be formed on very insufficient grounds'.[59]

Throughout the war there were numerous instances of poor military intelligence or, alternatively, no sort of intelligence at all. In 1805 the only available map of Hanover came from the King's library: there was none at all for the area outside the electorate. In 1806–07 naval Captain Dunbar twice visited Copenhagen, each time reporting that the Danish fleet was being prepared for sea and would soon be ready; Lord Pembroke, accompanying Dunbar on the second occasion, supported this conclusion. Yet after the city's capture, although a part of the fleet was quickly readied for sailing, much of it took six weeks of intense effort to make seaworthy. In 1808, with a force soon to be sent to Sweden, Castlereagh confessed an almost complete ignorance of the region in which it was to operate, his lack of knowledge including fundamental questions relating to the strength, positions and morale of the Swedish, Norwegian and Russian armies. In the same year Arthur Wellesley led his army to Portugal and hoped to fight in the environs of Lisbon: there was no map of the area outside the capital. That he was sent at all was in part due to a report from Rear-Admiral Cotton that Junot had only 4,000 troops in the country: in fact the French were considerably stronger.[60]

Notes

1 The army's organisation and tactics are well covered in H. C. B. Rogers, *Wellington's Army*, London, 1979, and P. J. Haythornthwaite, *Wellington's Military Machine*, Kent, 1989. For a brilliant study of naval matters see Lavery.

2 R. Glover, *Peninsular Preparation*, pp. 46–61. Buckinghamshire R.O., Hobart Papers, D/MH/H/War C96. P.R.O. ADM 2/1361.

3 Leeds R.O., Harewood Collection, Canning Papers, 31, Canning to Chatham, 11 July 1809. Canning had raised the matter on 23 July, 17 and 30 September and 21 November 1808; and on 14 January, 9 March, 11 and 20 April and 23 June 1809.

4 Sherwig, pp. 191–2, 237 n, 276–7, 280, 305–7, 310 n. and 316 n. B.M. Add. Mss 37051, Bunbury Papers, ff. 82–3v.

5 Northern Ireland R.O., Castlereagh Papers, D3030/1857.

6 G. Marcus, *The Age of Nelson*, London, 1971, p. 281. Devon R.O., 152m, Sidmouth Papers, C1803/ON. Northern Ireland R.O., Castlereagh Papers, D3030/1902.

7 R. Morriss, *The Royal Dockyards during the Revolutionary and Napoleonic Wars*, Leicester, 1983, pp. 18–25 and 44.

8 Morriss, pp. 78–83. R. G. Albion, *Forests and Sea Power*, Cambridge, Mass., 1926, particularly pp. 318–22, 375 and 388. B. Pool, *Navy Board Contracts, 1660–1832*. London, 1966, pp. 117 and 135. By 1812 15 per cent of timber imports came from North America.

9 Albion, pp. 323–4 and 382–3. Marcus, pp. 231–41. R. Glover, 'The French fleet, 1807–14: Britain's problem; and Madison's opportunity', *Journal of Modern History*, 39, 1967, p. 237.

10 Albion, pp. 392–5 and appendix D, p. 420.

11 P.R.O. ADM 2/1363, ff. 113–14 and 130–2. James, IV, appendix 15, p. 506.

12 P.R.O. ADM 109/105.

13 Ward, pp. 81–2. G. E. Watson, 'The United States and the Peninsular War, 1808–12', *Historical Journal*, XIX, 1976, pp. 870–1. National Army Museum, Marsden Papers, 7701–36–84 and 7701–36–92.

14 P.R.O. ADM 109/105 and WO 1/882, pp. 455–9.

15 P.R.O. ADM 109/106 and 107.

16 P.R.O. WO 1/904, pp. 374–5. D. W. Davies, *Sir John Moore's Peninsular Campaign, 1808–09*, The Hague, 1974, pp. 71–2.

17 Oman, p. 313. National Army Museum, Kennedy Papers 1811–13, 7807–22. Marsden Papers, 7701–36–24.

18 Ward, pp. 70–3. Castlereagh Correspondence, VI, p. 396. E. Herries, *Memoir of the Public Life of the Right Hon. John Charles Herries*, London, 1880, I, pp. 25–6. For some interesting examples of the sorts of embezzlement indulged in by commissaries on campaign see R. N. Buckley (ed.), *The Napoleonic War Journal of Captain Thomas Henry Browne, 1807–16*, London, 1987, pp. 202–3.

19 Ward, pp. 77–9. Herries, pp. 37–41.

20 Ward, pp. 82–3 and 89–90. P.D., XIV, pp. 609–21. Sir C. Oman, *History of the Peninsular War*, London, 1902–30, IV, appendix XX, p. 647. R. Glover, *Britain at Bay. Defence against Bonaparte, 1803–14*, London, 1973, pp. 36 n. – 37 n., erroneously says that the 'happy-go-lucky' system of hiring waggons had been abandoned in 1762: the Waggon Train as constituted was far too small to act as a replacement.

21 Ward, pp. 84–9. B.M. Add. Mss 58948, Dropmore Papers, f. 110v.

22 Ward, pp. 90–1. M. Glover, pp. 105–9. Oman, *Wellington's Army*, pp. 307–16. Gurwood, IX, p. 319. P.R.O. WO 1/632. Fortescue, *British Army*, 5, pp. 392–3, 399, 400 and 404.

23 Ward, pp. 97–101. Fortescue, *British Army*, 7, p. 380.

24 Sandon Hall, Harrowby Papers, XXIX, f. 49v.

25 Greenwich Maritime Museum, Victualling Papers, ADM/D 46.

26 P.R.O. ADM 110/53, pp. 163–5, 374–6 and 435–44.

27 Greenwich Maritime Museum, Victualling Papers, ADM/C 702.

28 P.R.O. ADM 1/3743, List of Victuallers, 1 January 1803. ADM 1/3751, Transport Office abstract, 7 February 1807. WO 1/812, p. 127. Greenwich Maritime Museum, Victualling Papers, ADM/D 45.

29 P.R.O. ADM 2/1385, pp. 287–91 and 319. Also R. Glover, *Britain at*

Bay, pp. 73–5.

30 P.R.O. ADM 109/106. The whole matter began with a complaint to the Transport Board about its delays, the explanation pointing to problems of repairing and then victualling its vessels: see P.R.O. WO 6/156, p. 336, and WO 1/803, pp. 249–52.

31 Leeds University Library, Brotherton Collection Box VII, Mulgrave Papers, 20/30.

32 Pope, p. 259. Harvey, p. 247.

33 Leeds University Library, Brotherton Collection Box VII, Mulgrave Papers, 19/29. *Castlereagh Correspondence*, VI, p. 254. Craufurd's force for South America in 1806 sailed with the provision of two and a half tons per man: P.R.O. ADM 1/3751.

34 B.M. Add. Mss 59289, Dropmore Papers, f. 62. *British Sessional Papers, Accounts and Reports*, XII, f. 67, and XIII, p. 261. P.R.O. WO 1/802, p. 73.

35 P.R.O. WO 6/156, p. 348. ADM 1/3751 and 3752.

36 P.R.O. WO 1/814, pp. 73–4 and 363–6.

37 P.R.O. WO 1/803, pp. 77–83 and 141–5.

38 P.R.O. WO 1/813, pp. 173–8. WO 1/814, pp. 73–5 and 363.

39 C. N. Parkinson, *The Trade Winds. A Study of British Overseas Trade during the French Wars, 1793–1815*, London, 1948, p. 84. P. Mackesy, *Statesmen at War. The Strategy of Overthrow, 1798–99*, London, 1974, p. 112. P.R.O. WO 1/814, p. 74. *Castlereagh Correspondence*, VI, p. 256.

40 B.M. Add. Mss 49482, Gordon Papers, ff. 65–6. Leeds University Library, Brotherton Collection Box VII, Mulgrave Papers, 19/29.

41 Leeds University Library, Brotherton Collection Box VII, Mulgrave Papers, 19/29.

42 Greenwich Maritime Museum, Yorke Papers, YOR/2, letter 14. See also P.R.O. WO 1/808, pp. 416–17.

43 Greenwich Maritime Museum, Papers of Henley, Michael & Son, HNL/13/20, letter 16. J. Kincaid, *Adventures in the Rifle Brigade and Random Shots from a Rifleman*, London, 1981, p. 3. M. Roberts, *The Whig Party, 1807–12*, London, 1939, p. 138 n.

44 Leeds University Library, Brotherton Collection Box VII, Mulgrave Papers, 19/29. Greenwich Maritime Museum, Papers of Henley, Michael & Son, HNL/14/5, letters 5–8. *The Naval Miscellany*, III, p. 235. *H.M.C. Bathurst*, p. 149. Greenwich Maritime Museum, Yorke Papers, YOR/2, letter 20.

45 For the enthusiastic views of Perceval, Melville and Berkeley see, respectively, Leeds University Library, Brotherton Collection Box VII, Mulgrave Papers, 19/29; *P.D.*, XVII, pp. 89–104; Historic Manuscripts Commission Report on the Manuscripts at Cirencester Park, 1923, p. 149 (afterwards referred to as H. M. C. Bathurst). For Mulgrave's doubts see *P.D.*, XVII, p. 115.

46 Leeds University Library, Brotherton Collection Box VII, Mulgrave Papers, 27/1. P.R.O. ADM 2/1370, p. 394. Over a hundred military transports, carrying some 24,000 troops, were employed in the Walcheren cam-

paign, but the short distance involved meant that this was an isolated example: *Castlereagh Correspondence*, VI, pp. 254–6 and 276.

47 Greenwich Maritime Museum, Journal of Sir Pultney Malcolm, MAL/104, pp. 38–9.

48 B.M. Add. Mss 49495, Gordon Papers, ff. 62–4v. P. Mackesy, 'Problems of an amphibious power: Britain against France, 1793–1815'. *Naval War College Review*, spring 1978, p. 19. A. Ludovici (ed.), *On the Road with Wellington*, London, 1924, pp. 1–8. Sir R. Henegan, *Seven Years Campaigning in the Peninsula and the Netherlands from 1808 to 1815*, London, 1846, I, pp. 12–14.

49 P.R.O. WO 6/13, pp. 8–9 and 132–3. Fortescue, *British Army*, 5, p. 296n. Greenwich Maritime Museum, Duckworth Papers, DUC/13, 38 MS 2136. Oman, *Peninsular War*, IV, appendix XX, p. 647.

50 M. Glover, *The Peninsular War, 1807–14. A Concise Military History*, Newton Abbot, 1974, pp. 173–4.

51 James, IV, p. 29; V, pp. 349–50; VI, appendix 17, p. 507. Lewis, pp. 356–60. *Castlereagh Correspondence*, VI, p. 125. Sir William Stuart, *Cumloden Papers*, Edinburgh, 1871, I, pp. 71–2; II, Brigadier General Stewart to Wellington, 11 March 1810.

52 *Castlereagh Correspondence*, VI, p. 43. *S.D.W.*, VII, pp. 414 and 450.

53 *Castlereagh Correspondence*, VI, pp. 157–60.

54 J. H. Leslie (ed.), 'The diary of First Lieutenant William Swabey, Royal Artillery, 28 July to 31 October 1807', *Journal of the Royal United Service Institution*, 61, no. 441, February 1916, pp. 67–72.

55 P.R.O. FO 933/4, Thornton Papers, no. 56, pp. 87–9; no. 57, pp. 91–3; and no. 60, pp. 99–100.

56 P.R.O. WO 6/1, pp. 226–7.

57 R. Glover, *Britain at Bay*, pp. 51–2 and nn. 48 and 49.

58 *Naval Chronicle*, XXIII, London, 1810, pp. 116–17, 119 and 121–2.

59 *P.D.*, XV, pp. cclii–ccliv. R. Glover, *Peninsular Preparation*, p. 22. *Castlereagh Correspondence*, VI, p. 302.

60 R. Glover, *Peninsular Preparation*, pp. 20–2. A. N. Ryan, 'The causes of the British attack upon Copenhagen in 1807', *English Historical Review*, LXVIII, 1953, pp. 43–5. N. A. M. Rodger (ed.), *The Naval Miscellany*, V, London, 1984, p. 301. B.M. Add. Mss 57539, Moore Papers, Castlereagh to Lt.-Colonel Murray, 20 April 1808. Aspinall, V, p. 93.

3

The political background

The political framework and condition of any nation fighting a war inevitably have a great impact upon the way strategy is formulated and pursued. Britain in 1803–15 was no exception, and to modern eyes the most immediate and obvious shortcoming at the time was the absence of any formal, wide-ranging political unity with which to face the French threat. Both world wars in the twentieth century eventually saw the formation of such coalitions, yet the years of struggle against Napoleon, though lasting longer and witnessing crises of equal magnitude, did not see any sort of unity among the warring political factions in Parliament. Even the so-called 'Ministry of all the Talents', however cynically that misleading title was bestowed, did not constitute any sort of political grand alliance, excluding as it did the Pittite faction, the war's most dedicated proponents. This situation is all the more surprising bearing in mind the greater degree of unity in the previous decade after the Portland Whigs had joined Pitt in 1794. The notion of national unity in the face of external threat was not an alien one to early nineteenth-century Britain, but it never took shape after 1803.

Not only was there no political coalition but, more importantly, once individual ministers achieved office they showed few signs of retaining their post for any length of time. During the twelve years under consideration there were no fewer than six different ministries, these incorporating six different Prime Ministers, nine Foreign Secretaries and seven Secretaries for War. For a more detailed illustration of how the primary strategic offices of state changed hands again and again, see appendix 1.

Such fluidity did not help ministers become fully acquainted with the individual demands of their particular departments. Nor did it, in the whirl of political manoeuvring, necessarily bring those most suited to positions of strategic responsibility into positions of power. Indeed, as will be shown later, many individuals of ability were actually driven out of office for varying lengths of time. A coalition would not, of course, automatically have given the most crucial positions to those best suited to hold them, but it would have increased the chance of it and would, at least, have given men of mediocre ability some security of tenure and the opportunity to accumulate experience and skill. As it was, Pitt returned to power in 1804 having to put figures like Harrowby and Mulgrave at the Foreign Office, appointees who reflected Pitt's political weakness rather than their ability. Similarly his first colleague at the War Office, Camden, has been described as a mere cypher.[1] Windham displayed great powers of intellect, but in office also showed a propensity to unpractical flights of military fancy. Two others, Chatham and Richard Wellesley, were prominent in government but also notoriously indolent – though Wellesley was far from incompetent when he did stir himself – and Ryder brought neither great talent nor practical experience to the Home Office.[2]

However, there is one very positive aspect to be discerned in all this. If offices changed hands regularly, it at least tended to happen within the same group of politicians, so bringing a measure of continuity to the Cabinet's overall composition. Thus Hawkesbury, second Earl of Liverpool from 1808, served in all Cabinets of the period except that of the Talents in 1806–07. Castlereagh spent eight of the twelve years in ministerial positions and Mulgrave did even better with a total of ten years' experience. Another holder of an assortment of posts was Bathurst, a Cabinet fixuture from 1807. These men accumulated great experience with the passage of time and could bring their knowledge to bear in discussion of strategic matters. Alongside them, moreover, were some other figures who had reserves of experience dating back to periods in office in the previous century: prominent among these were Pitt, Melville (the former Henry Dundas), William Grenville and Portland.

From the fluctations previously noted it will be apparent that the period saw moments of high political drama and turbulence. In 1804 Pitt returned to office amidst the dissatisfaction at Addington's seeming strategic lassitude. Yet, for all his reputation, Pitt brought no politicians of substance with him, other than Melville; nor could the new ministry secure a larger Commons majority than the one

Addington faced when he resigned.[3] When the Portland Cabinet collapsed in 1809 the country was without an effective government for three weeks while the politicians bickered and intrigued. Not until October, when Perceval became Prime Minister on the 4th, did any sort of order return, and then the new ministry was weak and not expected to survive long. Perceval experienced great difficulty in persuading people to serve, one stating that he would not embark 'in a crazy vessel' that would be 'wrecked . . . at the commencement of the Session'. Just as significant, Richard Wellesley joined the Cabinet only in the confident expectation that it would be easy to dominate.[4] Though Perceval, with growing stature, held his ministry together, it was beset by constant crisis: from the Walcheren inquiry, through the bullion reports and attacks on policy towards the United States, to Wellesley's eventual resignation. Such a political base was far from ideal when fighting so dangerous an enemy as Napoleon. Wellington scathingly remarked in 1810 that 'The Government are terribly afraid that I shall get them, and myself, into a scrape. But what can be expected of men who are beaten in the House of Commons three times a week?'[5] Following Perceval's assassination in May 1812 a state of chaos returned similar to that which had marked the demise of Portland's ministry. After an initial decision to remain in office, the incumbents resigned after the loss of a Commons vote. Then for two and a half weeks there was no government in being at all while the bargaining process between the factions continued, the final outcome being the ludicrous one of Liverpool and his self-same colleagues returning to the positions they had just vacated. Once again it was the received wisdom that the government would not survive long: it lasted, in the event, until 1827.[6]

In part the political weaknesses that impinged on strategy may be ascribed to the relationship between monarchy and Parliament. Although George III was a constitutional monarch, because the Commons included many independent-minded backbenchers from country seats, men who saw themselves, when bothering to attend, as loyal supporters of the King's government, the royal attitude could not be ignored. George III inspired both loyalty and respect, factors stemming from his social position and from the longevity of a reign begun in 1760: with his power to dismiss ministers and enjoy influence in the Commons those seeking office had to be wary of his opinions. The royal will could not fly in the face of a Parliament which had made up its mind, as when Addington's ministry collapsed despite continued royal support, but it was an important political factor to cultivate.

Certainly the King was no mere rubber stamp when it came to military policy. If Rose is to be believed, George III vigorously supported the notion of pursuing the war in an energetic manner and in 1804 put his weight behind the strategy of seeking European allies.[7] Prior to this he had expressed his views on lesser military matters, urging Hobart to order the capture of any French West Indian islands which might be vulnerable to attack. Such interests continued, the King urging in 1807 that careful logistical arrangements be made in the event of any force being sent to northern Germany. He also suggested that units in the Mediterranean intended to be positioned at Gibraltar as a strategic reserve might be better placed in Britain, where they would not suffer from cramped quarters and limited provisions. George III even took the liberty at one point of reminding Castlereagh that the terms of service for the King's German Legion precluded its use outside Europe.[8] In general he took an advisory and cautionary approach to military matters, not as a rule trying to press his views even when he felt them strongly. Judging from the urgency with which he exhorted Castlereagh to withdraw the troops from Egypt in 1807, for example, one can suspect that the venture had not been to his taste. However, he had not tried to thwart the Talents over their original dispatch.[9] He also felt grave moral reservations and some practical fears respecting the Cabinet's Danish policy in the same year, but again he did not try to force it to change its decisions other than by force of argument.[10]

Where the King became a more serious obstacle was when his personal prejudices came into play, this happening twice during the period and with significant results. That no widespread coalition was ever formed to fight the war was in part due to George III. Some such administration had seemed to be forming in the early part of 1804 as the Foxite and Grenvillite sections of the opposition drew closer to each other, the Foxite leaders increasingly moving away from their demands for reform and civil liberties, two issues formerly putting them beyond the pale in aristocratic Grenvillite eyes, while over the questions of Catholic Emancipation and reform in Ireland the two groups were in agreement. The Foxites also shared some of William Grenville's economic theories.[11] Although mutually suspicious, the two groups did pose a threat to Addington's government, and adding to this danger was the attitude of Pitt. He had initially avoided open opposition to Addington, but became increasingly critical of the war's conduct and moved slowly towards definite hostility. As the Premier's authority began to crumble the possibility grew of a replacement ministry comprising the followers of Pitt, Grenville and Fox. This would have included most of the active politicians in Parliament. Canning wrote in March 1804, 'Much talk about Fox: P[itt]'s mind softened towards him. Great hopes of his consenting to propose to the K[ing] to make a Govt.'[12] This prospect was shattered by George III's loathing of Fox and his resistance to any idea of Catholic Relief, an issue which had prompted Pitt's resignation in 1801 and which, although regarded as necessary by the three political groups, was a matter in which the royal hostility was very much in line with the prejudices of many independent MPs. When holding an audience with Pitt in May, George III made it quite clear that he would not accept Fox, thought he would agree to some of his followers and the Grenvillites. Despite his professions in support of national unity, however, William Grenville would not lead his faction into a coalition without Fox, an attitude his followers endorsed. Consequently Pitt was left to form a very narrow administration and the chance of a broader-based government had been lost.[13]

When Pitt's ministry collapsed with his death in January 1806, the King had no alternative but to accept a Cabinet including the hated Fox. But if his presence was briefly tolerated (Fox died in September 1806) there was still no willingness to compromise over the Catholic question, a suggestion George III interpreted as flying in the face of his role as head of the Church of England. For the new ministers, though, Ireland was a matter of vital stategic importance. Fox had hoped in 1803 that Catholic Emancipation would be introduced, writing that such a step 'might certainly if steadily pursued, have a very good effect, because . . .' the Irish 'probably would be less inclined to France and less willing to join in any rash attempt at risings, etc'.[14] At the other end of the Talents' thinking Grenville held similar views. Writing soon after they had left office, he grimly expressed forebodings that Britain could never prevent a France that controlled the coasts from Stockholm to Alexandria from landing troops in Ireland. In such circumstances little resistance could be expected from the Irish themselves, the Catholics there having previously avoided action against Britain only because of their hope of emancipation. With the Talents' fall that hope had disappeared. To hold Ireland, he believed, Britain had to win the sympathies of the majority of her people. 'Unless this be done, they will still believe that in resisting French invasion they are fighting your battle and not their own.' Such arguments had been pressed unavailingly on the King.[15] The Talents wanted to throw commissions in the armed forces open to Catholics and to allow Catholic troops freedom of religion. This would have eliminated religious discrimination and reduced Irish discontent, so allowing British governments more effectively to tap Irish manpower for military recruitment.[16] George III, however, maintained his adamant veto on the proposal, following it up by an insistence that his ministers refrain from raising the subject again. Faced with this the Talents resigned, the King thus removing one set of ministers and profoundly influencing strategy. He had restricted Ireland's value, had ensured that that country remained an uncertain area requiring garrisons at occupation levels, and had effectively eliminated the one ministry in the period that had tried to alter some of the fundamentals of British strategy.

The Monarchy's power was felt in other ways as well. George III's mental instability returned in 1804 and permanently afflicted him from 1810, the latter bringing with it all the uncertainties of a regency. To ministers directing the war there was, therefore, the additional worry of a monarch who could suddenly become incapable of conducting business. This was an embarrassment at the best of times, but when a government was trying to appear as a credible ally in the eyes of the rest of Europe, the collapse, or potential collapse, of the head of state was a disaster.[17] The King's condition also obliged ministers to tread warily with him for fear of a relapse, although his stubbornness over the Catholic question illustrated that he could still maintain his views when he wished. From 1811 relations between monarchy and government were to become even more uneasy with the presence of the Prince of Wales as regent, a figure previously associated with the opposition in general and Fox in particular.

For all the pressures working on government, though, there was no general administrative collapse. Despite their supposed weakness, the ministries of Perceval and Liverpool gained in stature and strength with the passage of time. That the Pitt and Perceval governments fell at all was due only to the death of the Premier, and the Portland Cabinet shattered only because of a mixture of the Premier's incapacity and the bickering of his ministers. The essential feature which must be stressed in these years is that, if ministries were often uncertain and weak, the condition of the opposition groups in Parliament was even worse. With politics lacking the more rigid party structures of the twentieth century, there was tremendous scope for division and dissent among the assorted factions which loosely constituted the 'opposition' and which did not have the cement of office to bind them together. Ministries had to win and maintain the support of the general body of parliamentary opinion, a support that could not be mobilised by the dictates of party dogma or the discipline of the three-line whip. With the exception of their brief tenure of office in 1806–07, the opposition bodies were never able to project themselves as a credible alternative to those in power. This failure was linked to a great extent with their inability to put forward ideas for a convincing strategy against Napoleon, an inability that allowed incumbent ministers to retain power by default at moments of setback and crisis.

Although the Foxites and Grenvillites formed a powerful group opposing Addington in 1804, they could not force themselves on a King able to turn to Pitt. Even on coming to office in 1806 they could not completely eliminate their factional differences. William Grenville had become disillusioned with Continental alliances after his experience in the 1790s and in this at least he agreed with Fox, who had feared in 1804 that luring Austria into war might destroy that country, and who had felt the following year that the Third Coalition would 'end in making Bonaparte as much in effect monarch of Germany as he is in France'.[18] However, such unity of thought was not shared among their followers. Windham and Thomas Grenville tended to veer from supporting the strategy of seeking allies, to an attitude, after Austerlitz, of greater caution. Even then Thomas Grenville was never completely opposed to what might be termed a 'European orientation'. Similarly Grey, although Fox's disciple and heir to his leadership, was an advocate during the Talents' administration of the value of European allies, urging support for both Russia and Prussia. The entry of Sidmouth into the Cabinet after Fox's death furthered such divisions: he went along with the isolationist strategy, but had sought Continental allies when he was Premier.

It was also a problem that the Grenvillites in 1806 were unwilling to launch attacks on Pitt, a former political ally – a reluctance not shared by the Foxites, to whom he had always been anathema. It was a constant source of embarrassment to the two groups that William Grenville in particular had been so closely associated with Pitt and his followers in the 1790s. Grenville tried to end factional politics in 1804 and once that has failed did not quite know how to proceed. For his part Fox always felt a measure of contempt for his new allies which was doubtless mirrored by his close followers. 'I have,' he commented on his Grenville partners, 'a dread of arguing with obstinate men, lest one rivet them faster in their absurdities.' On an earlier occasion he had noted the 'strong impression which many of my friends entertain against Windham, and everything of the name of Grenville'.[19]

Peace was also a bone of contention, there being differences not only over strategy but over whether the war should be fought at all. For Fox peace was an immediate necessity, but it meant accepting Napoleon's rule of France, an uncomfortable notion for Grenville's supporters. They preferred the removal of the emperor and a restoration of the European equilibrium of 1789; Windham in particular favoured a Bourbon restoration, an ideal quite alien to Foxite thinking. Fox was able to persuade his Cabinet colleagues that peace was essential in the wake of the Third Coalition's collapse, but the attempt got nowhere and the Talents were quickly back among the dilemmas of their military policy. Certainly their period in office did nothing to lessen their differences, and the eventual inclusion of Sidmouth and Erskine, as Lord President of the Council and Lord Chancellor respectively, though reinforcing retrenchment and home defence, placed a fifth column of opposition within the Cabinet to any idea of Catholic Emancipation.[20] Nor should social strains be ignored among these divisive elements. The Grenvillite nobility and their prudish wives were disgusted by the hard-living, hard-drinking style of many Foxites; they also sneered at the humble origins of men like Whitbread and Sheridan.[21]

The Whigs left office in 1807 in some disarray, their disunity getting worse in opposition and their leadership being very poor. The death of Fox deprived them of their best orator, and their Commons position was further weakened by Howick's elevation to the Lords in November 1807 as Earl Grey. Thereafter in the lower House they were something of a rudderless ship. The natural successor to Howick in terms of ability was Whitbread, but he was detested by the Grenvillites. In consequence the leadership mantle fell on Ponsonby, a compromise candidate who satisfied nobody. A failed

Irish Chancellor, he aroused the suspicions of the independent members while winning the support of neither the radical nor the moderate Irish members. Personally he was clumsy and slovenly and no figure to rouse the Commons against the government.[22] Overall opposition leadership rested with Lords Grenville and Grey, yet neither applied much energy to the task. After 1807 Grenville viewed any prospect of a return to office with distaste as a reimposition of 'fetters' which he found 'galling'. Both were markedly reluctant to leave the comfort of their country estates, Grey, in Northumberland, being notorious in this respect: Fox had pestered him repeatedly in 1804–05 to come to Westminster, observing in exasperation to Lord Holland that 'Grey, at Howick, is as difficult to fetch to town, as you from Spain.' During the regency crisis in 1810 Grey would remain on his estate despite the vulnerability of Perceval's government.[23]

Yet another problem was the uncertain relationship between the opposition leaders and their main royal ally, the Prince of Wales. Although he had been cultivated by Fox, William Grenville detested him and both he and Grey avoided him whenever possible. Matters were further soured when Grenville supported the restrictions placed on the Prince's powers in Perceval's Regency Bill, his hand being forced when the *Sun* printed his speeches of 1788 supporting then the sort of restrictions presently being proposed by Perceval. This did not stop many of his opposition colleagues being furious. Weak and vain as he was, the Prince Regent was infuriated by the arrogant and unbending tone adopted towards him by the two opposition peers, their dislike of Sheridan, a close ally of the Prince's, also doing nothing to smoothe ruffled royal feathers. This all helped to ensure that the Whigs were unable to oust Perceval following George III's final collapse at the end of 1810, or thereafter once the Prince Regent had assumed full royal powers early in 1812. That the government was not dismissed during 1811 caused great surprise, but, although never very comfortable with his Prime Minister, the Prince Regent did move close enough to abandon his previous sympathy for Catholic Emancipation.[24]

Alongside these failures was the obvious bankruptcy of the opposition's military ideas. After 1807 they had to labour under the disadvantage of their failures while in office, particularly the defeats at Buenos Aires, in Egypt and at Constantinople. Such a record did little to convince MPs of their suitability for office. There also remained the question of war or peace, for although Fox's demise removed the chief pacifist, Whitbread kept the flame burning. Yet, like so many such idealists since, he tended to go too far and to regard the enemy in too favourable a light, the ceaseless wails for a negotiated peace verging on the unpatriotic and tending to tar other, more realistic, opposition members with the same brush. That similarly facile sentiments were repeatedly expressed by Whig journals like the *Edinburgh Review* and the *Morning Chronicle* only furthered doubts respecting the Whigs' motives and competence.[25]

In terms of their actual strategic ideas, the opposition were a shambles. Their criticisms early in 1808 of the decisive steps taken against the Danish and Portuguese fleets merely made them look churlish. Privately William Grenville admitted that Denmark had appeared hostile to Britain while the Talents were in office, and he blundered when attacking the forced evacuation of the Portuguese court, the ministry being able to show that the Talents had had a similar step in mind in 1806.[26] Over the more protracted struggle in the Peninsula the opposition were similarly inadequate. Initially most Whigs saw the Spanish uprising as some sort of crusade of light against darkness and were among the most enthusiastic proponents of aid and support for the Spaniards. This ardour rapidly cooled after the disappointments of the Convention of Cintra, the routing of the Spanish armies at the end of 1808 and Moore's retreat to Corunna. By early 1809 William Grenville, one of the few who had a jaundiced view of the revolt from the beginning, began to receive support in his pessimism from some of the leading opposition figures, men like Grey, Horner, Lauderdale and Fitzpatrick. But this just widened the gulf between those opposition members who backed the campaign and those who did not. Grenville himself did not want to exacerbate these divisions by making a parliamentary issue out of it. Against this the Foxites were eager to see Moore, a good Whig, absolved from any blame for the Corunna failure while simultaneously loading any odium for the setback on the ministers. While Windham and Fitzwilliam wanted an inquiry into the retreat, and did not automatically condemn the idea of British troops in Spain, Ponsonby and Moira also tended to be critical of the way expeditions were conducted rather than of the strategic thinking which lay behind them. Finally, at the opposite extreme, Holland was to remain staunch in his support for the Spaniards and Sidmouth approved of 'continuing to support Spain so long as any hope remained', desiring 'a vigorous prosecution of the war'. Such divergences became more blatant as 1809 progressed. Grey described Talavera as a disaster, a view supported by Ponsonby. William Grenville, though, concerned not to offend the politically powerful Wellesleys, would not be drawn into criticisms of the new Viscount Wellington. For his part Windham compared Talavera to Crécy. Whitbread was to condemn the Austrian declaration of war in 1809 and as a result would be challenged by Ponsonby, yet Creevy was furious that Whitbread would not attack Wellington. Domestic resentments fuelled these fires, there being opposition divisions over the scandal of the Duke of York and over the question of reform. Both matters were zealously pursued by the Foxites, though Grenville and his followers were more cautious, in particular fearing that any reforms might cost them their sinecures.[27]

The rout of the opposition was completed with the Walcheren inquiry in 1810. Despite all the suggestions of mismanagement attached to the expedition, despite having strong parliamentary support, and despite having widespread backing in the country at large, the Whigs were unable to overturn the ministry. Certainly attacking a wartime administration, with all the suggestions of a lack of patriotism that it implied, was not easy, but even so the opposition's complete lack of credibility over their military policies disgusted many members. The inquiry itself would not have proceeded had not Castlereagh and four of his allies voted for the production of papers and the questioning of participants, their intention being to free Castlereagh from any blame for the disaster. That Canning and Castlereagh had already resigned made assaults on the government via them more difficult, and although many Whigs enjoyed ruining Chatham, brother of the hated Pitt, this did little political damage. Despite all the failure and ineptitude revealed by the inquiry, Perceval refused to resign and his ministry enjoyed majorities in the votes on the matter that ranged from twenty-three to fifty-one, a vote of censure being defeated by 275 votes to 277.[28] Horner summed it all up in April 1810:

> In the late vote on the Walcheren question, there were many members, I doubt not, who voted with the ministers, though they condemned the whole of their conduct in that fatal expedition, from a sincere conviction of the superior fitness and excellence of the present set of ministers, for holding the government, in the present circumstances, above any other set of public men.[29]

Such were their defeats in 1809–10 that thereafter the opposition made no frontal assaults on the Peninsular strategy. There were many criticisms, usually over points of detail, but few divisions. The Whigs remained as divided as ever. Grey enraged his immediate followers in 1810 by observing that the prospects of peace were illusory, and, in 1811, he was obliged even to praise Peninsular operations, despite this amounting to a confession of previous error. The pessimistic Auckland also swung round to support the campaign until eventually Grenville found himself virtually alone once again in opposing it. Even his brothers, the Marquess of Buckingham and Thomas Grenville, did not share his views, the latter writing in 1814 that 'I cannot but think that Lord Wellington's success had told very powerfully indeed upon the general favourable result that we see in the present moment.'[30] By 1812 organised parliamentary opposition had virtually ceased. Windham had died in 1810 and Buckingham was to do so in 1813. Grey, William Grenville, Spencer and Fitzwilliam hardly ever attended the sessions.

So it was that opposition weakness negated ministerial frailty, allowing governments to escape the worst consequences of their failures and permitting the maintenance of a much greater degree of strategic continuity than would otherwise have been the case. It should also be noted that, despite the shuffling around in the higher echelons of government, the lower tiers remained relatively undisturbed. Only the Talents brought a whole new set of politicians to power, yet even then, as one of their supporters wrote:

> The change of the inferior Offices of Government at the coming in of Ld Grenville and Fox did not extend near so far as at any former total change such as when Sir R. Walpole went out in 1742. When Ld North went out in 1782 or when the Coalition came in in 1783.[31]

Ministries in 1803–15 did not appear strong, but their various falls and readjustments did not prompt the sort of radical changes in military policy that had been evident in 1710, 1762 and 1782. With the brief exception of the Talents, the cornerstone of strategy remained pursuing European campaigns against Napoleon whenever they seemed viable, and doggedly keeping the struggle going when such opportunities were not available. Although having all the appearances of a political maelstrom, the period contrived to retain hidden depths of stability and the surface turbulence interfered with strategy much less than might have been imagined.

Looking in a sense from the general to the particular, it must be observed that the interaction of war and politics inevitably gave rise to individual scandals and attitudes that made the usual political rivalries more intense. Such sentiments tended to act to the detriment of both political and military activity.

When Pitt returned to office in 1804 his only colleague of political substance was Melville, the former Henry Dundas, who had been Pitt's main ally and Secretary for War in the 1790s. As an avid collector of political power and lucrative sinecures Melville was distasteful in many respects, but he was a valuable man to have in Cabinet, being well versed in strategic and administrative affairs. However, in February 1805 the commissioners appointed by St Vincent to investigate naval administration published their tenth report, a bombshell, showing that when he had been Treasurer of the Navy one of Melville's subordinates had misappropriated public funds. Out of a knowledge of the intricacies of naval administration, or perhaps out of a fear that some of their own misdeameanours might be revealed, some of the opposition had little desire to pursue the matter. However, for many Foxites the chance to savage Pitt's hated lieutenant was too good to miss. A motion of censure was moved and, in April, passed on the Speaker's casting vote; Melville immediately resigned. A. D. Harvey questions Melville's precise standing in Pitt's Cabinet, but even so admits that the Premier had lost his most experienced coadjutor, and certainly his position at the Admiralty at such a time of danger implies that Pitt had a high regard for his ability. As it was, Melville's departure prompted the search for a replacement, the Admiralty finally going to Middleton, an octogenarian of limited capacity whose primary interest was in being raised to the peerage as Lord Barham. If this were not damage enough, the battle over Melville opened a rift between Pitt and Sidmouth, the latter having supported the censure motion. The whole affair weakened the government at a moment of extreme national peril.[32]

A more serious victim of the interrelationship between war and politics, though fortunately for a shorter period, was the Duke of York. In January 1809 an MP named Wardle charged the duke with having connived in an unofficial traffic in commissions conducted by one Mrs Clarke, York's former mistress. This was the culmination of a vicious campaign of rumour and innuendo that had been directed at York for some time, his royal position and his efforts at military reform both having earned him enemies. The debates on York's private affairs in January–March 1809 saw the Commons packed with members eager to enjoy the scandal and, for some, to relish the Duke's discomfiture. The handling of the whole affair brought disrepute on the Portland ministry and dented its prestige, but as was so often the case the opposition could make little real progress and their own reputation suffered from the way in which some of their number harried the duke. As with all questions of reform, some leading opposition politicians had fears that the process might lead to their own activities coming under unpleasant scrutiny, but Auckland and Rosslyn had valid complaints when they grumbled about how such a scandal distracted from the main issue of the time, the conduct of the war. When a censure motion on the Convention of Cintra was voted on in February 1809 only 355 members were present in the Commons, the govermnent winning with ease: yet houses of nearly 500 divided on some of the debates about York. In March he was found innocent of corruption, but with 196 votes going against him he determined to resign nonetheless.[33]

At a time when Moore's army had just been expelled from Spain with heavy losses, and when Austria was about to declare war on France, the army was deprived of its most capable administrative brain. Since becoming Commander-in-Chief in 1795 York had laboured hard to improve all aspects of the army's training, discipline and supply; a hard-working government servant, he had consistently provided ministers with sound, if conservative, advice. Even Fortescue, usually critical of all those directing the war in London, describes York as 'the best Commander-in-Chief that has ever ruled the Army'.[34] Despite such a record York was the victim of cynical political faction and, as with Melville, his successor was aged and ineffectual, the septuagenarian Sir David Dundas contributing little to the position before York was restored to it in May 1811. By that time both Wardle and Mrs Clarke had been exposed as dubious characters, but even so his reinstatement provided another chance for the opposition to display its fragmentation. Some vitriolic members tried to oppose York's return despite its acceptance by the Grenvillite leadership, an act further alienating York's brother, the Prince Regent, from his erstwhile political friends.[35]

Outside these two great scandals, the interplay of war and politics sharply increased natural rivalries. Undoubtedly the most dramatic, and the most ludicrous, example came with the spectacle of two Cabinet members, Canning and Castlereagh, engaging in a duel in

September 1809. It was the climax of a rivalry stretching back several years. Canning, a close protégé of Pitt's, was a brilliant orator, with a quick and lively mind: he was also supremely ambitious and thoroughly unprincipled. Castlereagh in comparison was a poor speaker whose tortuous ramblings gave the impression of a ponderous clod: however, this lack of charisma belied a hard-working and capable minister. In March 1809 Canning began intriguing to have Castlereagh replaced in Cabinet by Richard Wellesley, a political ally. Canning threatened resignation on several occasions unless Portland agreed to sack his rival, machinations of which Castlereagh was kept in ignorance. New impetus was lent to Canning's moves when Portland suffered a stroke in August, the obvious pending vacancy in the premiership making Canning, significantly stressing to his colleagues how a replacement ought to come from the Commons, all the keener to remove his rival. Further muddying the waters were Perceval's amibitions for the top job, and in September, when Portland resigned, George III indicated his preference for Perceval by accepting Canning's own offer to resign. Not until this moment did Castlereagh discover what Canning had been up to, vacating his own Cabinet position in fury and, thus freed, issuing the challenge. Whatever Castlereagh's intentions, Canning's enforced acceptance of the meeting (what else could a gentleman do in 1809?) effectively destroyed his hopes of the premiership.[36]

Differences over military policy had intensified the rivalry. Canning had sought to abandon the generals responsible for the Cintra agreement in 1808 in order to protect his own position. Similarly he entertained a strong dislike of Moore and his Whiggish opinions, urging Castlereagh to throw all the blame for Corunna on the general. Castlereagh's inclinations were more to back his commander's decisions, even when, as in the case of Moore's withdrawl from Sweden in 1808, it caused political embarrassment. The scandal of the duel effectively deprived Britain of two of her foremost political talents, Canning not serving in Cabinet again during this period, while Castlereagh was out of office until 1812. Their quarrel ensured that future Prime Ministers, intent on forming a government, could only offer Cabinet posts to one or the other; they would not serve together.

Political disputes had a military impact in other, less theatrical, instances. In March 1810 Mulgrave threatened to resign if Chatham remained in the wake of Walcheren, being enraged at the way

Chatham had tried to pin blame for the failure on the Admiralty and the naval commander, Rear-Admiral Strachan. Shortly after this Mulgrave succeeded him as Master General of the Ordnance.[37] Richard Wellesley entered the Cabinet in December 1809 in the firm hope of being able to dominate his colleagues, but there was mounting tension between him and Perceval. It was prompted not merely by conflicting ambitions and temperaments but also by differences over military policy. Wellesley finally resigned in 1812, complaining that his:

objections to remaining in the Cabinet arose, in great degree, from the *narrow* and imperfect scale, on which the efforts in the Peninsula were conducted. It was also stated to him by Mr. Perceval, that it was *impracticable* to *enlarge* that system.[38]

Equally the war's conduct proved a barrier between Wellesley and the opposition leaders (see p. 18). Even with his indolence, sexual over-activity and arrogance, Wellesley was still an important loss: he had extensive administrative experience gained while Indian Governer General and was, when stirred, a man of ability.

A final mention may also be made of Canning, this time in connection with Sidmouth. Just as with Castlereagh, Sidmouth felt an extreme personal dislike of Canning, dating back to the way he had goaded the Addington ministry in 1801–04. Once again those seeking to construct governments had to think in terms of either Canning or Sidmouth; they would not serve together.[39]

Politics further intruded into strategy because many senior officers of both services were closely involved in parliamentary affairs as members of one House or the other. This inevitably spread political rivalries into the military sphere, to the detriment of all concerned. It was not a new phenomenon, and at least the nation was spared political wrangles like that between Keppel and Palliser which had split the navy after 1778, but even so political motives did intrude into the actions of military men.

One such was Captain Pellew, a leading frigate commander in the 1790s and, from July 1802, an MP and supporter of Addington. Pellew left the blockade of Ferrol in January 1804 to speak in the Commons in support of the beleaguered Premier, a step rewarded the following April when the newly promoted Rear-Admiral Pellew was given command of the East Indies station. Although Addington fell shortly after, Pitt retained Pellew in his new post in return for the sailor's resignation from Parliament and his agreement to support a Pittite candidate in his constituency. Soon after Pellew sailed for India Addington, now Viscount Sidmouth, joined Pitt's Cabinet and was eager to see his followers advanced. Pitt responded by dividing the India station and giving the more lucrative part of it to one of them, Rear-Admiral Troubridge. At a stroke Pitt had satisfied Sidmouth, while also putting two opposition admirals, each of a fiery disposition, in a situation where confrontation was inevitable. When the two finally met in September 1805 Pellew refused to acknowledge the validity of Troubridge's instructions, the two thereafter refusing to co-operate in the management of an important station. For twelve months, until Troubridge was drowned, British naval forces in Indian waters were hamstrung, while local merchants did not know to whom to apply for convoys.[40]

A more public example of political/service rivalries concerned the dispute between Cochrane and Gambier. The former was a radical member of Parliament, elected for the Westminster seat in 1807, as well as one of the navy's most dashing frigate commanders. Poles apart from him was the fervently evangelical Gambier, an Admiralty Lord and a man connected to the families of Pitt and Barham. The two clashed after the assault on a French squadron in the Basque Roads in April 1809, an operation commanded by Gambier but in which Cochrane had played a leading role. Cochrane considered the attack had been handled with too much timidity, insisting that more enemy vessels could have been destroyed over and above the five ships of the line that were actually eliminated. This resentment turned to fury when Gambier's after-action despatch made no mention of Cochrane's role in the assault at all. Prompted by personal rage and political animosity, Cochrane took the unheard-of step of opposing a parliamentary vote of thanks to Gambier. The latter immediately demanded, and got, a court-martial on his conduct, this fully acquitting him in August. Cochrane continued his campaign, however, trying and failing the following year to get the papers pertaining to the attack laid before Parliament.[41] This unseemly affair did nothing for the navy's reputation and marked the end of Cochrane's nautical career in this period.

Elsewhere political influence was blatantly applied to the preservation of Sir Arthur Wellesley's reputation after Cintra, though, however visible the double standards that sacrificed his co-signatories, Dalrymple and Burrard, while saving him, they did at least preserve Britain's foremost soldier of the time. Sir John Moore was also probably influenced in his attitude to his instructions by his political hostility towards most ministries, and certainly some politicians fully reciprocated the feeling. Canning disliked him intensely and Portland believed him a man of 'Intrigue and duplicity of Conduct'.[42] Such resentments can happen at any time in human relations, but that some military men were committed to particular political factions made antagonism all the more probable. A more obvious example still of this fact came in the shape of Chatham, both Cabinet member and commander of the Walcheren expedition. One reason for giving him the command in the first place may have lain with Canning's hope of installing the pliant and indolent Chatham as Premier in place of the ailing Portland. Were Chatham to enjoy a military success beforehand, any such manoeuvre would have been greatly facilitated.[43]

Before completing this consideration of political matters, some mention must be made of the nation's general sentiment regarding what was a long and arduous war. In this respect successive governments enjoyed a substantial measure of popular support. Just before the outbreak of hostilities Hobart could reflect that 'notwithstanding the eagerness with which peace was universally demanded, there exists at this moment as great and as cordial a disposition to support the Government in a war . . . as ever has been manifested upon any former occasion'.[44] Even those who felt that Britain rushed precipitately into war in 1803 found their views overwhelmed by the general determination to resist invasion. Many of those, in fact, who had opposed war in the 1790s became prominent figures in the Volunteers. Not until after 1807, and particularly in 1810–12, did the combination of a seemingly endless conflict with a variety of religious, social, economic and political factors start to revive the clamour for peace in some areas.[45] Most people for most of the time recognised that Napoleon had to be fought, no ministry having to face the sort of groundswell of pacific feeling that had, for instance, confronted North in 1782.

The domestic problems that did arise came in the shape of Ireland and the economic dislocations due largely to the Continental System. After the brief flaring of Emmet's rebellion in 1803, Ireland remained a dormant volcano. Irish governments felt the country to be freer from internal threat than at any time in the preceding decade. What indications ministers could gather from their sources of intellegence in Ireland suggested that disaffection would not become active until the French were actually able to land troops, something Napoleon could never manage.[46] Although no political solution of Irish grievances was ever achieved, and a garrison of varying strength had to be kept there, in part at least to preserve internal order, British governments were fortunate that the country remained essentially quiescent.

More generally, they were also spared economically based disorders for much of the conflict, although London always remained an area where politically inspired disorder could occur. The Burdett riots of April 1810 were a reminder of this and York, for one, was unwilling to see the capital's garrison reduced to a single battalion in 1808.[47] Widespread internal trouble did not become manifest until 1811–12. There had been peace petitions from commercial areas as early as 1807, but real trouble stemmed from the economic slump of 1810. One consequence was a series of Luddite attacks, chiefly in Nottinghamshire, Lancashire and the West Riding, tying down 12,000 troops in the affected areas by the autumn of 1812. More widespread disorder was caused by food price rises and shortages after the poor havest of 1811, troops having to be committed to these domestic problems and to guarding the tens of thousands of French prisoners-of-war scattered about the country. Bathurst stated in March 1813 that domestic security needs were tying down five regiments of cavalry and that a further 40,000 infantry were scattered around Britain and Ireland.[48] However, the situation might have been a lot worse. Prior to 1810 economic problems did not provoke serious violence, while from 1813 the decline in French power brought some relief to businessmen contemplating the reopening of extensive European markets. Distracting internal disorders were, in consequence, short-lived and their strategic importance more limited than might have been expected.

Notes

1 Harvey, pp. 154 and 157. More recently Camden has been described as decisive and zealous, though there is little supporting evidence: A. Schom, *Trafalgar. Countdown to Battle, 1803–05*, London, 1990, p. 41.

2 Harvey, pp. 117, 253 and 266–7.

3 Harvey, pp. 151–3.

4 Gray, pp. 254–77. Harvey, pp. 262–4.

5 Harvey, pp. 261–4. Gray, chapters 16–22, for Perceval's difficulties: Wellington's comment is quoted on p. 346.

6 Harvey, pp. 296–9.

7 L. V. Harcourt (ed.), *The Diaries and Correspondence of the Rt. Hon. George Rose*, London, 1860, II, pp. 176–7.

8 Aspinall, IV, pp. 94, 588, 617–18 and 662.

9 Aspinall, IV, p. 590.

10 Aspinall, IV, p. 607 and n.

11 J. J. Sack, *The Grenvillites, 1801–29*, Urbana, Ill, 1979, p. 71.

12 Leeds R.O., Harewood Collection, Canning Papers, diary entry for 2 March 1804.

13 Harvey, pp. 145–50. R. Reilly, *Pitt the Younger*, London, 1978, pp. 325–8.

14 Durham University Library, The Earl Grey Papers, 2nd Earl, Fox to Howick, 18 August 1803, no. 53.

15 G. Hogge (ed.), *The Journal and Correspondence of William, Lord Auckland*, London, 1861–62, IV, pp. 310–13. B.M. Add. Mss 38737, Huskisson Papers, ff. 197–v and 204–v. St Vincent had similar opinions: J. S. Tucker, *Memoirs of Earl St. Vincent*, London, 1844, II, p. 317.

16 A. D. Harvey, 'The Ministry of all the Talents: the Whigs in office, February 1806 to March 1807', *Historical Journal*, XV, no. 4, 1972, p. 644.

17 Sir A. W. Ward and G. P. Gooch (eds.), *Cambridge History of British Foreign Policy, 1783–1919*, Cambridge, 1922, I, p. 300. J. Holland Rose, *William Pitt and the Great War*, London, 1911, p. 508.

18 Lord Russell (ed.), *Memorials and Correspondence of Charles James Fox*, London, 1853–57, IV, pp. 58–9 and 123.

19 Harvey, *Britain in Nineteenth Century*, pp. 166–7. Russell, IV, pp. 6 and 128.

20 W. B. Taylor, 'The Foxite Party and Foreign Politics, 1806–16' University of London, Ph.D. thesis, 1974, pp. 52 and 56–9. F. A. Walker, 'The Grenville–Fox "junction" and the problem of peace', *Canadian Journal of History*, XII, 1977, pp. 52–6. Harvey, *Britain in Nineteenth Century*, p. 194.

21 Taylor, pp. 131–2.

22 Taylor, pp. 172–4 and 178–9.

23 Harvey, *Britain in Nineteenth Century*, p. 207. Russell, IV, pp. 37, 66, 71 and 73–4. Gray, p. 405.

24 Gray, pp. 404–19. Harvey, *Britain in Nineteenth Century*, pp. 273–9.

25 Roberts, pp. 106–10.

26 B.M. Add. Mss 58947, Dropmore Papers, f. 71v. *P.D.*, X, pp. 16–23 and 537 ff.

27 Taylor, pp. 217–302. Roberts, pp. 118–25 and 140–1. G. Davies, 'The Whigs and the Peninsular War, 1808–14', *Transactions of the Royal Historical Society*, II, 1919, pp. 113–31. *P.D., XII, pp. 10–11.. L. Horner (ed.), Memoirs and Correspondence of Francis Horner, M.P.*, London, 1843, II, pp. 69–70 and 114.

28 Taylor, pp. 320–1. Roberts, pp. 146–7. Harvey, *Britain in Nineteenth Century*, p. 268.

29 Horner, II, pp. 36–7.

30 Taylor, pp. 325–32. Roberts, pp. 153 and 160–1.

31 Harvey, *Britain in Nineteenth Century*, pp. 175–6, quoting from National Library of Wales, 4814D. Only in Scotland was there a purge as those who had enjoyed Melville's favour were removed: p. 176.

32 Harvey, *Britain in Nineteenth Century*, pp. 155–6. Melville's sinecures are listed in Pope, pp. 259–61.

33 Harvey, *Britain in Nineteenth Century*, pp. 233–43. R. Fulford, *The Royal Dukes*, London, 1973, pp. 77–85.

34 Fortescue, *British Army*, 7, p. 31. York's reforms are detailed in R. Glover, *Peninsular Preparation*. The only modern biography, A. Burne, *The Noble Duke of York*, London, 1950, is concerned with his campaigns in the 1790s to the exclusion of other aspects of his career.

35 Harvey, *Britain in Nineteenth Century*, pp. 278–9.

36 Harvey, *Britain in Nineteenth Century*, pp. 251–61.

37 Leeds University Library, Brotherton Collection Box VII, Mulgrave Papers, 28/3.

38 B.M. Add. Mss 37296, Wellesley Papers, f. 201v; the emphasis is Wellesley's; he concluded by saying that Perceval was 'incompetent': f. 206. For a more detailed account of his complaints see ff. 265–94.

39 Harvey, *Britain in Nineteenth Century*, p. 272.

40 C. N. Parkinson, *Edward Pellew, Viscount Exmouth, Admiral of the Red*, London, 1934, pp. 284–5, 303 and 310–26. C. N. Parkinson, *War in the Eastern Seas, 1793–1815*, London, 1954, pp. 278–9 and 287.

41 D. Thomas, *Cochrane*, London, 1980, pp. 109–19 and 147–89. Also Marcus, pp. 337–8.

42 Leeds R.O., Harewood Collection, Canning Papers, 32, Canning to Castlereagh, 31 December 1808; Canning to Portland, 30 December 1808. 33, Portland to Canning, 31 December 1808.

43 Harvey, *Britain in Nineteenth Century*, p. 255.

44 L. Melville (ed.), *The Wellesley Papers*, London, 1914, I, p. 164.

45 Cookson, pp. 173–85.

46 M. Elliott, *Partners in Revolution. The United Irishmen and France*, New Haven, Conn., and London, 1982, pp. 340–9.

47 Aspinall, V, pp. 107–8.

48 Emsley, pp. 154–8. Fortescue, *British Army*, 9, pp. 15–16. *P.D.* XXV, pp. 71–2.

4

Strategic options and pressures

There were certain inescapable factors confronting British military planners in 1803–15 which had a profound impact on strategy. First and foremost was Britain's insular situation. That this, whatever its defensive benefits, prompted headaches when assessing offensive possibilities has already been observed. A further difficulty in an age lacking rapid means of communication was that of co-ordinating military movements as part of an overall strategic scheme. A classic instance can be witnessed in the latter part of 1807.

In August that year the Cabinet decided to reduce the total forces in the Mediterranean. However, with the continuing need to apply pressure on the Turks, and with the growth of French power in the wake of Tilsit, ministers changed their mind early in October and decided to keep their forces intact. Unfortunately the change in instructions did not reach the commanders on the spot in time: on 24 October Moore, with the final evacuation of Egypt completed, left Sicily with a contingent of 7,258 troops. By early November ministers in London were starting to lose control of events, not being sure where Moore's force was and being worried in case Sicily had been left inadequately defended. These fears prompted the dispatch of 5,000 men to reinforce the island. Then the chaos worsened when Moore reached Gibraltar early in December to find orders telling him to assist in moving the Portuguese royal family to Brazil and to secure the island of Madeira. Yet in their own uncertainty ministers had already sent 3,000 troops under Major General Beresford to achieve the latter task. Someone in London also realised in December that, if Moore remained on Sicily, the additional 5,000 men going to that place would make the island's garrison embarrassingly large. Again fresh orders were issued, stating that of the 5,000 men for

Sicily only two battalions were in fact to go. Unfortunately the whole body had already sailed! Not until 29 December, when Moore's command finally reached Britain, did ministers begin to get a grip on the situation, their position aided for once by a gale, which prevented the Sicily-bound force from sailing from Falmouth; this permitted the implementation of their amended instructions.[1]

This tortuous tale of order, counter-order, disorder, has been cited to show not so much that controlling the war from London could be difficult as that at times it could be downright impossible. Ministers could not safely attempt complicated and protracted operations because that meant tying up resources for months at a time, during which circumstances could change radically and the forces involved might be desperately needed elsewhere. Rarely were bodies of more than 5,000–10,000 men sent abroad in one group, an exception being the Walcheren expedition, where the short distances involved in a cross-Channel assault meant that it could be controlled easily by ministers, i.e. quickly recalled, and could be supplied without obvious difficulty.

That as a rule units sailing abroad had to be committed to operations many weeks ahead, and that all too frequently ministers were acting on uncertain information in the first place, meant that it was customary for military commanders to be given extensive discretion in their instructions. This practice has caused confusion in the minds of some authors. In 1805, for example, when ordering Lieutenant General Craig to take reinforcements to the Mediterranean, Camden issued instructions directing the soldier to secure British control of Sicily but also mentioned the possibility of operations on the Italian mainland, of an attack on Alexandria, or of an occupation of Sardinia. According to Sir Henry Bunbury, who served on the expedition, this variety displayed no 'sound plan of operations'. For a later writer, Lewis Butler, they illustrate the ministers' 'utter incompetence to direct military operations'.[2] Neither view is sustainable and Bunbury in particular should have known better: unable to keep in direct communication with their subordinates, ministers had no choice but to inform them of the overall objectives of policy and then leave it to the judgement of the man on the spot. In Craig's case, therefore, it was stressed that the government's priority was the defence of Sicily, other objectives depending upon local circumstances. This practice was certainly realistic. Precise orders that had to be obeyed to the letter were unpractical when the officer concerned might take two or three months to sail to his area of operations, a period during which the whole basis of his instructions could have altered. Nor could ministers in London promptly react to the changing circumstances of a long campaign such as that in the Peninsula. Even where there was a definite instruction, such as that forbidding operations in Spain in 1809, the requests of the man in local command would usually be listened to favourably. Any doubts as to the wisdom of this system can be dispelled merely be examining the chaos caused in the French command by Napoleon's efforts to direct the Peninsular campaigns from Paris.

Another feature pressing strongly upon British strategy were the requirements of an empire. This provided the great benefits of commercial and economic strength, an influence over affairs in many parts of the globe, and leverage over other European nations nervous for their own, lesser, colonial holdings. However, this return required the investment of a considerable proportion of the nation's military means to colonial guard duties. Something like a quarter of the army's available regular strength would be tied up in colonial garrisons at any one time. On top of this must be added those troops stationed at key points in the European theatre, places like Malta, Gibraltar and Sicily, whose freedom of manoeuvre, i.e. whose offensive capacity, was very limited. The colonies also absorbed much of Britain's naval strength, both in terms of squadrons stationed as direct protection and in terms of other vessels appointed to escort the convoys which sailed to and fro.

The net strategic result of all these factors was that rarely could island Britain assemble armies of more than 40,000 men on the Continent: a total surpassed only on Walcheren and, eventually, in the Peninsula. In the light of this it was a fundamental tenet of British thinking that if Napoleon, who controlled armies numbered in hundreds of thousands, was to be defeated, then the support of those European nations who controlled equally large forces was essential. There was nothing new in such ideas, of course, they having been a feature of British strategy for centuries, but it has caused misunderstanding. Writing in 1932, Basil Liddell Hart, the military prophet of the twentieth century, considered British strategy to have traditionally been one of indirect assault. Reviewing the eighteenth century, he thought he saw British campaigns of colonial triumph and Continental failure. By the Seven Years War (1756–63), he believed, the strategy of indirect assault had reached its zenith, a time when 'direct military effort on the Continent was largely replaced by subsidy to our Allies'. After 1793:

> The struggle against Revolutionary France and against Napoleon saw a renewal, and a renewed success, of our traditional grand strategy. This was applied by sea-pressure on the enemy, by financial support to all possible allies. And no turn of ill-fortune induced us to deviate from it towards larger military effort. It was by lending sovereigns to sovereigns that we chiefly fought France on land.

Despite acknowledging the importance of Wellington's Peninsular campaigns, Liddell Hart still does not interpret them as a Continental commitment on a massive scale.[3]

This interpretation of eighteenth-century British strategy is fundamentally flawed. Whatever the scale of the colonial conquests, nevertheless a very large proportion of Britain's military means was invariably tied down in European operations. Even in 1760, when triumphs in Canada, the Caribbean and India might seem to support the theory of the indirect approach, Britain still employed over 20,000 of her own soldiers, plus over 68,000 hired foreign troops, under Ferdinand of Brunswick in Germany.[4] Similarly, in 1783–1801, despite Pitt's West Indian campaigns, Britain sent troops to attack France in Europe. In the Low Countries in 1793–95 and 1799; to encourage French royalist revolts in 1793, 1795 and 1800; to raid the enemy's coast, as with the Ostend attack in 1798; and to preserve British interests in Portugal and the Mediterranean in 1800–01.[5] For ministers reflecting on the past – and previous experience always exerts a profound impact on current planning – the conclusion was the opposite of the one proposed by Liddell Hart and success was, in fact, closely bound up with direct assaults on France. Certainly the lion's share of such campaigning would fall to European allies, but the with significant British participation.

Reinforcing such thinking after 1803 was the bankruptcy of the colonial strategy that had been part of policy in 1793–98. Then the heavy scale of commitment to the Caribbean had achieved little, at enormous cost, Britain's armed forces suffering around 100,000 casualties, half of whom died. Most of the losses were from disease.[6] This constituted a powerful argument in favour of a European strategic orientation. In 1810 Liverpool would tell Lieutenant General Beckwith, the commander of the Leeward and Windward Islands garrison, that no further reinforcements would be sent to him because of the extent of Britain's Continental commitments. Five months earlier Beckwith had been told to avoid any effort to take Guadeloupe were this to lead to a protracted campaign, i.e. one that would risk heavy losses through disease.[7] The implication of almost all colonial ventures after 1803 was that ministers had learned of the attendant dangers to the forces concerned, British planners frequently being prepared to accept what amounted to a live-and-let-live strategy with their enemies in colonial regions. Nor did it apply only to the disease-ridden Caribbean. In 1803 Richard Wellesley, then Governor General of India, was instructed to follow a policy of no further Indian conquests. Although the government wanted to preserve Britain's Indian position, the restriction of expenditure on colonial matters was seen as more important than seizing regions under French control: any such captures would merely consume both money and troops tied up in garrisons.[8] Even when Canada was menaced by the United States from 1812, the Cabinet responded by sending battalions in ones and twos, sufficient only for defensive duties. Not until after Napoleon's abdication were large reinforcements sent.

Working alongside these pressures towards a European-based strategy was an appreciation of the particular danger posed by Napoleonic France. During 1803–15 Britain faced an enemy with all its traditional power and skill, but one now including the vigour released by the Revolution harnessed to the energy and willpower of a military genius. With the failure of peace efforts in 1796–97, 1802–03 and 1806, British governments faced a fight to the finish. One contemporary observer got to the root of the matter when dismissing any idea of a peace with Napoleon. For Palmerston, in August 1806 a backbencher rapidly making a name for himself:

> If in this state [of possible peace] we venture to remonstrate at any injury or insult offered to us or to Europe, our mouths will be immediately stopped by the threat of invasion, and should we begin to arm in defence . . . the flotilla will have safely deposited a French army on our coast, with which we shall have to contend under every disadvantage of hurry and confusion.[9]

In such a conflict the fate of sugar islands was secondary. Of necessity the decisive battles had to be in Europe and the revolution in military practice generally during the period only served to emphasise the fact. In 1757 royalist France had an army in Europe and her colonies numbering 187,000; at the height of the Seven Years War the maximum number of soldiers she could field would not exceed 330,000.[10] Compared to this in 1805, in Europe alone Napoleon fielded just under 280,000 French, Dutch and Italian troops, to which a further 21,500 Bavarians may be added. By 1812, excluding Prussian and Austrian contingents, the emperor could lead 400,000 men into Russia while leaving more than 250,000 others in Spain and other parts of his empire.[11] The combination of large-scale domestic recruiting for citizen armies and the use of foreign manpower as well meant that Napoleon could campaign over wide areas and sustain losses on an unprecedented scale without defeat. When combined with the French practice of local requisitions for supply, the net result was that warfare was no longer a tortuous process of protracted campaigns and long sieges conducted by armies rarely exceeding 50,000 men. In the Seven Years War Prussia, together with Ferdinand's Anglo-German army, simultaneously fought off the armies of France, Austria and Russia, though the margin of survival was a narrow one. In 1806 France alone smashed Prussian military power and occupied Berlin in a campaign lasting twenty-four days.

This was quite unlike any previous conflict for ministers in London watching their allies being bowled over in a series of lightning campaigns, only that in the Peninsula seeing long periods of fighting in the same areas. It was impossible to think in terms of a peace with Napoleon based on colonial exchanges in return for a balance of power in Europe. A depressed Castlereagh reflected in 1805 that only control of Spanish America would serve as an adequate recompense for the exclusion of Britain from the Mediterranean which Napoleon seemed to be securing.[12] Napoleon's power in Europe extended too far and too fast, and even ministers of a more pacific disposition had to bear in mind the failed Peace of Amiens and the collapse of talks in 1806. A Europe dominated by France was a Europe in which Britain could never feel safe.

To this point emphasis has been placed on the objectives which British ministers wished to pursue, but it must be stressed that, to a not inconsiderable degree, Britain's strategy depended upon Napoleon's first moves. For most of the period Britain fought alone or allied to only minor military powers. In these circumstances the initiative lay with Napoleon, and British ministers had either to react to his actions or try to pre-empt them. If Britain could put a low priority on colonial operations, for instance, it was only because France was unable or unwilling to launch serious attacks upon her empire. It is worth noting that the escape in 1805 of the Rochefort and Toulon squadrons and their heading for the Caribbean saw the Cabinet taking immediate steps to preserve British interests in the region. Early in April, learning of the French attack on Dominica, the government decided to send two battalions from Ireland to Barbados; continuing nervousness prompted plans by the end of the month to increase this force to some 5,000 men under the command of Lieutenant General Coote. Preparations continued during the early summer, though in July, on hearing of the French ships' return to Europe, the whole scheme was dropped. The interesting aspect of all this was that the Cabinet was responding to a perceived threat to the colonies, this despite hopes of European operations in the shape of the nascent Third Coalition. As it was, five extra ships of the line were sent in pursuit of the Rochefort squadron in April and a further eight in May; on top of this the Toulon squadron was being pursued by Nelson.[13]

The constant blockade of Napoleon's ports reduced the danger of major French colonial campaigns, but the probability never became certainty. In 1798, despite Nelson's presence, the French had shipped 38,000 troops to Egypt and there always remained the threat of a repeat performance. Although the voyages of the Rochefort and Toulon squadrons in 1805 were the only serious alarms that actually materialised, British ministers could rarely relax. Mulgrave observed in 1804 that some areas, such as the Cape of Good Hope, were of little intrinsic value to Britain but would constitute a menace to her interests if controlled by France.[14] The mere threat prompted that area's capture in 1806. Just as significant was the survival of the French islands in the Indian Ocean until they became a serious commercial threat. Other instances of Cabinets reacting to dangers, real or imagined, will emerge in the chapters that follow.

Yet another outside restriction on strategic options came from the diplomatic necessity felt by most Cabinets to tie at least a portion of their military policy to the expectations of their allies. In this respect Liddell Hart's theory of 'sovereigns to sovereigns' is particularly fallacious, as is the more recent offering of another author to the effect that the British 'hired the Kings and Emperors of Europe as casually as they had hired mercenary regiments from minor German princelings during the American Revolution'.[15] The business of co-operating with European allies, especially the more powerful ones, was never as straightforward as this suggests. It was invariably the case that such powers sought not only huge financial support for pending campaigns, but also direct military action into the bargain. For ministers to be tardy in such operations was to incur the suspicion that they were unwilling to hazard British lives in the common cause, feelings that only fuelled the already sharp resentments at British colonial and maritime power. The appearance of inactivity in 1806–07 was to prompt the Tsar to fury and encourage him to seek terms from Napoleon. Prior to this, in 1805, basic Russian mistrust had been made clear by the repeated insistence that British troops should join in a campaign in southern Italy. In 1809 Cabinet worries about Austrian sensibilities, and a desire to keep that country fighting, encouraged the dreadful retention of Walcheren.

While for all these reasons British military planning had a pronounced European orientation, it was channelled into particular areas, and the reasons must now be reviewed. First and foremost in ministerial thinking was the overriding necessity of maintaining naval supremacy, the primary factor in domestic, imperial and commercial security. The most direct means of achieving it was the destruction of enemy warships at sea, most dramatically and famously managed at Trafalgar (October 1805) with the capture of eighteen French and Spanish ships of the line. In other encounters four more French ships of the line were captured a fortnight after Trafalgar, five were taken off St Domingo in February 1806, five more were destroyed by fireships in the Basque Roads in April 1809, and two were eliminated in the Mediterranean in October 1809.[16]

Such opportunities – five occasions in twelve years – were rare. Napoleon's strategy consisted chiefly of keeping his fleets in port, a constant threat, and one which steadily increased as newly constructed vessels were added. For most of the time the Royal Navy was confined to keeping powerful squadrons blockading the main enemy arsenals – Antwerp, Brest, l'Orient, Rochefort, Cadiz and Toulon – in an effort to constrict Napoleon's strategy, to keep his squadrons divided while being on hand to defeat them if they ventured out. This wearisome, never-ending task was the navy's chief strategic duty, and such ports became tempting targets for direct assaults of the kind that were aimed at Copenhagen and Walcheren, which helped prompt the sending of a squadron to Constantinople, and which caused continual interest in the fate of Portugal. Other attacks were considered or prepared before events prompted a change of direction. In 1804 Pitt actively contemplated sending 15,000–20,000 troops to seize Ferrol and its sheltering French squadron, only dropping the scheme when it was declared impracticable. Castlereagh was keen in 1805 and again in 1807 to attack Cadiz, Collingwood pouring cold water on the notion on both occasions. Sidmouth also suggested Cadiz as a target in 1806 and the following year Windham was talking of an Anglo-Russian assault on Toulon. In 1808 Canning wondered about the possibilities of an attack on the Texel and there were orders to Saumarez in the Baltic to consider an assault on Cronstadt or any other port in which the Russian fleet might be lying. A small squadron sheltering at Vigo attracted Castlereagh's attention in 1807 and the following year he proposed assailing the Spanish squadron at Port Mahon. In 1809, while Walcheren was high on the government's agenda, the Admiralty was exploring possible operations against two ships of the line in Cherbourg.[17]

In similar vein much attention was paid in the early war years to schemes aimed at damaging or destroying the French invasion flotilla. It made evident sense to reduce the invasion threat at source, but the measures taken were largely marked by impracticality and failure. In September 1803 Dieppe, Granville and Calais were all bombarded from the sea, but with indifferent results. Then came the stone ships expedition against Boulogne, a plan to block that harbour by scuttling a trio of vessels loaded with stone at its entrance. The preparations for it went ahead in March and April 1804 amidst a blaze of publicity, but in the event chaotic arrangements and bad weather prevented the attempt and it was abandoned in a flood of mutual recrimination. From that time onwards Boulogne was the focal point of Napoleon's invasion preparations and consequently of Britain's counter-efforts. In October and November 1804 the place was attacked by catamarans, a cross between a mine and a torpedo, and by rockets; another effort was launched in November 1805. Nothing worthwhile resulted from any of these attempts, Admiral Keith for one pouring scorn on the use of rockets and Barham preferring that the vessels so employed should be used on convoy duties – though, contrarily, Barham did favour using rockets against Cadiz. In the face of these setbacks the only remaining option was that of direct amphibious assault. This was a definite possibility, Mulgrave arguing in January 1805 against Russian requests for more British troops in the Mediterranean on the grounds that it would render ineffectual any assault on the Channel coast. Unfortunately such direct action was prevented by the strong defences in the Boulogne area and the dangers of landing and re-embarking troops, particularly in bad weather. Memories of the Ostend disaster in 1798, when 1,400 men had been lost in an attempt to destroy the canal, and of the problems of such operations in the Seven Years War may have played their part in scuttling these hopes.[18]

Thereafter Cabinets had to live with the threat, such as it was, posed by the Boulogne flotilla. With the Royal Navy never losing control of the Channel, combined with the fact that it would have taken several tides to have got the flotilla to sea, the danger was a limited one. Nevertheless as late as 1808 Castlereagh was still thinking of attacking it, sounding out the views of Commodore Owen, the commander of the blockading squadron there, as to whether such a step were viable. With French forces moving to Spain, Castlereagh envisaged a rapid descent on the place by 12,000–15,000 men. However, the plan was blocked by the Duke of York, who pointed to the overall shortage of troops, and thereafter all talk of an assault on the harbour was abandoned.[19]

It is not surprising that most of these naval-oriented schemes were in 1803–09, years when Britain often fought alone and had to look to a strategy of survival. In later years the danger of invasion lessened, despite the scare of 1811, with Napoleon's armies committed to trying to subdue the Peninsula and hold down Europe. The need to preserve naval supremacy, however, remained, in late 1813 Bathurst telling Lieutenant General Graham, commander of British troops in Holland, of something 'in which the British Interests are deeply involved, I mean the destruction of the naval armament at Antwerp'. Were this to be accomplished Graham would 'perform an essential service to your Country'.[20]

Alongside this need to chip away at Napoleonic naval might, British policy was also impelled towards specific geographical areas of Europe as well. Without question the most sensitive of these areas in British eyes were the Low Countries in general and the Scheldt estuary in particular. French control of Holland meant a permanent threat to George III's Hanoverian electorate, a danger that materialised in 1803 and expanded Napoleon's influence over northern Germany. It also gave the French access to the Dutch colonial empire, particularly in the East Indies and at the Cape of

Western Europe
N
Gothenburg
Copenhagen
Heligoland
Hamburg
Weser
Elbe
Cork
Thames
London
Antwerp
Portsmouth
Plymouth
Boulogne
Rhine
Cherbourg
Meuse
Danube
Seine
Brest
Lorient
Loire
Rochefort
Rhône
Genoa
Garonne
Corunna
Toulon
Vigo
Ebro
Oporto
Ciudad Rodrigo
Barcelona
Madrid
Tagus
Lisbon
Badajoz
Cartagena
Cadiz
Gibraltar
miles
0
200
400

Good Hope, from where France could challenge British dominance in India and endanger her valuable trade with the East. Holland also provided Britain with a link in her communications with the other powers of Europe, allowing relatively rapid overland contacts that were not as vulnerable to interference from winter weather as were communications via the Baltic. Most important of all, though, was the direct threat to Britain's security posed by Low Countries that were hostile. In terms of defending against invasion, England's southern coast, which faced France, was high in places and relatively difficult to attack. The sea off the south coast was also deep and allowed cruisers to sail more easily within its protection. Compared to this the east coast was flat, particularly that of Essex, while the sea and the strength of the winds made its seaward defence difficult. The Low Countries were situated directly opposite these vulnerable points, and the estuaries of the Scheldt, Maas and Rhine could shelter large fleets of transports ready to sail across the North Sea at any moment. Even without the invasion threat, the Low Countries' ports were still close to London and the Thames estuary, Britain's main commercial artery.[21]

In British minds this menace concentrated itself in the shape of the Scheldt estuary and its ports of Antwerp and Flushing. These, together with Terneuse, were the centres of enemy shipbuilding: to them, from northern France and Germany, via the Meuse and the Rhine, timber and assorted naval supplies could be brought and converted into warships. In 1804 the *Naval Chronicle* was reporting extensive activity in Antwerp, including the building of three ships of the line and five large frigates. There was supposed to be timber enough to more than double this construction and it was believed that the place was being converted into a naval base on a par with Brest and Toulon.[22] West of Antwerp stood the smaller port of Flushing, which it was understood could hold twenty large warships in its basin and which was very difficult to blockade because of the surrounding sandbanks.[23] Vessels at Antwerp enjoyed a safe haven because of its navigation and fortifications, while Flushing, although more vulnerable to attack, allowed vessels there to put to sea quickly. Another worry was that Antwerp, unlike such ports as Brest or Toulon, could not be observed by the blockading squadrons, an aura of secrecy heightening British fears. In 1808 Vice-Admiral Campbell was exhorted to find a reliable smuggler to provide information on the Scheldt squadron. Six months later the Admiralty repeated the request, observing that it was impossible to reconnoitre Flushing in winter and confessing that at that time they had no idea exactly where the squadron was.[24] Effectively Napoleon's warships in this area enjoyed both security and the initiative.

Britain had had a concern over the fate of the Low Countries ever since the time of Elizabeth I, but after 1803 the region became a subject of obsessive worry. Descents on Walcheren were discussed in 1803, 1805, 1807 and 1808 before the great expedition of 1809 was finally launched.[25] The wider question of Holland figured in planning when troops were sent to Germany in 1805–06, and forces were sent there when French power collapsed at the end of 1813. In the latter year Castlereagh wrote to a subordinate:

> I must particularly entreat you to keep your attention upon Antwerp. The destruction of its arsenal is essential to our safety. To leave it in the hands of France is little short of imposing upon Great Britain the charge of a perpetual war establishment.

Right to the end of hostilities the concern remained. As late as the end of February 1814 Castlereagh was urging Liverpool, 'Pray lay your shoulders to Antwerp: till that is secured, we run a risk in case of disaster.'[26] It should also be remembered that Napoleon's escape from Elba in 1815 was met by Britain concentrating all her available troops, under Wellington, her best commander, in the Low Countries. It was entirely appropriate that Britain's last battle of the period should have been fought on the road to Brussels and to Holland.

After this area, Britain's strategic priorities were chiefly directed to the Mediterranean and the Baltic. Neither posed the immediate threat of invasion, but there were still great interests involved in both. In the shape of Malta the Mediterranean theatre provided the immediate *casus belli* in 1803, the island's retention reflecting the growing British fear of French expansionary intentions towards Egypt and the Levant. Writing in February 1803, Governor Ball stressed that continued control of Malta would preserve the neutrality of the Barbary States, particularly Tunis and Tripoli, while to abandon the island would undermine the confidence of both Austria and Turkey. In effect he believed that leaving Malta would create a vacuum that France would immediately fill. Ball also dwelt on Malta's naval importance, it replacing the now French-controlled Italian ports as a haven for supplies and repairs. Another, unsigned, memorandum the same year pointed out that merely retaining Gibraltar would not offset Malta's loss. For the squadron blockading Toulon the sailing time in summer to either place was roughly the same, but in winter the prevailing westerly winds made the voyage to Gibraltar three or four times as long as the one to Malta.[27] The island was therefore of great strategic value, but it had one serious drawback: it could not feed itself. Because of this, and as a reinforcement to its security, it was crucial to ensure that Sicily did not fall to France. In effect there would be a chain reaction. To guard against unwelcome French expansion in the Mediterranean required a squadron to blockade Toulon and any other harbours used by the enemy. To facilitate this naval presence required Malta's retention as a naval base, while to feed and protect Malta involved the securing of Sicily.

From early 1806 onwards Britain was to maintain a substantial garrison on Sicily, serving both to guard the island and offer a threat to French control of the Italian mainland. From Sicily British forces raided Italy in 1806, threatened to repeat the performance thereafter, maintained the independence of the Neapolitan court as a challenge to the Bonapartist rulers of Naples, provided a military base for operations against the Ionian Islands and eastern Spain, and, finally, helped to expel the French from Italy altogether in 1814. For all this, though, ministers rarely looked to the Mediterranean as an area of extended offensive operations, being prepared only to tolerate pre-emptive strikes designed to thwart Napoleon's perceived intentions, as with the seizing of Alexandria in 1807 or the Ionian Islands in 1809–10. A defensive strategy suited British needs. 'With respect to our General Policy in the Mediterranean,' Castlereagh observed,

> looking to the Maintenance of our positions in Gibraltar, Malta, & Sicily, the Inclination of my opinion in the present State of the Continent, is strongly against undertaking any offensive operations in that Quarter. So long as we hold the two latter Islands as Naval Stations, I apprehend we possess every necessary accommodation for maintaining our Superiority in those Seas, and that the use of no third Station would repay us for the Garrison that would be locked up defending it.[28]

Ministers were keen to maintain their strong position on Napoleon's southern flank, but overall the theatre's value was not on a par with that of the Low Countries or the Baltic. In 1796 the whole Mediterranean up to Gibraltar had been abandoned without

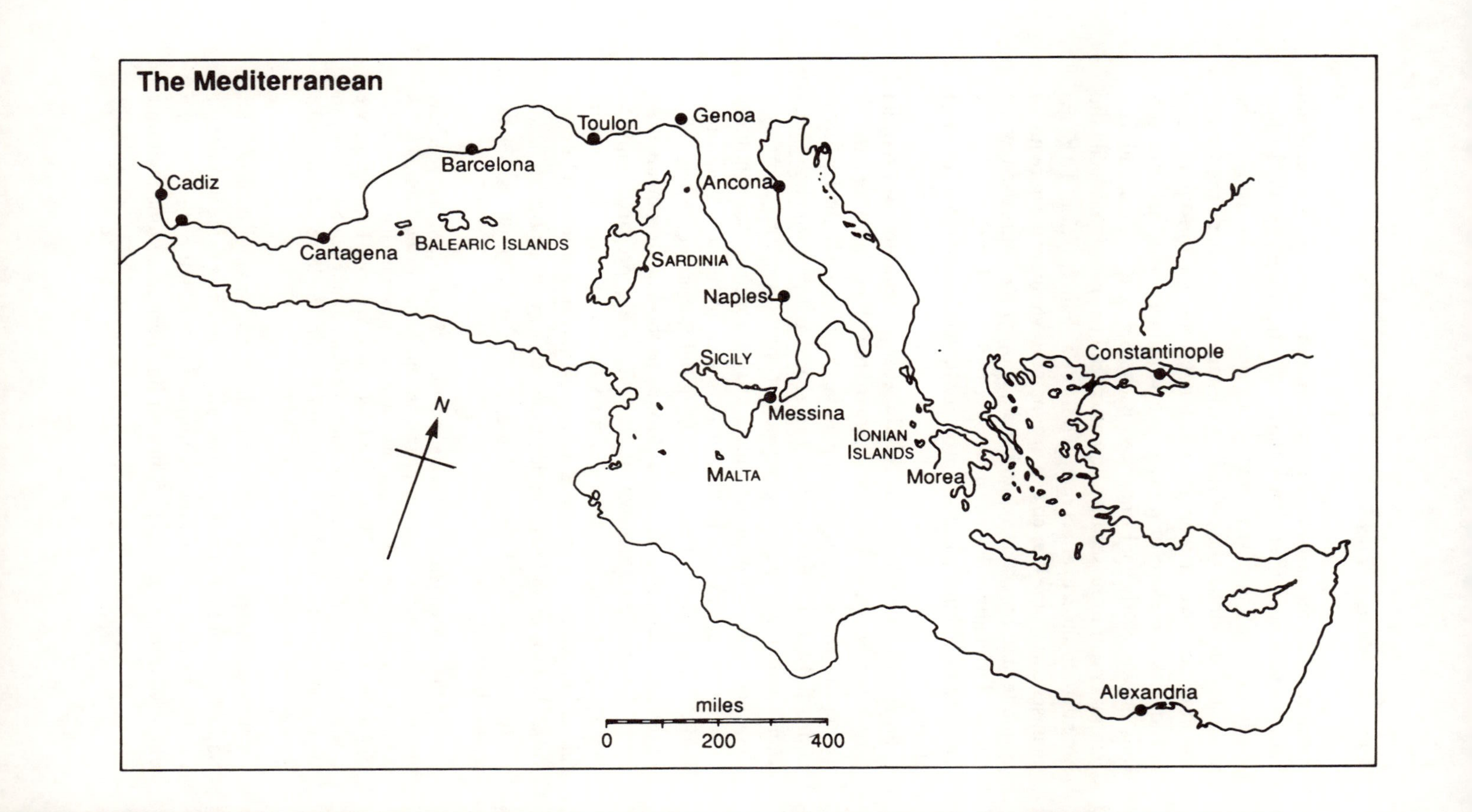
The Mediterranean
Cadiz
Barcelona
Toulon
Genoa
Cartagena
BALEARIC ISLANDS
Ancona
SARDINIA
Naples
SICILY
Messina
MALTA
IONIAN ISLANDS
Morea
Constantinople
Alexandria
N
miles
0
200
400

Britain's war effort being wrecked. It was an area of potentially serious military, diplomatic and economic reverses, but not one where the war would be won or lost.

Where Britain could suffer crippling blows, though, was in the Baltic. Brief challenges in this area had been encountered in 1780 and 1801, but that which materialised after the collapse of Prussia in 1806 was much more serious. The collapse made Napoleon the dominant force on the Baltic's southern shore and he was to remain so until the retreat from Moscow in 1812 marked the end of French authority. For Britain the seriousness of the situation lay in the Baltic's importance as her primary source of naval supplies. The best timber for medium-sized masts came from Russia; there was heavy reliance on Baltic oak for underwater planking and on Russian fir deals for vessels' decks; Russia also supplied most of Britain's tallow, over half her linseed, and almost half her pitch, tar and iron. Sweden also provided large quantities of iron, pitch and tar, and much of the timber purchased in the region was loaded at the Prussian ports of Memel and Danzig. There were alternative sources of such items, but like North American timber, they tended to be of inferior quality. More important than all those, however, was the question of hemp. This was a vital commodity for both the military and the merchant marines, and 90 per cent of Britain's needs were supplied by Russia, no other area being able to provide it on such a scale. In short 'the continued flow of imports from the Baltic was regarded as a national necessity'.[29]

Circumstances threatening interference with this commerce had a profound impact on military planning, and even when naval stores were still being obtained the uncertainties of Baltic politics could cause sharp price rises. In 1807 the amount of shipping passing through the Sound fell by almost half and prices, because of increased freight rates, started to rocket. In the autumn of 1806 Memel fir timber jumped from 15*s* to over £7: by 1809 it had risen to £16. Danzig plank cost £12 in 1806: by 1809 it had jumped to £24 and could scarcely be obtained. The freight rates for hemp also sharply rose from a peacetime rate of £2 per ton to £30 per ton or more in 1809, though the increase in its price attracted substantial quantities to Britain and by the end of 1809 there were supplies sufficient for approximately three years.[30] The scale of the trade was very large, some 11,537 ships sailing through the Sound in 1805, over half of them going to Britain. So precise a figure is not available for later years, but nevertheless one list noted that 1,675 vessels sailed through the Great Belt in a sixty-day period in 1810.[31]

Together with these raw materials, the Baltic also offered a means of communication with Russia and Sweden that would have been hard to maintain had Britain been excluded, an exclusion that would have been made all the worse by the sharp increase it would have meant in French standing. Finally to be considered was the question of the maritime power of some of the Baltic nations: fear of the potential hostility of the Danish and Russian navies was a profound influence on British military thinking in 1807–08.

All these factors weighed heavily, being most apparent in the shape of the expeditions sent to the region in 1807–08, but just as significant was the presence during the ice-free summer months of 1808–12 of a large Baltic fleet under Saumarez. In May 1810 this was the second largest such force maintained by the Admiralty, with a strength of twenty ships of the line and thirty-eight frigates and sloops. Even during the winter months in 1808–10 small squadrons were left behind at Gothenburg to support the Swedes.[32]

It is a singular fact that, despite the strong interests in the regions already considered, Britain's main strategic effort from 1808 was centred in none of them, but in the Iberian Peninsula. That this was so was prompted by several factors, the first of which was that it permitted, initially at least, a continuation of the policy of striking at Napoleon's naval power. Supporting the Peninsular revolt meant that the French emperor lost the use of Spain's navy and the refuge, repair and building facilities provided by the assorted Spanish ports. A further bonus was the elimination of the five French ships of the line that had been sheltering in Cadiz since Trafalgar, plus another one in the port of Vigo; these surrendered to the Spaniards in June 1808. Once the isolated French troops in Portugal had been removed, moreover, Britain could liberate those Portuguese warships not secured in 1807, could secure the eight Russian ships of the line sheltering in the Tagus while on their voyage from the Mediterranean to the Baltic, and could gain the use of important Atlantic ports like Lisbon and Oporto.[33]

Almost as important was that, as long as the revolt in Spain continued, Napoleon could make no credible claim to control that country's New World colonies. This nightmare prospect had haunted ministers' minds for many years and when the French first flooded into Spain in 1808, initially facing no Spanish resistance, the

Cabinet was very alarmed. With the King of Spain as Napoleon's puppet, 'the Interval may be short between the seizure by France of the Spanish Government at Home, and the Occupation by the same Power of its Colonies abroad . . .'.[34] The eventual Spanish revolt relieved ministers from this and spared them from any necessity for direct military action of their own in the New World. During the course of 1808 British policy moved rapidly from encouraging independence among Spain's colonies to encouraging them to remain quiescent and supportive of the mother country against the French invader. Francophobic propaganda was disseminated in these territories and they were further guarded from any attempts at French influence by British naval power.[35] In the event the colonies' stirrings towards liberation made them completely unsympathetic to French imperialism, the main British problem being a delicate diplomatic balancing act between their requests for help in their struggle for independence, calls to which Britain naturally felt responsive, and the need to preserve all of Spain's available power for the struggle against Napoleon. At one point a furious Richard Wellesley complained of Spain's diverting her forces to the New World in an effort to crush her rebellious colonies. His ire was particularly venomous because part of the Spanish action consisted of a blockade, a measure harming Britain's trade and which was possible only because the Spaniards were employing warships repaired in Britain at Britain's expense![36] Despite these irritations, Britain was fortunate in seeing the removal of Spain's colonies from Napoleon's grasp, a situation that would be maintained as long as the Peninsular conflict consumed the energies of both France and Spain.

Fighting Napoleon in the Peninsula also provided a large measure of relief from fears of French attack elsewhere in the world. Castlereagh was concerned at the end of 1807 about the possibility of French operations against India, but could reflect by 1809 that any such schemes would have been shelved with the commitment of so many French troops to Spain. Similar comfort could be felt about Canada, Liverpool writing to Craig, then Governor General, in the summer of 1810:

> With respect to any military attempt by Bonaparte upon Canada, I can assure you that at present his hands are too full for any such operation. It is evident that he has not the military means of making as large an effort in Spain and Portugal as his interests and reputation require. As long as the

contest can be maintained in that quarter upon its present scale we need be under little apprehension for more distant objects.[37]

Beyond these defensive benefits, fighting in the Peninsula also provided the opportunity of undertaking offensive operations against Napoleon on a scale that was not, prior to 1813, viable elsewhere. Surrounded on three sides by water, the Peninsula was a region where British naval power could be used to maximum effect, harassing French communications, supporting guerillas and permitting strong military landings on different parts of the long coastline.[38] Invariably unable to supply their troops locally from requisitions, Napoleon's commanders found it difficult to concentrate their usually superior forces into large armies, or at least to concentrate them for any length of time. Elsewhere in Europe the more powerful French armies, particularly with their superiority in cavalry and artillery, would have destroyed any British forces thrown against them. In the Peninsula a war of smaller bodies enabled Britain to fight with advantage. Moreover, as long as Britain fought, so would Portugal and Spain. Chronically short of her own troops, Britain found in Portugal a ready-made auxiliary with a tradition of having her troops led by foreigners. Placed under the command of Lieutenant General Beresford, and with the tactical leadership of a cadre of British officers and NCOs, by 1810 the Portuguese soldiers displayed a proficiency and *élan* which put them on a par with their British allies. By October 1810 Wellington's army was one-third Portuguese, they numbering some 27,000 men. This figure remained roughly constant during 1811–12, reaching a peak of 30,000 in 1813: thereafter numbers declined with the reluctance of the Portuguese to fight at any distance from their own borders.[39] Similarly valuable were the Spaniards. Although poorly trained and led, they persistently maintained substantial forces in the field to challenge the French despite repeated defeats. Added to such regular forces were the ubiquitous guerillas, ceaselessly pursuing their ruthless brand of cruel warfare and tying down thousands of Napoleon's troops in the process.[40] Both these advantages would have been lacking in any other theatre of military operations.

The Peninsula had wider ramifications for Britain's war effort besides this immediate provision of allies because its influence extended into diplomatic relations with other powers. By campaigning with and for the Iberian nations Britain could demonstrate to the rest of Europe that any enemy of Napoleon became, in Canning's phrase, 'instantly our ally'.[41] Such a stance was excellent propaganda in dealing with countries like Russia as clearly illustrating Britain's determination to fight. Perceval expressed the view that British troops in the Peninsula kept the Spaniards fighting, which in turn made France insecure all over Europe; similarly for Richard Wellesley it gave 'the others powers of the Continent the means, not only of recruiting strength, but of employing their strength for the purpose of relieving themselves from the dominion and influence of France'.[42] That Napoleon could not crush Iberian resistance drained his strength and his reputation, the fluctuating campaigns of 1812–13 illustrating that the French hold upon Spain was being eroded and the complete rout at Vitoria (June 1813) having serious repercussions for a French emperor trying to prevent Austria joining the allied campaign in Germany.[43]

With thousands of her troops committed to the Peninsula Britain could rebuff any charges that she was not pulling her weight in the war militarily. Despite the arrogant recalcitrance of the Spaniards, ministers could regard the area as one in which their strategy and their commanders prevailed, a position confirmed when the Cortes offered Wellington the position of commander-in-chief of the Spanish armies in 1812. Such pre-eminence would have been impossible while fighting alongside the huge and well organised armies of Russia, Prussia or Austria. In this respect Britain enjoyed the best of both worlds, seeing, in due course, heavy blows delivered in northern and central Europe while able to direct her own southern campaign without allied criticism or interference. In 1812 Castlereagh could blandly express regret at the fall of Moscow while simultaneously stressing that the scale of the Peninsular commitment prevented any direct aid to Russia. The following year the same argument could be used to fend off unwelcome Austrian ideas about the use of British troops in Italy.[44]

Yet another attraction of the Peninsula was the potential commercial benefit of a campaign that was a major wound in the Continental System, trade following the bayonet if not the flag. The official value of exports to the region rose from just under £1·7 million in 1807 to just over £6·7 million in 1809. By 1812 it was absorbing 19·3 per cent of all British exports. 'During these two years [1811 and 1812] in Britain's resistance to the Continental System', according to one authority, 'the Peninsula played a part that was as important commercially as it was from the military and political viewpoints'.[45] Access to Spain and Portugal was matched by commercial penetration of their colonies as well. Although Spain always resisted a commercial treaty, one was agreed with Regent John after the Portuguese royal family had fled to Brazil. This document, signed in February 1810, threw the whole area open to trade, and the official value of exports to South America increased from almost 1·2 million in 1807 to almost £2·7 million by 1812: this despite the glut of 1810–11.[46]

Against all these advantages, however, the Peninsula did suffer from one strategic drawback in that none of Britain's primary objectives was at stake – at least, not once the Iberian navies had been secured. The area did not pose an invasion threat, was not a source of vital imports, served no link in the chain of communications with other powers, and offered no direct barrier to French attacks on the Middle and Far East. Apart from the crucial links with Central and South America, the Peninsular campaign made little sense once Britain's political, as opposed to her military, interests took precedence. As long as ministers faced a Napoleon dominant in Europe the military advantages of the campaign outweighed all other considerations. However, once French power started to crumble, the commitment of so great a proportion of Britain's means to the southern theatre was less convenient. By the end of 1813, with dramatic changes in European political arrangements on the cards, it was most unwelcome to ministers to reflect that their only powerful army was in the Pyrenees. By December Bathurst had concluded that 'if we had our option, it would be better for us to throw our whole force as much as possible to co-operate with the Allies in the Netherlands'. Preventing this were the difficulties and dangers of moving a large army by sea in the middle of winter: as Bathurst lamented to Wellington, 'we could move you, but not your army'. Even had transport not been a problem, the question of Britain's suspicions of her allies would still have been an obstacle. When talking of aid for 1814, Castlereagh spoke of 'the contingency of being abandoned by the Continental Powers, [when money and supplies sent to them] would be required to sustain a protracted contest in the Peninsula, from which neither the honour nor the interest of Great Britain will permit [the British government] to withdraw'.[47] If Britain were abandoned once again by her European allies in the north, there was the consolation of knowing that the Peninsular War could at least be maintained. Fighting south of the Pyrenees became politically inconvenient as ministers became increasingly concerned to ensure a strong British voice in any peace settlement, but it did ensure a large measure of military independence.

One striking feature of strategy in 1803–15 was that there was little emphasis on extending Britain's imperial position. Although large resources were committed to guarding the nation's colonies and the trade that flowed from them, there was little interest for most of the time in attacking enemy islands and territories. Part of the reason for this has been considered already, namely the recognition that France had to be fought in Europe, and the relative inactivity of Napoleon himself in the colonial sphere, permitting Britain to be similarly inactive. Outside Spanish America, which will be reviewed shortly, only one large expedition actually sailed from Britain with a colonial objective: the 6,500-strong force sent to seize the Cape of Good Hope in 1805. There was a steady flow of replacements and reinforcements to the scattered imperial garrisons as required, but outside the dispatch of, say, two or three battalions in specific circumstances, no substantial formations were sent out to implement an aggressive policy. In stark contrast to previous eighteenth-century wars, no expeditions were sent to the West Indies, even the capture of the strongest French islands in 1809–10 being accomplished by local troops and others from Nova Scotia and Bermuda: none were sent out from Europe. Similarly the conquests in Africa and the Indian Ocean in 1809–11 were undertaken by troops already in those regions.

This resistance to imperial campaigns was maintained despite the frequent use of enemy colonies as bases for attacks on British trade. Such activities were a constant irritant: in the Caribbean one solitary Spanish privateer inflicted over £200,000 of damage to the Guinea coasting trade in 1805 and some forty-eight enemy privateers were captured in this sea in the period January 1806 – January 1807. In the Indian Ocean French vessels operating from Mauritius prompted a howl of anguish from the underwriters, merchants and shipowners of Calcutta in 1808: the former had to pay out £290,000 in claims in a two-month period for losses due largely to French attacks.[48] As a rule ministers would be prepared to tolerate such damage, and the resulting political pressure, aware that counter-measures would be costly in terms of manpower and uncertain in terms of success. Convoys would protect most of the trade for most of the time.

Part of this passivity can also be explained by the fact that the commercial gains to be anticipated from further colonial conquests were limited. By 1803 Britain was already a massive re-exporter of colonial crops such as sugar, coffee and rum. Renewed hostilities made selling these products to Europe increasingly difficult, a problem worsened by Napoleon's triumphs and the spread of the Continental System. Sugar, the most important single re-export, had sold for 73*s* per cwt in 1798: the price had fallen to 32*s* per cwt by 1807 and thereafter hardly rose above 50*s* until 1813. Overall the value of Britain's re-export trade, largely colonial in origin, fell from £14,419,000 in 1802 to £7,862,000 by 1808, rising only slightly to £8,278,000 in 1811.[49] Nothing in all this made the acquisition of further sources of supply attractive: a suggestion in 1812, for instance, that Denmark's African settlements might be seized was dismissed by the Duke of York on the grounds of lack of commercial viability.[50]

Governmental uninterest in capturing colonies was matched by a similar attitude when it came to selling colonial produce in Europe and defeating the Continental System. With only two major exceptions, governments in this period showed little inclination to mould their strategy directly to commercial needs. When Heligoland's potential was being assessed in 1807, for example, those advocating its capture did anything but stress its commercial value, yet its usefulness as a depot for goods being smuggled into northern Europe was considerable: one seven-day period in 1809 saw cargoes worth £300,000 being shipped out for the neighbouring coasts. As the Continental System waned Heligoland's value continued. In April 1813 2·5 million lb of sugar and coffee, as well as other items, were dispatched to the German ports.[51] Similarly when assessing the value of Malta (see pp. 86–7) commercial factors were not taken into account, yet the amount of goods sent to Europe via the island increased elevenfold in 1806–08. Again in the case of Walcheren its convenience for commercial purposes played no part in prompting its capture and was mentioned only once its retention or otherwise was under review.[52]

One of the two exceptions to this policy comes in the instructions to occupy the Dutch colonies of Demerara, Berbice and Essequibo in 1803, discussed in the next chapter. Much more profound was the question of Spanish America. Since the time of Drake this part of the world had been attracting British ambitions and greed, feelings heightened by the region's fabled wealth. In 1803 some eyes again began to turn towards the area; one unsigned memorandum to Addington spoke of the great colonial and maritime resources possessed by the Iberian powers because of their control of South America, remarking how in the sixteenth century this 'had nearly crushed the political independence and the civil and religious liberties of Europe'. Vansittart, later to be a Treasury Secretary, exhorted the Premier to encourage the Spanish colonies towards independence via an assault on Vera Cruz, from which point, he believed, most of Central America could be brought under British influence. He wanted another expedition to attack Chile as well.[53] In November 1803 the ubiquitous Popham reflected many opinions when expressing the view that South America sent $50 million *per annum* to Spain and that to deprive her of those provinces would, moreover, destroy her as a maritime power. Two months later Mulgrave was writing to Pitt anticipating that a French withdrawal from St Domingo 'might be made to lead very naturally to the completion of the great & extended views upon South America which we often discussed at Bath'.[54] In September 1806 Windham reflected that with Britain established in the region, combined with a supposed Calabrian revolt in Italy, Napoleon's power might begin to collapse.[55]

In fact this appreciation of Spanish America's value as a market has been questioned, one expert making the point that its inhabitants were far too poor to be of much commercial worth. Most of their needs were met by local craftsmen, and the abysmal state of South American communications was not at all conducive to trade. As it was opened up as a market there was a strong initial demand for manufactures, the region previously having been starved of such items because of the war, but this level of interest could not be sustained. After the fall of Montevideo roughly 2,000 businessmen and adventurers flocked to the place, their cargoes producing an immediate glut. Similarly the first fleet of merchantmen arriving at Rio de Janeiro in July 1808 served to flood the market. South America was unquestionably a useful addition to British commerce, particularly respecting sales of cotton goods and manufactures, but it was not the crock of gold that some imagined.[56]

During 1806–07 British strategy was to become enmeshed in efforts to pursue the dream of New World expansion, with disastrous consequences, though even before the final defeat at

Buenos Aires Castlereagh was starting to wonder whether the region was worth all the effort. 'The policy', he believed, 'upon which we are now acting will be productive of little commercial or political benefit, and must be felt as a great waste of our military means.' Wanting to cultivate good relations with the colonists, he wished to avoid direct conquest or any encouragement of their stirrings for independence, for fear of creating a political vacuum. Castlereagh hoped that some sort of local autonomy, perhaps under a Bourbon prince, might be possible, but did not speculate on how it might be brought about, wishing only that Britain's trade might be secure. Canning had similar opinions: although doubting the idea of a Bourbon prince, he wondered whether it would not be better to withdraw Britain's forces, except for a few military and commercial posts, and try to secure a peace with Spain.[57] On the one hand ministers came fully to appreciate the problems of military campaigns in South America, but on the other felt attracted to them by the dread that Napoleon might otherwise gain command of the region himself. By April 1808, with the French seemingly in control of Spain, Portland wrote of the Cabinet's grave alarm at the possibility of Napoleon ruling the Spanish colonies via his control of Spain herself: 'whatever orders France may think fit to dictate with respect to the Spanish Colonies may now be issued in the Name of His Catholic Majesty . . .'. Two days later Castlereagh was reassuring the Premier, after worries by George III on the same score, that the sending of Moore's expedition to Sweden would not compromise any effort in the Americas, i.e. the Cabinet was already actively considering military intervention. This was evidently going to be on a large scale, for in an undated memorandum (from its contents, probably penned in May 1808) Castlereagh spoke of South America being liberated by her inhabitants but with substantial British support. This took the form of almost 14,000 troops being sent to Caracas or Mexico, with a further 9,000 going to Montevideo. After the latter's capture some 4,000–5,000 of the force involved would move to support the assault on Central America.[58] Quite clearly Portland's Cabinet did not relish the thought of such a strategy, but felt that a French take-over of Spain made it unavoidable. Only the sudden Spanish revolt and the arrival of representatives seeking aid served to alter policy. Suddenly Britain was provided with an opportunity to try and seize the initiative and fight Napoleon in Europe. While Spain was in revolt Napoleon could make no credible claim to rule that country's colonies, so removing the need for British action against them: such an attack was anyway impossible while Britain and Spain were allied against the common enemy.

Notes

1 Aspinall, IV, pp. 617–19, 636–7, 644–5 and 662. Sir J. F. Maurice (ed.), *The Diary of Sir John Moore*, London, 1904, II, pp. 193–6 and 200. *Castlereagh Correspondence*, VIII, p. 96. P. Mackesy, *The War in the Mediterranean, 1803–10*, London, 1957, pp. 261–4.

2 P.R.O. WO 6/56, pp. 2–10 and 19–22. Sir H. Bunbury, *Narratives of some Passages in the Great War with France, 1799–1810*, London, 1927, p. 120. L. Butler, 'Minor expeditions of the British army from 1803 to 1815, *United Services Magazine*, CLI, 1905, pp. 510–11.

3 B. Liddell Hart, *The British Way in Warfare*, London, 1932, pp. 24–36.

4 Fortescue, *British Army*, 2, pp. 454–5, 499 and 501. R. Whitworth, *Field Marshal Lord Ligonier. The British Army, 1702–70*, Oxford, 1958, pp. 229–73. Sir W. D. Bird, 'British land strategy in four great wars', *Army Quarterly*, 30–1, 1930–31, p. 50. Sir R. Savory, *His Britannic Majesty's Army in Germany during the Seven Years War*, Oxford, 1966.

5 For these operations see Fortescue, *British Army*, 4.

6 Fortescue, *British Army*, 4, p. 565. For a more recent assessment: M. Duffy, *Soldiers, Sugar and Sea Power*, Oxford, 1987.

7 P.R.O. CO 318/40 and 36.

8 J. S. Owen (ed.), *A Selection from the Despatches, Memoranda, and other Papers relating to India, of the Marquess Wellesley, K.G., during his Government of India*, London, 1877, pp. 581–2.

9 K. Bourne (ed.), *The Letters of the Third Viscount Palmerston to Lawrence and Elizabeth Sulivan, 1804–63*, London, 1979, p. 64.

10 The 1757 figure is from J. Corbett, *England in the Seven Years War*, London, 1907, I, p. 203 n. Total of 330,000 from C. Duffy, *The Military Experience in the Age of Reason*, London, 1987, p. 17.

11 The 1805 figures are from A. Horne, *Napoleon, Master of Europe, 1805–07*, London, 1979, pp. 80–1. For 1812, from Chandler, appendix G, pp. 1108–14.

12 Durham R.O., Castlereagh Papers, D/Lo/C3, unsigned memorandum, but in Castlereagh's handwriting.

13 Fortescue, *British Army*, 5, pp. 240–9 and 255–61. Aspinall, IV, pp. 310, 320, 323, 326–7, 334 and 340–1. *Castlereagh Correspondence*, VI, pp. 128–9.

14 P.R.O. 30/58/5, Dacre Adams Papers, letter 122.

15 Elting, p. 505.

16 A general account of these actions can be found in Marcus, pp. 287, 296, 337–8 and 348. More detailed descriptions of all naval engagements in the period are in James, III ff.

17 The schemes are outlined in a whole variety of sources. Maurice, II,

pp. 97–108. *Castlereagh Correspondence*, V, pp. 127, 141–3 and 153–60; VIII, pp. 101–3. B.M. Add. Mss 37883, Windham Papers, ff. 54–5 and 259–v. Leeds R.O., Harewood Collection, Canning Papers, 31, Canning to Mulgrave, 15 October 1808. A. N. Ryan (ed.), *The Saumarez Papers. Selections from the Baltic Correspondence of Vice-Admiral Sir James Saumarez, 1808–12*, London, 1968, p. 13. P.R.O. WO 6/185, pp. 17–20. ADM 2/1369, pp. 188–9.

18 James, III, pp. 178–81. T. H. McGuffie, 'The stone ships expedition against Boulogne, 1804', *English Historical Review*, LXIV, October 1949, pp. 488–502. Buckinghamshire R.O., Hobart Papers, D/MH/H/War C137, 143, 149, 150 and W1–7. Lloyd, *Keith Papers*, III, pp. 89–90 and 101–6. *Castlereagh Correspondence*, V, pp. 85–131. Sandon Hall, Harrowby Papers, XXXII, ff. 85–6v. Aspinall, IV, p. 359. B.M. Add. Mss 49482, Gordon Papers, ff. 14–16.

19 *Castlereagh Correspondence*, VI, pp. 384–5. Aspinall, V, pp. 106–8.

20 P.R.O. WO 6/16, p. 20.

21 Marcus, p. 216. G. J. Renier, *Great Britain and the Establishment of the Kingdom of the Netherlands, 1813–15*, London, 1930, pp. 8–15. Sir H. Richmond, *Statesmen and Sea Power*, Oxford, 1946, p. 216.

22 *Naval Chronicle*, XII, London, 1804, p. 150. According to James, V, p. 131, Napoleon spent £2,640,000 on Antwerp in 1805–09.

23 *P.D.*, XV, pp. ccxlvi–ccxlvii. Lloyd, *Keith Papers*, III, pp. 51–2.

24 P.R.O. ADM 2/1365, pp. 328–9; 2/1367, pp. 120–1.

25 Buckinghamshire R.O., Hobart Papers, D/MH/H/War C107. *Castlereagh Correspondence*, VI, pp. 44–5, 82, 188–9 and 384–5.

26 *Castlereagh Correspondence*, IX, pp. 75 and 299.

27 P.R.O. CO 158/7, pp. 34–6. B.M. Add. Mss 59282, Dropmore Papers, f. 113–v. Richmond, pp. 221–2.

28 Leeds R.O., Harewood Collection, Canning Papers, 34, Castlereagh to Canning, 31 December 1807.

29 A. N. Ryan, 'The defence of British trade with the Baltic 1808–13', *English Historical Review*, LXXIV, 1959, pp. 443–4. Crouzet, p. 128.

30 Albion, p. 337. Crouzet, p. 398. *H.M.C. Bathurst*, pp. 137–8.

31 Crouzet, p. 129. P.R.O. FO 22/44, ff. 21–5. Ryan, *Saumarez Papers*, p. 144.

32 Leeds University Library, Brotherton Collection Box VII, Mulgrave Papers, 19/30.

33 M. Glover, *Britannia Sickens*, London, 1970, pp. 40–1. *P.D.*, X, p. 144.

34 Nottingham University Library, Portland Papers, PwF 4117.

35 *Castlereagh Correspondence*, VI, pp. 364–7 and 374–5.

36 P.R.O. WO 1/164, R. Wellesley to H. Wellesley, 4 May 1811. I. A. Lagnas, 'The Relations between Britain and the Spanish Colonies, 1808–12, University of London Ph.D. thesis, 1938–39, particularly chapters VII and VIII.

37 Leeds R.O., Harewood Collection, Canning Papers, 34, Castlereagh to Canning, 31 December 1807. *P.D.*, XIV, pp. 35–6. C. D. Yonge, *Life and Administration of Robert Banks Jenkinson, Second Earl of Liverpool*,

London, 1868, I, p. 314.

38 Marcus, pp. 335–7 and 350–60.

39 S. A. Vichness, 'Marshal of Portugal: The Military Career of William Carr Beresford, 1785–1814', University of Florida Ph.D. thesis, 1971, particularly pp. 117–326. Oman, *Peninsular War*, III, appendix XIV, p. 556. B.M. Add. Mss Loan 57, 6, Bathurst Papers, ff. 614–15. B.M. Add. Mss 49481, Gordon Papers, ff. 161–2v.

40 An excellent study of the Spanish side of events is C. J. Esdaile, *The Spanish Army in the Peninsular War*, Manchester, 1988.

41 *P.D.*, XI, pp. 890–1.

42 *P.D.*, XVI, pp. 15–16. Melville, II, p. 44.

43 C. Buckland, *Metternich and the British Government from 1809 to 1813*, London, 1932, pp. 525–6.

44 P.R.O. FO 65/78, ff. 64–6. Sir C. K. Webster, *British Diplomacy, 1813–15*, London, 1921, p. 96.

45 Crouzet, p. 688 and appendix II, p. 884. Heckscher, pp. 174–80.

46 Crouzet, pp. 478–9 and appendix II, p. 884. W. W. Kaufmann, *British Policy and the Independence of Latin America, 1804–28*, New Haven, Conn., 1951, pp. 55–6.

47 *S.D.W.*, VIII, pp. 414–15. Webster, p. 28.

48 C. Dowling, 'The Convoy System and the West India Trade, 1803–15', University of Oxford Ph.D. thesis, 1965, pp. 155 and 158–9. Parkinson, *War in the Eastern Seas*, pp. 308 and 311. P.R.O. ADM 2/1366, pp. 166–70. *The Times*, 14 and 22 December 1808. The largest single reinforcement sent from Britain to the Caribbean in this period was three regiments dispatched to Barbados at the end of 1807: P.R.O. CO 318/31, Instructions to Lt.-General Bowyer, 13 November 1807.

49 Sugar prices from Dowling, p. 55. Trade values from Crouzet, appendix II, p. 887. Detailed statistics for all crops are in Mitchell and Deane; also E. B. Schumpeter, *English Overseas Trade Statistics, 1697–1808*, Oxford, 1960.

50 *H.M.C. Bathurst*, pp. 215–16.

51 Sir J. K. Laughton (ed.), *The Naval Miscellany*, I, London, 1901, pp. 380–5. Crouzet, p. 437. J. Holland Rose, 'British West India commerce as a factor in the Napoleonic wars', *Cambridge Historical Journal*, III, 1929–31, p. 46.

52 Crouzet, p. 385. Nottingham University Library, Portland Papers, PwF 7635.

53 Devon R.O., 152M Sidmouth Papers, C1803/OL and C1803/OZ.

54 Northern Ireland R.O., Castlereagh Papers, D3030/1845. Leeds University Library, Brotherton Collection Box VII, Mulgrave Papers, 17/42.

55 B.M. Add. Mss 58930, Dropmore Papers, ff. 19–20v.

56 D. C. M. Platt, *Latin America and British Trade, 1806–1914*, London, 1972, pp. 3–9.

57 *Castlereagh Correspondence*, VII, pp. 315–24. Leeds R.O., Harewood Collection, Canning Papers, 32, Canning to Castlereagh, 19 May 1807.

58 Nottingham University Library, Portland Papers, PwF 4117 and 8583. Aspinall, V, pp. 68–9. *Castlereagh Correspondence*, VII, pp. 385–9.

5

Addington and Pitt

The British declaration of war on 18 May 1803 was a response to the creeping expansionism of France, yet the ministers concerned were the same as those who had eagerly grasped the Peace of Amiens the previous year. They had concluded in the interim that peace with Bonaparte was too dangerous in the light of French power in northern Italy, Switzerland and the Low Countries, an authority made all the more menacing by the First Consul's obvious ambitions in the Mediterranean, the Caribbean and Louisiana.[1] Continuing the peace meant leaving France pre-eminent in Europe, evacuating Malta in line with the Amiens terms and so giving Bonaparte a free hand in the Mediterranean, and would have prolonged British uncertainty respecting French colonial intentions. With France trying to regain control of St Domingo, Hobart had already, in February 1803, warned Lieutenant General Nugent, the Govenor of Jamaica, to beware of an attack both from that island and from Europe. The Cabinet's problem was that France, legitimately trying to reoccupy her own territory, had every excuse to send ships and men to the West Indies, forces which could just as easily be directed against British islands. As long as the two nations were at peace Britain could take no 'decided measures' to intercept French vessels at sea or blockade them in their ports. All Hobart could do was promise to send reinforcements to Jamaica once the hurricane season was over and exhort Nugent to ceaseless vigilance. In the following weeks, with tension mounting, the Admiralty sent out a series of delicate instructions reminiscent of those issued in 1755 prior to the outbreak of the Seven Years War. At the end of March Rear-Admiral Thornborough was told to prevent military vessels sailing from Holland to Louisiana, though he was to use force only as a last resort and was somehow to avoid needlessly annoying the French. Five days later his orders were amended: vessels could now sail to Louisiana provided they were not carrying troops. Similar instructions were sent to the Caribbean, Commodore Hood being told at one point to prevent the arrival of French troops in the Leeward and Windward Islands, only to be informed four days later that small parties of troops were permitted but not large expeditions.[2] In short, ministers were dithering and loading heavy responsibilities on their naval commanders.

The whole nature of the problem was made clear in a communication to the Russian government shortly after the declaration of war. In it the Cabinet stressed that France had displayed no tendency towards reasonableness, while simultaneously trying to delay hostilities to a more favourable moment. France had the initiative while Britain had to maintain extensive forces merely against the possibility of action. Ministers did not trust Bonaparte and felt that continued peace brought the risk of war with none of the latter's strategic benefits. 'It is clear therefore that the delay arising from any new negotiations would, in the first instance, operate to the advantage of France and the injury of Great Britain, whilst its ultimate success would remain extremely precarious.'[3]

Once hostilities had openly resumed Britain enjoyed the psychological benefit of removing the uncertainty, could try to stop French naval movements, could continue to hold Malta, and was free to reopen the whole question of French power in Europe. The Cabinet was also aware that its declaration of war enjoyed general support in the nation at large (see p. 70) and in Parliament. On 23 May Addington, with Pitt's support, won a Commons vote of confidence by 398 votes to sixty-seven.[4]

Without question the most decisive military step taken by Addington was the declaration of war itself. It set up an immediate naval barrier to French colonial activity and allowed Britain to take advantage of Bonaparte's naval weakness. The latter's dockyards were only partially restocked after the draining away of stores during the previous war; furthermore his naval dispositions were vulnerable, with half France's warships commited to supporting operations on St Domingo. Bonaparte had maintained in January that war would not be resumed until the autumn of 1804; instead, during the summer of 1803, his arsenals were blockaded, his trade was swept from the seas and most of the warships recalled from the Caribbean were forced to seek an isolated refuge at Ferrol. French naval power 'had been dealt, at the outset of war, a crippling blow from which it was never to recover'. For one French historian 'it was an initial success, and a major one, for our enemies . . .'.[5] Nor was this shrewd blow some sort of fortuitous accident. Four days before war was declared Castlereagh had observed that 'Their [the French] navy has been getting rather worse than better since the peace, being chiefly employed in transporting troops to the West Indies, and I do not understand that their arsenals have been replenished.'[6] In June 1803 there were fifty British ships of the line blockading ports from the Texel to Toulon that contained only thirty-seven equivalent vessels.[7]

Having gained this immediate naval advantage, however, Addington's strategy was of necessity defensive. This policy has prompted much misunderstanding over the years, authors interpreting it as either weak and ineffectual or, at the other extreme, as far-sighted and subtle. In the former category are writers like Fortescue, Reilly and Steven Watson, who see Addington as either unduly passive or too cautious financially.[8] Addington's more recent biographer, Philip Ziegler, is firmly of the other camp, seeing in the defensive policy adopted in 1803 an appreciation that no European power was ready to fight France and that Britain's best option was to lure Bonaparte into a failed invasion. This theory is summed up by the startling 'Victory would go to the side which could remain inactive the longest.'[9]

In reality the concentration on domestic defence was not something over which the government could exercise much choice. Although there has been some debate over the viability of the invasion threat,[10] it could not be ignored, especially in the light of the intense activity in Bonaparte's harbours. *The Times* spoke of an army of 200,000 men being assembled across the Channel in July 1803 and no ministry could ignore such a danger.[11] Concentrating its forces at home to meet the threat was a conventional response. In March 1803 there were 52,000 regular soldiers in Britain and Ireland: by January 1804 the number had risen to over 94,000 and there were also some 85,000 militiamen and 400,000 volunteers.[12] Combined with naval attacks in the Channel, it was the Cabinet's hope that these forces would repel any invasion attempt. Certainly the threat was taken seriously, and ministers were made aware that the blockade of ports like Brest could never be total – there was always the chance that escaping enemy warships might establish temporary control of the Channel and permit a landing. In general ministers felt that the preparations would defeat any such attempt, not least because of the awareness that any invasion would suffer delays due to contrary winds and tides.[13]

Such a concentration, of course, meant that few resources were available for operations in other areas as long as the French army remained concentrated on the coast. This put Addington in the uncomfortable political position of seeming lethargy in the face of Bonaparte's energy, with a consequent diminution in parliamentary support.[14] Nothing could be done to stop France overrunning Hanover in May and June 1803, while the brief flaring of Emmet's Irish rebellion in July also made the ministry appear weak. Compared to this its only obvious efforts at activity were the futile bombardments of French harbours culminating in the fiasco of the stone ships expedition (see p. 82) and some minor colonial conquests.

Strategic lethargy, though, was not something deliberately sought by the Cabinet. Early in 1804, keenly spurred on by Hobart, ministers were taking steps to form a disposable force in Britain of at least 20,000 men. No detailed proposals for its employment were drawn up, but the implication is obvious: the ministry wanted a body of troops ready to respond to any French moves and to pursue offensive operations. Although not formed before Addington fell, the possibilities were probably in Castlereagh's mind the following year when ordering 30,000–35,000 infantry and 8,000–10,000 cavalry to be ready for any chance of European service.[15] Other facts also indicate a ministry ready to take the offensive. In September 1803 Hobart expressed a wish to attack Walcheren, but 'our exertions have hitherto not enabled us to look much beyond defensive measures . . .'. At about the same time Nelson was also told that more troops might be sent to the Mediterranean, so many only having been removed in the first place because of the need for home defence.[16]

Just as thoughts about Walcheren and the Mediterranean anticipated the strategy of later ministries, so Addington's Cabinet also faced the sort of worries about the Iberian Peninsula that were to come to a head later on. During 1803 the Cabinet viewed with mounting alarm the way Spain was fawning on France and offering, in October, to pay Bonaparte a massive subsidy to preserve her tenuous neutrality. Ministers were concerned that Spain would be dragged into the conflict against them, a prospect worrying not merely in itself but also because it might in turn allow French pressure to be put on Portugal to become hostile as well. By September Bonaparte was demanding that Portugal should close her ports to British trade, and Hobart was fearful for the future of Brazil and Macao in the light of French influence. There was discussion among ministers about a pre-emptive occupation of Brazil, though Hawkesbury for one felt it to be impossible, given the scale of Britain's commitments in the Caribbean, the Mediterranean and Ireland. With no forces to spare, ministers were obliged to wait on Iberian events, feeling able only to urge the Portuguese to place their fleet under British command so that it, and their royal family, might be moved to Brazil. In return Britain promised to protect Portugal's coasts, a somewhat hollow reassurance, given that that country might be facing occupation. If Portugal would not co-operate, then Fitzgerald, the ambassador in Lisbon, was instructed to threaten British attacks on her colonies. Only the Portuguese accession to the Spanish treaty giving a subsidy to France in November 1803 eased the pressure for the moment. The Cabinet remained deeply suspicious of Portuguese assurances that there would be only one payment to France and that there were no secret territorial concessions, but felt unable to do more than apply diplomatic pressure. This was particularly the case while Portugal retained neutrality, of however dubious a nature, and while there were prospects of a new coalition against France, one that might drive Spain out of Bonaparte's control.[17]

Britain's isolation and the pinning of her military means to domestic defence were major strategic handicaps during the first months of the war, but, despite Ziegler's statements, Addington's ministry did try to revert to the traditional policy in such circumstances: the search for European allies. In July 1803 the Russian ambassador, Woronzow, was informed:

> The Emperor of Russia is placed in a situation which may enable him to render the most important services to Europe. It is in consequence of His Interposition that Europe can alone expect that the Cabinets of Vienna and Berlin should suspend their ancient jealousies, should Relinquish those lesser Interests which have hitherto divided them, and which, by dividing them, have left them successively at the mercy of the common Enemy. It is to Him that they look for that General Concert which can alone remedy those evils.

While professing pacific intentions the government pointed to

French ambitions in Europe and the Levant. The only way of restoring peace was:

> a combination of the Great Powers on the Continent, with his Imperial Majesty at their head, who shall be steadfastly determined to make new and extraordinary efforts for the purpose of circumscribing the Power, and restraining the Ambition of the Government of France.

This was a blunt request for another great anti-French coalition, and the day after it was written Warren, the ambassador in St Petersburg, was told to inform the Russians that Britain would provide subsidies for any military action, the hope that Austria and Prussia would participate again being stated. At the year's end Hobart summed up the Cabinet's attitude by remarking that 'we must always look to a combination of the great Powers on the Continent as calculated to be productive of the most salutory consequences'.[18]

Neither Austria nor Prussia offered much hope of such co-operation. The ambassador in Vienna complained that the Austrians had not even objected to the French occupation of Hanover and he doubted their claim that they had sought closer ties with Russia and been rebuffed. As for Prussia, that power displayed great nervousness of France and had hopes of controlling Hanover herself, an ambition to which Britain would never concur but to which Bonaparte just might.[19] This left Russia as the main target of British wooing, particular attention being paid to possible military co-operation in the Mediterranean. There Russia was already worried about Bonaparte's plans for the Ottoman Empire, having signed a defensive treaty with Naples in 1798 and viewing that kingdom as a barrier to French expansion in Albania and Greece. The Cabinet shared this view, Britain subsidising Naples to the tune of £170,000 p.a. in an effort to improve its defences. Woronzow was told in January 1804 that British warships were being sent to cruise off the Greek coast and that Britain's agents in the region were being instructed to work with their Russian counterparts. In March Hobart wrote that both countries wanted to preserve Naples and that Russia would not object to British actions aimed at thwarting any French schemes in the Morea.[20]

The ministry fell before these feelers came to anything more definite, but they explode the myth of Addington's diplomatic inactivity and also Holland Rose's claim that any contacts were 'indirect or semi-official'.[21] Nor do the suggestions respecting

Addington's supposed financial stringency hold water in the light of the proffered subsidies. That the attempt to form a new coalition failed at this time was due to several factors. Initially Russian suspicions of France were matched by similar sentiments towards Britain, resentment being felt at the retention of Malta, at British maritime laws aimed at gaining a monopoly of the carrying trade within the empire, and from bitter memories of failed Anglo-Russian co-operation in 1799. Addington's domestic position was also uninspiring, particularly with Pitt's absence from the Cabinet and the brief return of George III's mental instability. Woronzow confided to Rose in August that the Tsar had no confidence in the ministry.

> marked as they are throughout Europe for their utter imbecility; which, the Count said, occasioned no surprise to him, as he knew from all the foreign Ministers here, and from his correspondence with different parts of Europe, that they are held in universal contempt.

To what extent such feeling blocked any renewed coalition is hard to quantify, but certainly Woronzow had little confidence in the government, remarking on another occasion that 'If this Ministry lasts, Britain will not survive'.[22] If Addington's endeavours met with little success, he did at least lay the foundations upon which Pitt would later construct the Third Coalition.

Outside Europe the ministry had few resources to spare for any object beyond preservation of the *status quo*. In Jamaica Nugent vainly hoped that 3,000 reinforcements might be sent to him, but the Cabinet preferred to rely on a naval blockade to prevent any attack from St Domingo and earlier promises of more troops (see p. 102) were forgotten. In the Leeward and Windward Islands the outbreak of war saw a British garrison of only 8,999 troops scattered among the assorted colonies – in 1808 York estimated that its optimum garrison should number 14,000 – and any hopes of sufficient troops for an attack on Martinique were dashed. Lieutenant General Grinfield, the local commander, was told to make no attempt on the island unless its garrison was weak or the disposition of its inhabitants made success very likely.[23] In the East the prospects of offensive action were similarly limited. Informing Richard Wellesley of the war, Castlereagh ventured the opinion that France could do little to harm Britain's Indian interests, giving the governor-general a very broad hint as to the Cabinet's priorities by expressing the hope that the East India Company's finances would continue to improve. Such progress would be impossible were Wellesley to pursue costly military adventures. Only in India did financial considerations dictate, and then only because the ministry felt secure anyway. Just as Castlereagh was keeping the purse strings tight Hobart was telling Wellesley direct not to attack Mauritius or Dutch Batavia without specific permission from London. Even without such an injunction the shortage of military means would still have been a restriction: shortly after Addington's fall it was noted that the Indian military were 6,000 men short of their establishment.[24]

Despite these restrictions the Cabinet was able to score a series of virtually bloodless minor successes. Off Canada the small French islands of St Pierre and Miquelon were occupied, eliminating potential privateering bases. In the Caribbean, with Martinique not being deemed practicable, St Lucia was taken, an island to windward of Martinique and so valuable in its blockade: in Castries St Lucia had the best harbour in the region. Tobago was also occupied, being to windward of the whole island group and, having been British in 1793–1802 and prior to 1783, containing many British settlers and investments. It was, furthermore, because of its situation close to South America, potentially valuable as a centre for smuggling.[25] This commercial motive, which played a part in prompting Tobago's capture, was uppermost in prompting the seizure of the Dutch Guiana settlements of Demerara, Essequibo and Berbice. These had previously been taken in 1796 and had thereafter been the recipients of heavy British investment. One Liverpool merchant had loans totalling £200,000 tied up in Demerara and another, with £400,000 invested in the same place, told the government that a French takeover would ruin the leading merchant houses of Liverpool, Bristol, London and Glasgow. The total amount involved came to some £5 million, the colonies not only providing Caribbean staples like coffee and sugar but also significant supplies of cotton for the burgeoning Lancashire mills. All these pressures prompted orders in June 1803, once the Cabinet was sure that hostilities with France also meant war with Holland, for the settlements' capture. Such was their importance that ministers were even prepared to send a modest reinforcement, of 159 officers and men, to Grinfield from Britain, also putting one of the black regiments at Jamaica under his command.

Such undiluted commercial motives were virtually unique in the

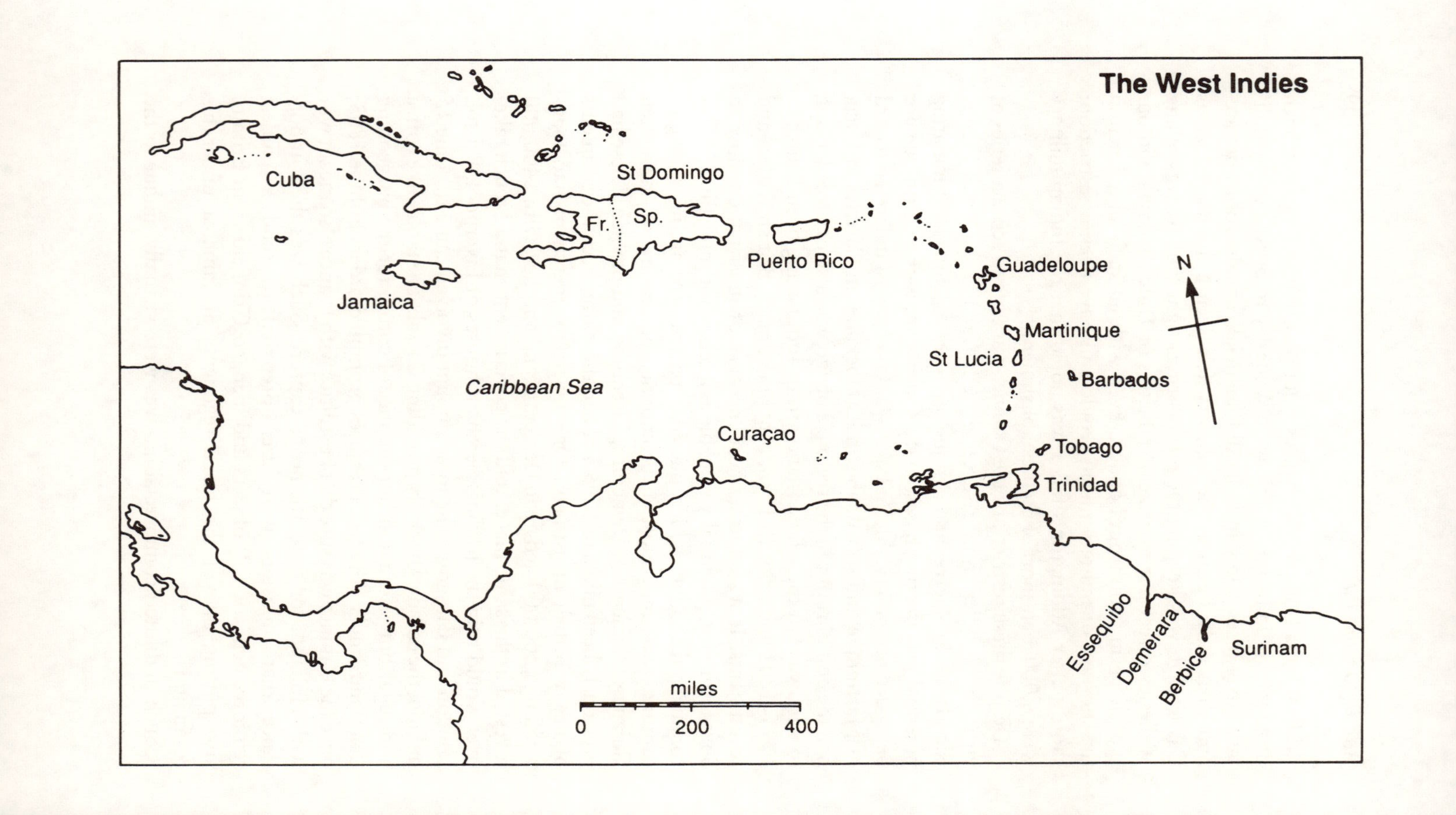
The West Indies
Cuba
St Domingo
Fr.
Sp.
Puerto Rico
Jamaica
Guadeloupe
N
Martinique
St Lucia
Barbados
Caribbean Sea
Curaçao
Tobago
Trinidad
Essequibo
Demerara
Berbice
Surinam
miles
0
200
400

period, for even the later involvement in South America had political and military considerations as well. However, it should be stressed that though this was the case it also involved little effort. Hobart felt that the colonies would be surrendered without a struggle, there being reports that their garrisons were mutinous and their inhabitants eager for a return to British rule. Such confidence, in the event, was to prove fully justified, Grinfield employing only 1,300 soldiers to capture the three areas easily in September. One may wonder whether the operation would have been launched at all had the Dutch defences appeared stronger and more capable of resistance. All the ministerial attitudes of the time suggest that, despite the financial interests at stake, the colonies would have been ignored had their reduction seemed likely to be troublesome.[26] Whether this be so or not, their fall left only one immediate object for the Cabinet in the region: Surinam. This was taken in May 1804 and was the last of the 'easy' Caribbean captures.[27]

There is no doubt that Addington's military thinking was overwhelmingly defensive in character, a trait that was to continue in later years: in August 1807 he would complain of reductions in the Militia's strength and, with British troops in the Baltic, of the danger of invasion if Napoleon quickly moved his troops back from Poland.[28] As long as no new European coalition was available to distract the invasion threat this concern made sense, and it is significant that even after Pitt's return to office there was no offensive strategy on the Continent until the Russian alliance had been secured. Addington had his failures as a war leader: the loss of Hanover, the inept anti-invasion operations in the Channel and the chaos in the navy's administration due to St Vincent's efforts at reform. But there were solid successes as well, ranging from the blow to French maritime power in the timing of the war to the augmentation of Britain's domestic defences[29] and the siezure of valuable enemy colonies. Unfortunately for the Prime Minister none of these triumphs carried with it the sort of dramatic impact that could have bolstered his flagging reputation in Parliament. In spring 1804 Pitt committed himself from political neutrality to outright hostility, the opposition in Parliament already enjoying the benefits of all the other oratorical big guns of the time, figures such as Fox, Canning and Windham. Against all this the ministry appeared singularly inept, Addington himself cutting a poor figure in the Commons with no juniors of stature to support him. It appeared that the demonic energy of Bonaparte was being confronted by a government capable of only a shambles like the stone ships project. The French navy may have been seriously wounded by the coming of war, but the damage was neither as obvious nor as reassuring as a major victory in open battle. Lacking such a public relations boost, the ministry's support in the Commons crumbled during March and April 1804 and finally prompted the Premier's resignation.

The eventual construction of a new government in May did not bring any changes in military planning. British activity was still most obviously visible in the Channel and Melville, the new First Lord of the Admiralty, was confident of repelling any invasion, though felt that 'jealousy and attention ought to be alive and chiefly directed to Boulogne and Ostend on the French and Flemish Coasts and to that of the Texel on the Coast of Holland'. These attacks achieved as little as the previous administration's efforts.[30] Only with respect to Melville's surrender to the timber monopoly was there substantial improvement in the general strategic position, and this was reduced by the additional responsibilities incurred in fighting Spain.

Anglo-Spanish relations steadily deteriorated during the course of 1804 and by September the Cabinet had become alarmed at reports of Spanish naval activity at Cadiz, Cartagena and Ferrol. Prior to this there had also been word that the French squadron in Ferrol was receiving supplies and recruits from France either overland through Spain or via Spanish coastal waters. Further annoyance was caused by attacks from privateers which used Spain's American harbours as their base; despite Spanish assurances, ministers believed that the Spanish would not or could not put a stop to the practice. Off Ferrol Cochrane expressed the view that Spain would declare war once her treasure ships from the New World had arrived safely.

Once again British strategy was to be jolted into a pre-emptive strike against a potential foe, Pitt ordering all Spanish vessels carrying military stores to be seized and her treasure fleet to be intercepted. Britain did not formally declare war, but after the bloody fight to capture the treasure ships in October its likelihood was obvious: Spain actually declared hostilities in December. Hawkesbury publicly summed up British policy in a chilling phrase that would be echoed at Copenhagen: 'We must not permit either the strength of one power, or the weakness of another, to be converted into a weapon for our destruction.' The ministry justified its actions by pointing to the activities at Ferrol and the scale of 'neutral' Spain's financial support of France, Pitt asking the Commons in February 1805 how Parliament would have reacted had the government remained idle and a united Franco-Spanish fleet effected an invasion of Ireland.[31]

Strategically the new enemy brought a substantial addition to French naval power, but to the Cabinet this appeared inevitable anyway and by striking first Britain was at least able to dent Spanish finances. A hostile Spain meant pressure on Portugal but possibly ministers were viewing that nation in a jaundiced light already. In July 1804 Britain had expressed displeasure at Portugal's participation in the financial support of France and fears that territorial concessions might in future be demanded from the Portuguese. However, by December Fitzgerald was reporting from Lisbon his confidence that Portugal would evade any further French demands, an opinion that hardened as the weeks went by. In March 1805 the Cabinet had become sufficiently impressed with the Portuguese determination to preserve their independence to consider sending them arms and ammunition to strengthen their defences, though it would not go so far as to supply money or a cadre of British troops to train the Portuguese army.[32]

Like that of Addington before him, Pitt's primary objective was to break the strategic straitjacket that bound Britain by the formation of a new coalition. Reports in April 1804 indicated that neither Austria nor Prussia showed any willingness as yet to fight France, Harrowby remaining pessimistic about them in July despite proffered subsidies of £250,000 to Prussia and £200,000 per month for three months to Austria.[33] Russia consequently remained the chief British hope, though mutual suspicion still remained a profound handicap. One problem was Tsar Alexander I's desire to gain control of Malta, an objective in harmony with the perennial Russian quest for warm-water ports. Another difficulty remained the Russian resentment of the maritime laws and annoyance at the new Anglo-Spanish war, the Tsar being offended when his offer of mediation was rejected and nervous that Britain would prefer to attack the Spanish colonial empire rather than co-operate with Russia in the Mediterranean.[34] On the Cabinet's part there were fears that Alexander I might try to enforce some sort of disagreeable Anglo-French peace in an effort to escape from the pressure for a military alliance – as would happen in 1807. The worry was heightened in September 1804 when both Austria and Prussia recognised

Napoleon's imperial title, it being feared that this might frighten the Tsar away from any alliance.[35]

Starting from such a fragile basis, it is not surprising that the actual Anglo-Russian negotiations were fraught with disagreements. Financially Britain was prepared to offer all her potential allies a total of £5 million. Russia was unenthusiastic and wanted more, while Austria, when she tentatively moved towards hostilities, wanted £6 million without any guarantee that she would fight at all![36] Just as awkward was the Russian determination to see British troops as well as British money committed to the cause. As early as April 1804 Czartoryski, the Russian Foreign Minister, pointedly observed that, keen though the Tsar was for financial help, 'His Majesty would be no less eager to learn also how Great Britain for her part would employ her land forces, which by well-directed diversions could do a great deal of damage to the enemy.'[37] Russia thought in terms of a joint force operating in Greece to protect that region from the French, though the preferred Cabinet option was a Russian force in southern Italy, propping up the Neapolitan court, while British troops held Sicily. By October ministers were prepared to send an extra 5,000–6,000 troops to the Mediterranean, but the Russians still regarded this as an effort to let their allies do the fighting. In November 1804 they offered a campaign in Naples provided Britain contributed 10,000 men, tartly, if correctly, pointing out that British troops on Sicily would do nothing to encourage Austria. By the end of that month Czartoryski was increasing the demand still further, pressing for 12,000–15,000 British soldiers, and December saw the Russians threatening to send no troops at all to Naples, they still complaining about the size of the potential British force. However, Leveson Gower, Warren's replacement in St Petersburg, did report that the Russians still seemed willing to fight, he suspecting that they were concerting plans with Austria. As this latter prospect began to take shape, and with it the chance of a large campaign in central Europe, Russian pressure about the scale of Britain's force for Naples began to ease.[38]

Nevertheless it was to be April 1805 before Leveson Gower was finally able to secure a formal Russian alliance, and even then he felt compelled to agree to a surrender of Malta. Few things are more indicative of the importance the Cabinet placed on the new coalition than the fact that Pitt was prepared to ratify such a concession. Under no circumstances was Britain prepared to yield over the maritime laws and Castlereagh for one thought that Russia would never agree to fight unless Britain gave ground over the other major bone of contention.[39] What chiefly propelled the nascent coalition, though, were Napoleon's actions rather than Britain's concessions. Already offended by his kidnapping and execution of the Duc d'Enghien in March 1804, both Russia and Austria were alarmed when he declared himself King of Italy (May 1805) and then annexed the Ligurian Republic (June 1805). Nor could Napoleon and Alexander I agree about the future of the, Russian-controlled, Ionian Islands. By August these differences had prompted the formation of a general coalition in which both Austria and Russia committed themselves to halting French expansion. Although the Cabinet felt obliged to pledge more financial aid to Austria than had been originally intended,[40] the strategic reward came on 26 August when the Grande Armée broke its camp on the Channel coast and marched eastwards. The military paralysis prompted by the invasion threat was lifted and, with the rapid pace of events, the surrender of Malta was not something that Britain had to implement.

Now the Cabinet could actively start assessing its own offensive options, though its choice still remained fairly limited. Destroying the invasion flotilla at Boulogne would have been an obvious step, but Napoleon left substantial forces behind on the coast to guard it, and a discouraging report on the inherent dangers of any amphibious assault on Boulogne prompted ministers to drop the idea. Similarly uninviting were prospects for any attack on the other coastal fortresses such as Brest or Toulon; not only would such operations be dangerous and difficult but they were unlikely to contribute much to the defeat of France.[41] All that remained, therefore, if Napoleon were to be directly attacked, were possible campaigns in the Mediterranean and/or northern Germany.

As already seen, there had been much negotiation with the Russians about a Mediterranean campaign. During the course of 1804 Malta's garrison had been increased by 1,000 men and on 28 March 1805 Lieutenant General Craig was ordered to take command of all Mediterranean units and to sail to the region with reinforcement of a further 4,000 troops. Initially Craig's instructions did not go beyond the objective of making sure that Sicily did not fall to Napoleon but, in view of the Russians' continuing distrust of Britain's intentions, they were amended. Now Craig was told to assist the Russians in Naples should they or Elliot, the British ambassador to the Neapolitan court, request it. However, Craig was not to allow his command to become so involved in Italian operations that he could not withdraw should the need arise, ministers wanting to keep their options open should attacks against Alexandria or Sardinia be deemed necessary. Later, in April, a further sop was thrown to the Russians when Craig was told not to occupy Sicily without the permission of the Russian commander, though he could act unilaterally if Naples became hostile and started closing her ports to British vessels.[42]

Ministers felt little enthusiasm for an Italian campaign, pursuing it primarily for the sake of Anglo-Russian relations, an objective in which it was successful.[43] Their determination to do all in their power to secure the alliance is illustrated by the fact that Craig and his reinforcements sailed on 17 April, a moment when the Tsar was still no more than a potential ally and when Villeneuve's Combined Fleet was loose at sea. The danger from the latter prompted the convoy of thirty-three transports to seek shelter at Lisbon at one point on their voyage, the force not reaching Malta until 18 July. That the politicians were indifferent towards the campaign has prompted severe criticism from Fortescue, who believed that Italy offered the best prospects for British military action prior to 1808. For him 20,000–30,000 British troops in the area, discounting possible allied contingents as well, would 'have embarrassed, and might wholly have wrecked, the plans of Napoleon'. Craig's force was part of 'Pitt's incurable failing – the passion for frittering England's little force away in minute diversions, instead of keeping it united at a single point'.[44] Such strictures have little to commend them. They assume that Napoleon's planning would have been distracted by a peripheral threat to his empire. Had the British army landed and remained in Naples, Napoleon could have ignored it; had it marched north to attempt to make some impact, it would have faced difficult sieges of the Italian fortresses and great peril on the north Italian plains from French armies better provided with both cavalry and artillery. Even if Fortescue's theory made more strategic sense, it still takes no account of the practical difficulties involved in transporting, say, 25,000 troops to Italy. Moving Craig's 4,000 infantry consumed 11,000 tons of shipping: how much more would have been required for a larger force, particularly if one included some provision for cavalry and artillery horses? How could such an army's commissariat have functioned, so far from convenient supply in

Britain and lacking large accumulated magazines on the spot? Could any ministry have risked sending so many men so far from home, with all the risks of wind and weather, at a time when they could have been needed to repel an invasion?

As it transpired the eventual Anglo-Russian campaign in southern Italy was to play only a marginal role in the destiny of the Third Coalition. Not until the end of October did the Neapolitan court, repudiating a newly signed treaty of neutrality with Napoleon, invite allied forces to land. Seriously delayed by the weather, the eventual disembarkation did not take place until 20 November; the united force, under the command of an aged Russian general named Lascy, finally comprised 5,000 British troops, 11,000 Russians and a body of Greek irregulars. This was much below the 25,000-strong contingent of which Leveson Gower had spoken in June, and furthermore the Russians were expecting their troops to be moved in British transports. The army was also short of draught animals for moving artillery and could muster only 300 cavalry. When the force, including Neapolitan units, eventually assembled on Naples's northern border in the middle of December 1805 it numbered some 30,000 soldiers.

By this time news of the allies' disasters in central Europe was filtering south, the Russians were reduced by sickness to only 8,000 effectives and the Neapolitan troops were recognised as militarily worthless. With the looming prospect of large French forces moving south, the allied commanders in Naples dithered and bickered, the *impasse* only being resolved early in January when Lascy received orders to take his troops back to Corfu. With the mainland campaign collapsing, Craig was able to secure Sicily in accordance with his primary instructions: his troops landed at Messina in February. The southern Italian campaign had ended without a shot being fired and the mainland, excepting the fortress of Gaeta, was abandoned to the French.[45]

The expedition had succeeded in causing some alarm to the French in northern Italy, prompting reinforcement of the garrisons of Ancona, Genoa and Leghorn and obliging Massena to delay his pursuit of the retreating Austrians and leave a strong force at Bologna. Against this, the French withdrawal from Naples before the allied landing meant that Lascy's army never engaged the enemy and in no sense managed to interfere with Napoleon's main strategic objective – the pinning of the Austrian forces in northern Italy. If

Massena had to use some of his troops to guard against the southern threat, then equally the allied cause lost the effective use of Lascy's army. From the British viewpoint the whole business was as much diplomatic as military and in so far as it showed a willingness to commit troops to the mainland it successfully reduced the Russian suspicions that were so evident in 1804–05. It also, eventually, secured Sicily and so went a long way to securing the whole Mediterranean position.

The chief British effort in 1805 came not in the south but in the north, in Germany. Several strands of thinking lay behind this strategy, the first, naturally enough, being a straightforward desire to recapture George III's Hanoverian electorate; this was not merely a question of prestige, but was also for the area's strategic value, positioned close to both Holland and Prussia. There was also the question already encountered *vis-à-vis* the Mediterranean of satisfying the Europeans' constant demands for active operations on the Continent. In September the Russians had been promised that once Continental hostilities had begun the Cabinet would prepare troops and transports for mainland service, pressure for this coming from Austria as well. Already in August the British ambassador in Vienna had reported that 'I have been besought in the most impressive Terms by Count Cobentzl to entreat his Majesty's Government . . . to the Succour of His Allies, by sending a Part of His Force into Holland, and thereby creating a powerful diversion . . .'.[46] With a direct landing in Holland or France deemed too dangerous, the Cabinet opted to send forces to northern Germany as a viable way of meeting such requests.

During much of 1805 the British plan was to secure access to Stralsund in Swedish Pomerania as a fortified base, the Russians particularly pressing for use of the port by one of their divisions. This situation obliged Pitt to agree to an exorbitant subsidy treaty with Gustavus IV of Sweden, covering both the use of Stralsund and 10,000 Swedish troops as well.[47] By the time the campaign opened in the autumn the allied plan was still to send a Russian force to Stralsund, though by that time the Cabinet had decided to land its own troops directly in Hanover. Stralsund was a good base but had the drawback of requiring a long sea voyage into the Baltic to reach it, an unpleasant thought with winter fast approaching. Early in October 1805 Lieutenant General Don, who was to command the vanguard elements of the expedition, reported that the passage to

Stralsund usually took from fourteen to twenty days and that some skippers regarded the route as unsafe from 15–25 October onwards. Just as this voyage became unattractive, though, the opportunity appeared of a more direct landing: from the middle of September the Cabinet had started receiving reports that Bernadotte's I Corps, Hanover's main garrison, was moving out of the electorate, leaving behind only a few troops to hold Hamelin.[48] The two elements prompted a decision, some time in the middle of October, to land in Hanover itself. With Bernadotte gone, British forces arriving would be secure from sudden counter-attack; such an assembly area was also closer to Holland – the ultimate objective – than was Stralsund and required a shorter sea journey to reach it. On 16 October Don was formally sent his instructions, these being to clear the electorate of the 3,500 enemy troops said to be still there, to gain recruits for the army, and to prepare Hanover as a base for future operations. To achieve this he was given 10,883 troops, with himself sailing on ahead to procure precise military and diplomatic information about local circumstances prior to the actual landing.[49]

As is clear from this, the Cabinet's hopes went far beyond a mere reoccupation of the electorate. A memorandum in September spoke of the Russians assembling a force of about 20,000 men at Stralsund, added to which it was hoped that there would be 4,000–12,000 Swedes available, plus the British contingent and, possibly, troops from Denmark as well. The ministry anticipated that by spring 1806 a polyglot army of some 100,000 men might be assembled, a force that would then set about the conquest of Holland.[50] York for one expressed severe doubts about the scheme, warning against a winter campaign plagued by poor logistics and based on faulty intelligence. He wondered about the army's command, particularly if it were led by the unstable Gustavus IV, and most especially he worried about the attitude of Prussia to the whole venture.[51] Although York's views were disregarded, he was correct in pointing to Prussia as the enigma that could wreck the whole plan. That power was geographically placed to menace both Hanover and Stralsund, so endangering allied communications, but ministers felt it reasonable to gamble on Prussian sentiments. It was noted in September that the Tsar would soon be meeting the Prussian king, Frederick William III, and that this would see Prussia either committed fully to the allied cause or at least to benevolent neutrality. By the end of the month Pitt, for one, was feeling very optimistic: 'The Prospect on the Continent is improving . . . The next accounts will probably bring the decision of Prussia, which I think will at least not be hostile.'[52] Having British troops in Hanover could only encourage Prussia to be amenable, it was felt, and further hope was sparked by Frederick William III's fury early in October when Bernadotte's corps, hurrying towards the Danube, blatantly violated Prussian neutrality by marching through Prussian-controlled Anspach. By the 25th the British representative in Berlin considered that a Prussian declaration of war on France was 'almost inevitable'.[53]

Very rapidly, though, these fine prospects started to vanish. On 20 October the forward Austrian army in Germany, surrounded by the sweeping advance of the Grande Armée, surrendered at Ulm, losing about 60,000 men in the capitulation and the break-out which preceded it. Thereafter Napoleon chased the Austro-Russian forces across central Europe, occupying Vienna on 20 November and Brünn, the capital of Moravia, five days later. In northern Italy the Austrians were also in full retreat, prompted by Napoleon's success and Massena's victory on the Adige. Only Nelson's destruction of much of the Combined Fleet at Trafalgar on 21 October brought a crumb of comfort to the allies.

With Prussia still wavering, on 27 October Harrowby was dispatched to Berlin to open direct negotiations, the main incentive he had to offer being a subsidy of up to £250,000 for the participation of 200,000 Prussian troops. The Cabinet still hoped for a Prussian invasion of Holland, but was ready to settle for a Prussian assault on the French in central Europe if that were preferred. Increasingly Prussian participation in the war was being regarded as essential.[54] From Berlin, however, Harrowby was able to offer little but gloom. His reports in late November spoke of a Prussia unwilling to forfeit her claim to Hanover, a hope moreover to which the Tsar had given his support, and reluctant to fight despite a display of martial energy. Harrowby feared the Prussians would try and impose an armistice that would give no thought to British interests. If they did fight there was, he believed, no chance of them campaigning in Holland. Nor were the lesser powers of whom the Cabinet had had hopes more encouraging: Denmark, Saxony and Hesse-Cassel declined urgings for them to join the conflict, while Sweden was proving to be a broken reed. Prusso-Swedish relations were extremely cool and Frederick William III refused to guarantee the safety of any Swedish troops on Prussian soil. Such a veiled threat effectively hamstrung the Swedes and placed a question mark against the allied use of Stralsund as a Russian base.[55] The hope of forming a large allied army in Hanover was rapidly evaporating.

While diplomacy faltered, the build-up of British troops in Hanover slowly went ahead. The vanguard of 10,883 embarked on their transports in the Downs in mid-October, a further 5,000 men being ordered from Ireland to assemble at the same point. Then the weather intervened, contrary winds preventing those in the Downs from sailing until 5 November, they reaching the Elbe on the 17th. On the day of their departure, in the increasing belief that Prussia would fight, the Cabinet decided to make an all-out commitment to the campaign and told York that the whole of Britain's disposable force would be going to the Continent, its strength being assessed in December as some 65,000 men. The first cavalry units sailed for Germany on 28 November, followed on 10 December by a second large group comprising nine infantry battalions and one cavalry regiment. This latter division met with disaster in the shape of a severe gale which caused the loss of 2,000 men and forced the surviving vessels to return home. Not until 22 December did this force sail again. By the early days of 1806 Britain, thanks to these efforts, had managed to assemble roughly 25,000 troops in Hanover.[56]

The persistence with which these troops were dispatched in the face of ever more depressing news from the Continent is the strongest sign that ministers still felt that the balance of probabilities favoured the coalition. On 7 November, reflecting on what looked like bellicose moves from Prussia, Pitt considered that 'Europe will still be saved by the end of the Year'. On the 28th Castlereagh wrote of the 'Convincing proof' that the provision of subsidies and soldiers should give to the allies of Britain's determination to recover Holland.[57] This underlying optimism persisted through most of December, Mulgrave responding on the 20th to ugly rumours of a French victory – it had happened at Austerlitz on the 2nd – by feeling that inevitable French losses and their scattered position would still prompt Prussian intervention. Had Napoleon been defeated or checked, of course, then Prussia would not hesitate.[58] Not until 29 December did reliable news arrive of the crushing Austro-Russian defeat on the 2nd. The natural reaction would have been to order an immediate evacuation of Hanover, but this was put off, Castlereagh worrying on 5 January that any such step would be seen as desertion of Prussia at a moment of crisis. Although deciding that no more troops would be sent to Germany, he still professed to believe that Prussia would never have a better opportunity to strike, with Napoleon committed to the south and a British army on hand and ready to co-operate.[59]

Such pious hopes could not survive. After Austerlitz the Austrians sought an armistice and dropped out of the coalition; the Russians meanwhile were in full retreat. By 11 January several ministers, namely Montrose, the President of the Board of Trade, Hawkesbury, Camden, then Lord President of the Council, and Chatham were urging Castlereagh to order a withdrawal. Outside the Cabinet, Canning had become disillusioned with the whole affair and York had opposed it from the start. Castlereagh now admitted defeat, telling Harrowby that, short of some dramatic Prussian move, the troops would come home, and telling Lieutenant General Cathcart, who had taken overall command of the expedition, that there were now 'convincing proofs' that Prussia was about to come to terms with Napoleon. York grimly pointed out the British predicament by stating the obvious fact that, free of Continental enemies, Napoleon could once more turn his attention to invasion plans.[60] In February 1806 the troops from Hanover returned safely home: like their comrades in Italy they had failed to fire a shot in anger.

There has been much criticism since of the ministry's handling of the expedition. Fortescue, with his usual vehemence, considers any plan that relied on Frederick William III misconceived, that monarch always displaying 'blindness, timidity, self-seeking and double-dealing'. The long-term objective, an invasion of Holland, is similarly damned:

> it was idle to suppose that England's part in the shaping of that destiny [Holland's] would be determined by a small party of redcoats on the spot rather than by successful operations of a strong British force against France in another quarter.[61]

Neither charge is fair. Although his assessment of the Prussian monarch's character is accurate enough, it relies heavily on hindsight. The very feature of 'double-dealing' might have prompted Frederick William III to ditch his tentative friendship with Napoleon and join the coalition. That Prussia would cling to neutrality while Austria and Russia took up arms, while British troops were on hand to provide support, while Britain was offering subsidies, and while

Napoleon's armies were scattered and vulnerable, was not something that Pitt might realistically have anticipated. It was senseless for Prussia to remain idle in 1805 and then fight alone in 1806, yet that is what she did. No minister could have foreseen such a chain of events. Nor did the Cabinet think in terms of liberating Holland with only a few soldiers: quite the contrary, it was planning for a large multi-national army being employed, one which would have included the whole disposable British force. Because of his Italian obsession Fortescue dismisses any strategy centred in a different area.

Another commentator, Lewis Butler, considers that the mistake in 1805 was not sending the force to Hanover sooner so as to have prevented Bernadotte's march south.[62] This idea is unsustainable. Given the speed of Napoleonic movements, it assumes that ministers could have assembled their diverse formations and then dispatched them at a similar pace. Such a theory makes no allowances for the cumbersome supply and transport arrangements, or for the hindering effects of the weather. Such a movement could not have been implemented before news of the Austrian declaration of war, the event that made a general European campaign possible, and as it was the Austrian entry immediately spurred the Grande Armée to march eastwards. If the British had somehow contrived their landing at the mouth of the Elbe on, say, 20 September, they would have found Bernadotte's corps 300 miles away. Had a landing been possible while the French were present in force Butler gives no thought as to how it could have been managed in the face of 30,000 enemy troops. Even the usually clear-thinking Piers Mackesy seems misled by this: 'If there was failure, it was in the North, where Bernadotte and Marmont were allowed to abandon Hanover and fall across Mack's communications in Bavaria.'[63] But how could this 'failure' have been avoided, given all the dangers of seaborne movement and landing?

In truth the strategy employed deserves much more sympathetic consideration. Faced with their allies' military demands, ministers sent their troops to where Britain's particular interests and the wider aims of the coalition generally could be best served. Hanover provided a secure base from where British troops could be reinforced or evacuated as circumstances demanded, and one where a friendly population could provide logistical support and possible recruitment.[64] Certainly the expedition had its risky aspects, but Pitt did everything he could to induce Prussia to fight, short of signing away the electorate itself. He could neither anticipate Prussia's hesitation nor the Austro-Russian blunders that would wreck the coalition. Had Prussia been more resolute, or had Napoleon been defeated or merely checked in Moravia, the whole strategy could well have appeared in a much more favourable light as 1806 unfolded. Then a large British army, probably alongside strong allied contingents, would have been poised to invade Holland, seriously endangering the whole French position in the Low Countries. Had Prussia also attacked Napoleon's long lines of communication in the Danube valley the French position would have been serious indeed. As it was, the British force, enhanced by new recruits raised in Hanover, was evacuated safely and no disasters accompanied the failure. The margin of error between astute strategic forward thinking and failed fiasco was very narrow.

During its lifetime Pitt's government laboured either to form or to maintain a coalition, leaving few resources for the country's imperial interests. In a marked alteration of his policy in the 1790s, Pitt made no attempt to conquer Caribbean islands: indeed, in 1804 there were specific instructions forbidding any attack on Cruaçao – in the previous war the island had required a 600-strong garrison and the government was unwilling to spare the troops. Similarly, although an attack on the small island of St Martins was ordered, it was only to destroy its defensive works and make the island useless as a privateering base: permanent occupation would again have required a garrison of 600 men. Finally, a request by Lieutenant General Myers in July 1804 for permission to attack Martinique, an objective the Commander of the Leeward and Windward Islands was confident he could capture, was turned down.[65] Minor expeditions were also avoided in other areas if reinforcements from Europe were required, as when Camden dropped plans to attack St Louis in the Senegal river in October 1804. Its capture would have removed the last French base in Africa, but its defences had been improved and any assault would have required more ships and troops than had been anticipated.[66]

Only two exceptions stand out from the trend. The first was the preparation to send Coote's force to the Caribbean in the summer of 1805, an intention prompted solely by a perceived French threat (see p. 80). The second was Pitt's only large colonial expedition during his final ministry, that sent to take the Cape of Good Hope.

Opinion respecting the strategic worth of this Dutch colony had undergone some fluctuation. In 1781 the directors of the East India Company had called it the 'Gibraltar of India', a view prompting its capture in 1795. However, by 1801 it had cost £1 million to hold and its potential as a source of danger seemed to have diminished; moreover the Egyptian campaign in 1798–1801 seemed to suggest that future threats to India would come via the Middle East rather than the south Atlantic.[67] Such opinions prompted the colony's restoration to the Dutch in 1802, though with the renewal of warfare there came a renewal of concern, ministers talking about its possible recapture in summer 1804 and Mulgrave expressing the view in December that in French hands it would endanger India. Such trepidation was enhanced the following year when the Toulon and Cadiz squadrons were able to unite, there being rumours in February and April that Villeneuve was heading for India by way of the Cape.[68] This alarming prospect prompted action, a stimulus encouraged by a belief that the Cape was poorly defended and would fall without difficulty.[69] Furthermore there was also an element of convenience in the Cabinet's planning, for, by early summer 1805, some 2,000 reinforcements were due to be sent to India. Given a modest addition to these troops, it seemed possible to seize the Cape by the use of some units that were heading to the East anyway. For all that, the final decision to send the expedition, eventually numbering 6,360 men,[70] was not an easy one. Not only did it deprive the European theatre of the soldiers involved, but it also meant their sailing at a moment when the Admiralty were uncertain as to Villeneuve's whereabouts: after some delay it did not finally sail from Cork until 28 August.

The Cape's only value lay in its position as an Indian outpost astride the sea route to the East, providing as it did a forward defensive position and depriving the enemy of a base for the inavsion of the subcontinent. British control permitted its use as a support for vessels in the Indian and China trades and removed another potential source of enemy privateering. It also served as a position from where troops could be drawn for India in the event of any sudden emergency. Castlereagh ordered that the Cape could, if necessary, be completely denuded of troops to deal with such a crisis; the only proviso laid down was that London was to be informed of such a step as quickly as possible so that the Cape could be reinforced or retaken as required.[71]

In the face of only negligible resistance the colony was captured in January 1806, thereafter being relegated to the status of a military backwater whose sheer size made any effective defence very difficult. Apart from serving as a base for attacks against the French islands in the Indian Ocean, it saw little future activity, though its importance was not underrated again, being one of the few captures retained by Britain after 1815.[72]

Pitt's death on 23 January 1806, and the rapid collapse of his ministry thereafter, marked the end of an epoch in British strategy. From 1803 efforts had been concentrated on finding European allies: the Third Coalition's demise threw Britain back upon her own resources, deserted by her allies and disillusioned at what were seen as the Europeans' shortcomings. The ministry that followed regarded the Continental powers with suspicion and those which came after 1807 were strongly to resist the notion, so prominent prior to 1806, that Britain's military policy should be subordinated to the demands of any alliance partners.

Notes

1 A review of French expansion can be found in J. M. Thompson, *Napoleon Bonaparte. His Rise and Fall*, Oxford, 1969, pp. 217–21.

2 Buckinghamshire R.O., Hobart Papers, D/MH/H/War C63. P.R.O. ADM 2/1360 – orders similar to Hood's were also sent to Duckworth on the Jamaica station.

3 P.R.O. FO 65/62, ? to Woronzow, 21 May 1803.

4 Reilly, p. 332.

5 J. Tramond, *Manuel d'histoire maritime de la France des origines à 1815*, Paris, 1947, pp. 713 and 715–16. Marcus, p. 221.

6 Martin, III, p. 300.

7 Albion, p. 385.

8 Fortescue lashes Addington in several works, viz. *British Army*, 10, p. 182; *County Lieutenancies*, pp. 7–8; *British Statesmen of the Great War, 1793–1814*, London, 1911, pp. 170–1. For the financial imperatives in strategy see Reilly, pp. 324–5; and Steven Watson, p. 414.

9 P. Ziegler, *Addington. A Life of Henry Addington, First Viscount Sidmouth*, London, 1965, pp. 197–8. His opinions are echoed by Emsley, p. 99.

10 R. Glover, *Britain at Bay*, tends to dismiss the suggestion of some earlier writers, like Desbrière and Corbett, that the threat was just a bluff, though Glover himself is confused, saying in 1967 that there was 'little to fear' in 1803–05 – 'The French fleet', p. 233 – and then in 1973 that 'There should, then, be no doubts about the reality of the danger England faced in 1803–05' – *Britain at Bay*, p. 15. A later writer has no doubts about the

danger: see Schom, particularly pp. 63–127.

11 *The Times*, 18 July 1803.

12 Bunbury, p. 133. Devon R.O., 152M, Sidmouth Papers, C1806/OM. *P.D.*, I, pp. 205–6.

13 Melville, I, pp. 168–9. *The Times*, 5 November 1803. R. Glover, *Britain at Bay*, p. 87. Similar feelings were expressed by Pitt, the Premier observing in 1804 that 'we may meet with confidence . . .' any French effort: P.R.O. 30/58/5, Dacre Adams Papers, 90, pp. 2–3.

14 Harvey, *Britain in Nineteenth Century*, pp. 143–4. G. Pellew, *The Life and Correspondence of the Right Hon. Henry Addington, First Viscount Sidmouth*, London, 1847, II, pp. 265–6.

15 Northern Ireland R.O., Castlereagh Papers, D3030/1833. P.R.O. WO 6/14, pp. 1–4.

16 Buckinghamshire R.O., Hobart Papers, D/MH/H/War C106 and C107.

17 For Iberian concerns see *P.D.*, III, pp. 61 ff. P.R.O. ADM 2/1362 and FO 63/41–3 and FO 72/48–51. Buckinghamshire R.O., Hobart Papers, D/MH/H/War B73, B74 and B78.

18 P.R.O. FO 65/63, ff. 14–17 and 32–3. Melville, I, p. 170.

19 P.R.O. FO 7/67, nos. 14, 19 and 22. FO 64/63, ? to Jackson (ambassador in Berlin), 28 June 1803; Jackson to Hawkesbury, 16 July 1803.

20 Sherwig, pp. 144–6 and 162. P.R.O. FO 65/64, ff. 61–4. Buckinghamshire R.O., Hobart Papers, D/MH/H/War C138. Anderson, pp. 28–34.

21 J. Holland Rose, *Napoleonic Studies*, London, 1904, p. 364.

22 Sir A. W. Ward and G. P. Gooch (eds.), *Cambridge History of British Foreign Policy*, I, Cambridge, 1922, p. 330. Harcourt, II, pp. 41–2. P. H. Stanhope, *Life of the Right Hon. William Pitt*, London, 1861–62, IV, p. 53.

23 P.R.O., CO 137/110 and 318/21. WO 1/904, p. 365. Buckinghamshire R. O., Hobart Papers, D/MH/H/War A53, C68, C116 and F18.

24 Martin, III, pp. 300–3 and 305–6; IV, p. 225.

25 P.R.O. CO 318/21. R. Pares, *War and Trade in the West Indies, 1739–63*, Oxford, 1936, pp. 198–9. St Lucia and Tobago were taken on 22 and 30 June respectively.

26 Devon R.O., 152M, Sidmouth Papers, C1803/OC2/14. P.R.O. CO 318/22 and 23. Buckinghamshire R.O., Hobart Papers, D/MH/H/War A65 and C87. S. Drescher, *Econocide. British Slavery in the Era of Abolition*, Pittsburgh, 1977, p. 94–100 and 147. Holland Rose, 'West India commerce', pp. 36–7. Mitchell and Deane, p. 28. Fortescue, *British Army*, 5, pp. 185–6.

27 P.R.O. CO 318/24. Fortescue, *British Army*, 5, pp. 186–92. British practice in this period was to maintain the primary striking force at Barbados, to windward of the other islands, from where it could move quickly to any threatened spot.

28 Pellew, II, pp. 476–8.

29 As well as its military defences, Addington improved the nation's finances by reviewing the income tax system. Aiming to tax at source, to reduce evasion and to simplify the whole procedure, the ministry levied the rate at 1*s* in the £ and in the first year raised £4·76 million. At the end of Pitt's

first term in office the rate had been twice this but had brought in only £5·3 million. The fundamentals of this tax were to remain unchanged throughout the rest of the period: see Ziegler, pp. 148–50.

30 Scottish R.O., Melville Papers, GD 51/2/179. Detailed accounts of these operations can be found in *Castlereagh Correspondence*, V, pp. 91–137; in Lloyd, *Keith Papers*, III, pp. 86–106; and James, IV, pp. 219–45 and 305–14.

31 The despatches relating to Spain were published in *P.D.*, III; Pitt's and Hawkesbury's speeches are on pp. 362–4, 371–3 and 467.

32 P.R.O. FO 63/44, 45 and 46.

33 J. Holland Rose, *Selected Despatches relating to the Formation of the Third Coalition*, London, 1904, pp. 4–5 and 29. Sandon Hall, Harrowby Papers, LXXXIII, ff. 12–14 and 127–8.

34 J. Holland Rose (ed.), *William Pitt and the Great War*, London, 1911, pp. 526–7. P.R.O. 30/58/6, Dacre Adams Papers, no. 29.

35 Holland Rose, *Selected Despatches*, pp. 35–6. Sir A. Paget (ed.), *The Paget Papers: Diplomatic and other Correspondence, 1794–1807*, London, 1896, II, pp. 136–7.

36 Sherwig, pp. 148–50.

37 Sandon Hall, Harrowby Papers, XXXII, f. 45.

38 Holland Rose, *Selected Despatches*, pp. 10–12, 44–6, 61, 72–3, 76–9 and 83–4. Sandon Hall, Harrowby Papers, XXXI, ff. 129–35.

39 P.R.O. 30/58/6, Dacre Adams Papers, no. 79. Durham R.O., Castlereagh Papers, D/Lo/C3.

40 The final figure came to £4 million per annum: Sherwig, p. 161.

41 For the report on Boulogne's defences see B. H. Add. Mss 49482, Gordon Papers, ff. 14v–16. Napoleon left 25,000 troops and 10,000–11,000 sailors to hold the place: *La Correspondence de Napoléon Iier*, Paris, 1863, XI, pp. 142–3, 159–60 and 254. For ministers' intentions see Aspinall, IV, p. 359.

42 P.R.O. WO 1/904, p. 365. WO 6/56, pp. 2–10, 19–22 and 35–6. Mackesy, *War in the Mediterranean*, pp. 60–1. The proviso about Alexandria reflected fears for Egypt and that about Sardinia a concern that the fleet could lose that island's supplies of fresh food and water: P.R.O. 30/58/6, Dacre Adams Papers, no. 123.

43 Holland Rose, *Selected Despatches*, p. 151.

44 Fortescue, *British Army*, 5, pp. 196–7 and 266–7; *County Lieutenancies*, pp. 7–8; and *British Statesmen*, pp. 170–1 and 178–80.

45 Detailed reviews of the campaign can be found in Mackesy, *War in the Mediterranean*, pp. 69–88; Bunbury, pp. 130–41; and Fortescue, *British Army*, 5, pp. 272–8. See also B.M. Add. Mss 49495, Gordon Papers, ff. 26–30 and 41–2; P.R.O. WO 6/56, pp. 23, 47, 49–50 and 63–7; Holland Rose, *Selected Despatches*, p. 179.

46 Sandon Hall, Harrowby Papers, XXXII, ff. 85–6, P.R.O. 30/29/387, Granville Papers, pp. 33–4. Leeds University Library, Brotherton Collection Box VII, Mulgrave Papers, 18/264. Also Paget, II, p. 233.

47 Fortescue, *British Army*, 5, pp. 284–5. R. Carr, 'Gustavus IV and the British government, 1804–09', *English Historical Review*, LX, January

1945, pp. 46–7. The subsidy was at the rate of £21 per man: the usual rate was £12 10*s*.

48 P.R.O. WO 1/186, pp. 1–3. FO 933/4, pp. 99–100. Lady Jackson (ed.), *The Diaries and Letters of Sir George Jackson, K.C.H.*, London, 1872, I, p. 324.

49 Holland Rose, *Selected Despatches*, p. 314. P.R.O. WO 6/13, pp. 10–15.

50 *Castlereagh Correspondence*, VI, pp. 6–8.

51 Aspinall, IV, pp. 357–8 and 367–9.

52 Sandon Hall, Harrowby Papers, XII, ff. 55–6.

53 P.R.O. 30/29/387, Granville Papers, no. 33. Jackson, I, p. 348.

54 Holland Rose, *Selected Despatches*, pp. 207–14 and 218–19. If Prussia stayed neutral, Harrowby was told to try and get those lesser states seen as dependant on her, viz. Denmark, Saxony and Hesse Cassel, to fight.

55 Holland Rose, *Selected Despatches*, pp. 216–17, 228–38 and 241–4. Carr, p. 47.

56 The build-up is best described in *Castlereagh Correspondence*, VI. See also P.R.O. WO 1/186 and WO 6/13.

57 Leeds R.O., Harewood Collection, Canning Papers, 30, Pitt to Canning, 7 November 1805. Sandon Hall, Harrowby Papers, XXIX, ff. 32–6.

58 *Castlereagh Correspondence*, VI, pp. 66–7, 70–2 and 87–90. Sandon Hall, Harrowby Papers, XXIX, ff. 244–5.

59 *Castlereagh Correspondence*, VI, pp. 94–5, 103–10 and 112–14.

60 *Castlereagh Correspondence*, VI, pp. 117–20. J. Holland Rose, *Pitt and Napoleon, Essays and Letters*, London, 1912, pp. 330–1.

61 Fortescue, *British Army*, 5, pp. 297–8.

62 Butler, CLI, p. 401.

63 Mackesy, *War in the Mediterranean*, p. 91.

64 The latter possibility was always in ministers' minds and, in the event, roughly 4,000 new recruits were secured during the brief occupation: *Castlereagh Correspondence*, VI, p. 105; P.R.O. 30/8/121, Chatham Papers, f. 215v; WO 1/186, p. 626.

65 P.R.O. CO 318/25, Camden to Lieutenant General Myers, ? November 1804. WO 1/629, pp. 133–6.

66 Aspinall, IV, pp. 237 and 242.

67 G. S. Graham, *Britain in the Indian Ocean. A Study of Maritime Enterprise, 1810–50*, Oxford, 1967, pp. 24–7.

68 Aspinall, IV, p. 214. P.R.O. 30/58/5, Dacre Adams Papers, no. 122. Northern Ireland R.O., Castlereagh Papers, D3030/1963, undated and unsigned memorandum, but in Castlereagh's handwriting. L. F. C. Turner, 'The Cape of Good Hope and the Anglo-French conflict, 1797–1806', *Historical Studies. Australia and New Zealand*, 9 (36), 1961, pp. 375–6.

69 Durham R.O., Castlereagh Papers, D/Lo/C3, unsigned memorandum in Castlereagh's handwriting. *Castlereagh Correspondence*, VI, p. 133.

70 Fortescue, *British Army*, 5, p. 306 n.

71 Martin, II, p. 405. *Castlereagh Correspondence*, VI, pp. 144–6.

72 Graham, pp. 36–7. For the details of its capture see Fortescue, *British Army*, 5, pp. 306–10.

6

The Ministry of the Talents

The only substantial change in Cabinet personnel during these years came in February 1806 – March 1807, the ministry derisively referred to as of 'All the Talents'. Only Sidmouth, as Lord Privy Seal, and later Lord President of the Council, provided any continuity between this administration and the others of the time. In the light of this it is not surprising that such a change in personalities should have brought with it a change in strategic thinking. Two particular individuals stand out as men who stamped their authority on the new government. One was the cynical, rather disillusioned William Grenville, the other the powerful figure of Fox, the pacifist who cherished hopes of a peace with Napoleon. The new attitudes were immediately apparent as strategy was directed away from Europe and the forging of anti-French alliances. Only objectives of obvious benefit to Britain were to be pursued, a policy avoiding direct confrontations with France on land while inaugurating the only attempt at large-scale colonial expansion during the period. This was encouraged by Britain's exclusion from the Continent and embarked upon in the hope of exerting a distant influence upon events that the Cabinet could not change directly. Pitt's strategy in 1804–06 had been largely shackled to the demands of the coalition: the Talents rejected such a policy and sought independence of action.

Coming to power at the moment when Austerlitz had shattered the Third Coalition, forcing Austria into peace and Russia into retreat, the new government's alienation from European alliances is easy to understand. Combined with this, in early 1806 Prussia occupied Hanover, a step marking that power as little more than a French satellite. Had the Talents' attitude been different there would still, initially, have been no potential allies for them anyway; indeed, the ministry felt obliged actually to declare war on the acquisitive Prussians. Such circumstances strengthened Fox's hand in pressing for a peace with Napoleon, those members of the Cabinet like Grenville, Windham and Sidmouth who felt more distrust of the emperor being unable to point to any convincing alternative way in which Britain could solve her problems by continuing hostilities. Reinforcing such sentiments was the Cabinet's feeling that some way had to be found to ease the financial strain being placed upon Britain. Such an objective made it clear that the government wished to husband the nation's resources so as to survive any long and costly struggle.

Nor did such retrenchment apply only towards impecunious allies. In his Army Estimates of May 1806 Windham announced his intention to reducing the strength of the cavalry regiments from 1,000 to 800 men, of cutting the Foot Guards from 140 to 130 per company and of reducing the numbers in the Waggon Train by 1,728. He estimated a saving of £363,000 from such measures, aiming also at curtailing expenditure on the Volunteers, a body that was his particular *bête noire*. In total he looked for a saving of £934,192 and simultaneously hoped to limit actual manpower losses by reductions in units' establishments rather than in the numbers with the colours. In March he had anticipated that any losses to the regulars would be compensated for by men joining the Militia. These measures did nothing to improve the army's efficiency, but nor did they achieve their aim of large savings. The army had cost £18,581,000 in 1805 and the figure fell only to £18,507,000 in 1806. In part this was due to diligent lobbying by the Duke of York, who managed to preserve the Waggon Train from Windham's intended emasculation, the minister having no understanding of the importance of an integrated supply system however limited its scale.[1]

Without doubt the leading question on the Cabinet's agenda during its first weeks in office was that of peace, the first concern being how Britain's allies might conduct any negotiations of their own. Talks briefly started in April, when Napoleon insisted on dealing with Britain and Russia separately, but when the talks were resumed the process rapidly ran into trouble. On 1 July Lord Yarmouth, the chief British negotiator in Paris, reported that Napoleon was demanding the occupation of Sicily as part of any agreement. The Cabinet had already ruled this out in March, with the proviso that any such step would be impossible without the consent of the Neapolitan court, an agreement that was hardly likely, and its surrender would have meant a return of all the fears about France's Mediterranean ambitions as well as consequent problems in feeding Malta. The heart of the matter, of course, was complete distrust of Napoleon, and on 4 July the offer of concessions in Germany, i.e. Hanover, in return for Sicily was rejected. The Cabinet emphasised its determination to retain the island by sending 6,000 reinforcements there.[2] Much of the discussion about the fate of Sicily was obscured by a smokescreen of talk about the Neapolitan Bourbons' future and of possible territorial compensations for them. Such niceties made the British position seem more inflexible as ministers sought to provide them with possessions which, were a surrender unavoidable, would serve Britain's Mediterranean interests. Howick for one wanted them to receive Sardinia and the Balearics, as potentially useful naval bases, rather than another suggestion that they receive the more distant Dalmatia.

Throughout the talks the Talents tried to preserve co-operation with Russia, despite the fact that D'Oubril, the chief Russian negotiator, agreed on 20 July to a separate treaty assigning Dalmatia and Sicily to Napoleon. The Cabinet, in the event correctly, surmised that such concessions would never be ratified by the Tsar, but all this took much time and did nothing in the interim to make an Anglo-French agreement more likely. Further inhibiting progress was Fox's last illness, he being increasingly inactive from August and dying the following month. As the summer progressed there were also rumours about a pending French invasion of Portugal and of British conquests in South America. William Grenville made a final effort in September, suggesting, against Howick's advice, that the Neapolitan court should exchange Sicily for Dalmatia, providing such a plan was agreed to by Alexander I. However, by then Napoleon was moving against Prussia and with the Tsar coming to support Frederick William III any chance of a general compromise and agreement was gone. Anglo-French talks finally ended on 6 October.[3]

Whatever its pacific tendencies, credit can be given to the ministry for not having been so strategically shortsighted as to surrender Sicily to Napoleon. It remained firm on this point during most of the negotiations and seemed to be yielding only when the one stipulation, Russian concurrence, was most unlikely. More awkward was the formal state of war with Prussia. Although no settlement with that country was likely, given its desire for Hanover, it was nevertheless faintly ludicrous that the two nations found it difficult to co-operate against the common enemy in the autumn of 1806 because they were supposed to be fighting each other. Despite his offer of the Dalmatia/Sicily exchange at the end of September, it seems unlikely that Grenville ever intended the suggestion seriously. While making it he was also writing of how a British take-over of Spanish America would be sufficient to oblige France to evacuate Naples in order to preserve the Spanish Empire. He believed that the peace which would spring from this would not only regain Hanover but would see Russia and Austria dividing Dalmatia while Sardinia was established as a separate kingdom in control of the Balaerics. His whole September offer appears to have been an attempt to make Britain seem more reasonable while embroiling France and Russia.[4]

Putting backbone into the Cabinet's determination to retain Sicily was the protracted resistance of the Neapolitan fortress of Gaeta during the first half of 1806 and the highly successful British raid on Calabria in July, the latter including the morale-boosting victory at Maida. Gaeta finally fell to the French on 18 July, but that month also saw them hustled out of Calabria and any preparations for an attack on Sicily were for the moment wrecked. The island was heavily reinforced during the course of 1806, its garrison numbering 17,500 troops by December.[5]

British suspicion of Napoleon's Mediterranean ambitions helped thwart the peace talks during the summer of 1806, and these sentiments were deepened by concern over the fate of Portugal. That country was suspected of being about to form an alliance with France and Spain and, more directly, there were reports of Napoleon forming an army at Bayonne preparatory to an invasion. Howick feared a French naval attack on the Tagus forts in preparation for a link-up with the Bayonne force and believed a British squadron ought to be situated to block it, William Grenville agreeing with him. Both Howick and Windham wanted to send troops to Portugal to stiffen her resistance and each was keen to secure the Portuguese fleet and keep it out of Napoleon's grasp. Windham believed the fleet to be a strong one of twelve ships of the line and smaller vessels.[6]

Early in August Howick badgered the Premier over this issue, dreading the consequences of delay and expanding his plans to include an occupation of Madeira and Teneriffe. Finally, on

9 August, orders were issued for approximately 10,000 troops to go to Lisbon to help fight a French army thought to number around 30,000. It was made clear that Britain would help Portugal resist, but were she to refuse and her royal family be unwilling to flee to Brazil, then her fleet would be attacked. The Cabinet chose to regard the French preparations as a violation of Portuguese neutrality and was also prepared, if necessary, to attack Portugal's colonies. Three days later, amidst reports from Paris that seemed to confirm Napoleon's Iberian intentions, Fox repeated that Portugal could receive ships, money and men if she would only defend herself, it being believed in London that, if the Bayonne force could be resisted, Napoleon would experience difficulty in reinforcing it.[7]

Suddenly, though, the danger started to ease. On 12 August Lauderdale wrote from Paris, where he led the peace mission, that the French preparations were not advanced and that he had received one report discounting the whole business. On the 17th Howick declared that a naval reconnaissance of Bayonne, Bilbao and adjacent ports had not found any boats capable of moving large numbers of troops, adding that, although there was a substantial French army in the region, the Spaniards would resist any movement into their territory. At last, on the 28th, the expedition to help the Portuguese was postponed pending further enemy action, and by early September Howick and Spencer, the Home Secretary, were expressing the view that more troops could now be sent to Sicily.[8]

The Talents were not lacking in determination and energy in their strategy respecting Sicily and Portugal, but Britain's interests were ill served by their sustained hostility towards potential European allies. At the heart of it lay a sense of distrust typified by the Prime Minister himself. In Grenville's case much of this was prompted by his frustrations and disappointments as Foreign Secretary in the 1790s, his feelings being made clear soon after he came into office. Responding to a winsome notion of Windham's to the effect that Russia might provide troops to help a British attack on Guadeloupe and Martinique, Grenville acidly observed that Russian inexperience would cause them to fail and 'if we engage for any co-operation, the whole failure will by their officers be thrown on our shoulders'. Later Grenville was to be similarly unenthusiastic about any idea of trying to cement the Russian alliance by giving way to the Tsar's demands respecting the Ottoman Empire and indifferent to a suggestion of colonial surrenders to France in return for a restoration of Prussian power.[9]

Britain's enforced state of war with Prussia in the early part of 1806 prompted little activity other than the blockade of German ports, but the ministers' attitudes continued to show them in a poor light. Fox naively wondered whether Russia might be induced to attack Prussia following the Hanover occupation. He felt that this would weaken Franco-Prussian harmony, but his belief was hardly likely to be tested in the wake of Alexander I's endorsement of Frederick William-III's Hanoverian aspirations at their meeting at Potsdam in November 1805. Fox ought to have appreciated that, with France already powerful in Germany, the alienation of Prussia was the last thing Russia would want. In September William Grenville displayed his own shortsightedness when objecting to Prussian efforts to form a German confederation. Although this would have involved a barrier being constructed against France, he felt that it could not proceed without involving Britain and Russia and including a surrender of Hanover. He believed the Tsar would back such a stance, but again, bearing in mind the Treaty of Potsdam, this seems unlikely.[10]

Such antipathy towards the Europeans became crucial for Britain as Franco-Prussian tension during the summer of 1806 turned into war in the autumn, a campaign that spread into Poland and involved the Russians. Although both Britain and Russia had remained in a state of war with France, there had been no planning for actual campaigning or for further British aid. Nor did Prussia's entry into the war bring a sudden change in relations: William Grenville noted on 22 September that Prussia had offered to return Hanover, but Morpeth, being sent as the British representative in Berlin, was given no instructions to encourage the Prussians. Grenville later expressed contempt for Prussian requests for financial aid that were not formally embodied in the shape of a subsidy treaty and condemned what he regarded as continued evasiveness over the question of Hanover. Howick coldly pointed out that Britain had been fighting for a long period and would provide aid only when Prussia had proved her need and had shown what advantages would flow to Britain from any support.[11]

Given the tortuous nature of communications, the simple process of proving need and making formal arrangements would have taken weeks, time during which the Cabinet was committed to nothing at all. This procrastination continued as Prussia plunged into catastrophe, her armies defeated at Jena–Auerstädt on 14 October and completely routed thereafter. On the 20th Prussia was informed that Britain was assembling a force on the coast for diversionary purposes, but at that time of year, with winter approaching and with the Hanover issue still unsettled, it was unlikely that any large-scale support would be forthcoming. Similarly over the question of subsidies the Cabinet believed that much discussion would be necessary before any agreement could be signed. For the present all it would do was permit Prussia to raise a loan of £500,000 which would constitute part of any eventual treaty. Part of the motivation behind this reluctance was suspicion that the Prussian treasury, rumoured to contain £2 million, was still intact. In November Hutchinson, the British military representative in Prussia, was told to discover the truth behind this, though he was still empowered only to dispense Treasury bills up to a value of £200,000 were Prussia in dire need.[12]

Ministers would have been less than human had they not felt a certain grim satisfaction at the treacherous Prussia's humiliation, but other factors contributed to their unhelpful attitude. Prominent among them was the desire to minimise financial expenditure, though this seems to have caused some debate at least, Windham observing towards the end of September that what aid could be sent to Prussia would have little impact. To support his view, and also ensure that resources were not diverted from South America to Prussia let it be said, he told William Grenville that to hire transports for 10,000 cavalry for three months would cost £2·4 million. A staggered Prime Minister replied that if troops did not go to Europe then more would be available for South America. 'The expense of transports which you state,' continued Grenville, 'is so very beyond any idea I could have formed, that I quite agree with you on the necessity of pausing before such a step is taken.'[13] This exchange has interesting implications, illustrating not merely the ministry's financial concern but also that Grenville, despite his extensive government experience, still had no notion of the costs involved in sending troops abroad. This allowed Windham to be disingenuous because of the huge tonnages required. Many battalions of infantry could have been sent to Europe, as they were to be sent to South America, for a fraction of the cost that Windham quoted.

Much less understandable than the antipathy towards Prussia was the approach towards Russia and Austria. As the fighting in Poland progressed in 1806–07 the pressure for British aid increased, the

Tsar pleading in December for 'a Diversion on the Enemy, in the North of Europe, by a powerful expedition to the Coast of France or Holland'. In January there were complaints about British inactivity.[14] The ministry was unwilling to commit troops, and the only aid it provided consisted of 60,000 muskets and £500,000 still outstanding from Pitt's subsidy treaty. A Russian request to raise a loan of £6 million in the City of London was stymied when the government refused to act as guarantor for fear of the Russians reneging on the debt. De Nicolay, the Russian ambassador, was reduced to asking pointedly whether Britain still intended to make common cause with his country. Howick coolly rejected any implication of desertion and considered that so large a country as Russia must have the means to defend itself. The Cabinet's position was that Russian troops were not being employed by Britain and that, as they were fighting to preserve their own territory and interests, they should look to their own resources. Facing the prospect of a long struggle with Napoleon, ministers wanted to hoard Britain's means.[15]

A similarly cheerless view was offered to the court of Vienna. Appearing unaware of Austria's menacing position along Napoleon's long lines of communication to Poland, the Cabinet seemed indifferent about whether that country re-entered the war or not. Adair, the British ambassador, was told that no financial help would be forthcoming merely for Austria to make military preparations. Were she to fight, matters would be different; but even then British policy would not follow previous thinking. The Cabinet chose to believe that previously Austria had been campaigning away from her own borders, but that in 1807 she would be defending them and would have to look to her own resources first.

> If the great Powers now at war, or threatened by France, cannot find in themselves the means of such exertion, it is vain to expect that this Country, by any supplies which we could afford, would be able effectually to support them. It is now indeed more than ever necessary that we should husband our resources, & you will therefore be cautious of holding out any expectation of pecuniary assistance . . .[16]

As for Prussia, by February 1807 she was not regarded as a power of importance. Looking at her broken condition, and at the seeming divisions among the Russian generals, the Cabinet was confirmed in its negative attitude: 'What hope could there be but that any pecuniary supplies furnished by H.M. would like the Magazines of

Dantzig and Königsberg be left to fall into the hands of the Enemy . . .?[17]

The government was not unaware of the importance of the campaign in Poland, it was merely that it would not commit British money or men and would play no part in trying to influence its outcome. Howick was full of exciting ideas for the use of Swedish troops to attack the French or Dutch coasts, but any British participation in such a venture would not go beyond the employment of the shipping to move them. He also pondered upon the possibilities of a Swedish–Danish diversionary attack on Holstein, though, again, without any British participants. With it becoming more and more obvious that Britain was not going to provide any active support for her allies, during February and March the Foreign Office was bombarded with hostile despatches clearly indicating the scale of Russian and Swedish fury.[18]

Windham later argued that no British aid was ever promised to the Europeans, a statement of doubtful honesty, as will be shown later, and that respecting financial support 'were we to be merely the great bank of Europe, on which the different nations should be empowered to draw in defence of their own existence? Was not the result likely to be that they would make no spontaneous exertions?' William Grenville was later to admit that a pervading sense of pessimism permeated Cabinet thinking about the fighting in Europe, that 'from the first opening of the campaign, neither he nor his colleagues were sanguine in their hopes for success . . .'.[19]

There were some Cabinet voices raised against this trend. Sidmouth, for one, wrote in October 1806 that troops should be sent to help Prussia and encourage Austria, believing that the latter would be lost if Prussia were defeated.[20] Thomas Grenville also had his doubts, feeling in December that more attention should be paid to Britain's Baltic interests and bemoaning the fact that, despite the possibility of a Franco-Russian peace, his colleagues remained indifferent. The following month he was thinking of sending ten or twelve ships of the line to the Baltic, though the later operation against Constantinople put paid to that.[21] Howick is quoted by his son as drawing up a memorandum in which he complained of distant operations while Napoleon overran Europe. He is supposed to have felt that troops should have been sent to the Continent, yet neither he nor any of the other 'Europeans' in the Cabinet felt the matter important enough to resign over it. The majority opinion was summed up in Parliament by Petty, the Chancellor of the Exchequer, soon after the Talents had left office:

> It was ridiculous to talk of saving Europe, if Europe could not save herself. It was not in the desperate affairs of the continent that England could step in and save her. No; she had only to look to better times. She could be most useful in following up victory, not in remedying defeat; and therefore was a government wise in keeping up and refusing to exhaust the resources of the country until they could be useful.[22]

This is superficially plausible, but lacks real credibility. The only guarantee of security lay in the defeat of Napoleon, but the Talents consistently turned away from the great powers who were the only means whereby the French emperor might be contained. Ministers tacitly recognised that Britain's danger stemmed from Europe when they hoped to check French expansion there via a trade-off for British success in Spanish America. Petty spoke of waiting for 'better times', but when would there be a better moment for exerting all means than when Napoleon was fighting a tough campaign in Poland and had lines of communication vulnerable from both the north (the Baltic) and the south (Austria)? It was easy to speak of 'following up victory', but in practice this was strategic Micawberism. Britain would wait for victory to turn up, but would do little to prompt it herself: a strategy that risked there being no victory at all. Turning away from the traditional Continental strategy against France, the Talents found no viable replacement. Had an opportunity to follow up victory appeared there is no evidence to suggest that the Talents would have known how to respond.

The failure became most obvious in spring 1807, when any British reluctance could no longer be blamed on winter weather. On 10 March Straton, the ambassador to Sweden, was told that the Cabinet was interested in Swedish suggestions for an offensive in Pomerania, a project about which it had previously been evasive. Now, however, promises of pecuniary support were made and, as it appeared that only a shortage of cavalry might inhibit the Swedes, a brigade of British dragoons 'might probably' be forthcoming.[23] In similar style the Russians, who had been told in February that the weather and the risks involved ruled out any British landing on the French coast, were informed on 10 March about possible British military action. There was talk of energetic preparations, but possible action in northern Germany was an option hedged in by provisos about inherent difficulties and the limitation of British means.[24] These hints were vague, but still appear to have been deliberately misleading. There is no reason to believe that ministers had suddenly become willing to provide direct military help, the statements seemingly being designed to try and keep the Swedes and Russians fighting. The evidence for this contention comes from two directions.

First, during its last weeks in office the ministry became increasingly committed to Spanish America. By March 1807 there were already 9,550 troops in that region or on their way, and on the 5th Lieutenant General Whitelocke was told to proceed with a further 1,630. Alongside this, numerous reinforcements had also been sent to the Mediterranean, numbers there having risen from 15,410 in March 1806 to 28,630 by early 1807. Given that York required 208,000 regulars and militiamen for the defence of Britain and Ireland, and that in March 1807 their actual number did not exceed 180,000, there was little spare capacity for Continental campaigning.[25] Of course, under similarly constraining circumstances the Portland Cabinet would still send troops to Copenhagen, but there is nothing about the Talents' attitude which suggests similar risk-taking. However, further supporting the charge that the Talents misled their allies deliberately is the fact that on 24 March 1807 there were only twenty-five transport vessels, totalling 7,807 tons, in home waters and fitted for foreign service. Allowing a ratio of one and a half tons per man moved, the size of any force sent to help the allies would have been small indeed. Within this total, moreover, there was sufficient tonnage for moving a mere 148 horses.[26] One may wonder how a brigade of dragoons could have been sent to Pomerania in such circumstances. The Portland Cabinet was able to send troops in June and July only after weeks of frantic transport hiring.

Two of the Talents Cabinet made their true feelings clear when speaking later on. In July Windham stated that he thought it unwise to send troops to Europe when they might be needed for home defence, while Grey spoke in February 1808 of there being too many obstacles in the way of sending a force to the Continent in the spring of 1807, and that anyway an expedition to Pomerania, even with Swedish help, could have achieved nothing. His despatch to Straton on 10 March, however, had adopted a completely different tone and its honesty must be questioned.[27]

In one respect alone can the Talents be said to have used British forces to help their allies directly, and that was the attempt to support the Russians via the squadron sent to the Dardanelles, though here as well British interests were clearly at stake. The roots of this operation went back to August 1806, when the Porte had removed the russophile Hospodars of the Danubian provinces, Russia responding by moving troops into those areas. These events were accompanied by growing French influence at Constantinople, a trend much encouraged by Napoleon's defeat of Prussia. It was in the allied interest to see the Russo-Turkish quarrel settled and Russia's troops freed for service in Poland; equally desirable was the expulsion of the energetic Sébastiani, the French ambassador, from Constantinople. For the Cabinet, action became more important still when it learned on 9 November that Sébastiani was demanding that the Turks should close the Dardanelles. Arbuthnot, Sébastiani's British counterpart, had already pressed in September for a squadron of warships to be sent to cow the Turks[28] and in November Collingwood, acting on his own initiative, sent three ships of the line and two smaller vessels to the Dardanelles. Shortly after this the Cabinet went still further, deciding to send Vice-Admiral Duckworth with a squadron to the Turkish capital. On 21 November he was instructed:

> to demand the immediate surrender of the Turkish Fleet, together with that of a supply of naval stores from the Arsenal, sufficient for its equipment, and he is to accompany this demand with a menace in case of refusal, of immediately commencing hostilities against the Town [of Constantinople].[29]

Delayed by the weather, Duckworth did not finally reach the Straits until 10 February 1807, by which time Arbuthnot had fled the capital and the Turks were preparing their defences. Upon reaching Constantinople Duckworth was able neither to intimidate the Porte nor to begin useful negotiations. Nervous of his exposed position, the admiral eventually retreated on 3 March, escaping through the Straits but being battered by some 300 Turkish cannon placed on shore as he did so. The attempt both to eliminate a potentially hostile fleet and to ease Russia's Balkan situation had failed miserably.[30]

Mackesy considers that the expedition's chief purpose was to effect a Russo-Turkish settlement, its diplomatic elements contributing to Duckworth's uncertainty and failure before Constantinople.[31] The mediation aspect, though, is easy to overstate. Duckworth's actions were subordinated to Arbuthnot's opinions, but the latter had been told to demand the surrender of the fleet, the right to garrison the Dardanelles and Alexandria, the expulsion of Sébastiani and the renewal of the treaties with Britain and Russia after a Russo-Turkish settlement.[32] Such a shopping list seems almost designed to provoke Turkish hostility rather than eliminate it.

From the expedition's inception in November it was plain that the ministers' priority was securing the Turkish fleet. When combined with the instruction to seize Alexandria as soon as hostilities became evident, the diplomatic aspects of Duckworth's mission seem yet more doubtful. That he failed was due not to any ambiguities in his orders, but rather to the inadequacy of his force and his misfortune in repeatedly meeting adverse winds. Certainly its lack of accompanying troops was the expedition's most obvious weakness, a shortcoming that meant that Duckworth could not secure the Straits behind him and so secure a safe retreat in case of need. In danger of being trapped before Constantinople, it was hard for him to appear simultaneously as a grave threat to the Turks.[33]

Whatever Russian goodwill was likely to be earned by this attempt, however, was immediately forfeited by the operation that followed it: the British occupation of Alexandria. On the same day that Duckworth had been sent his orders, Howick also issued instructions to Lieutenant General Fox, the military commander in Sicily. These instructed him to prepare a force of 5,000 men who were, in the event of hostilities with Turkey, to sail to Egypt. 'The object of His Majesty's Government, in Determining upon this measure, is not the conquest of Egypt, but merely the capture of Alexandria for the purpose of preventing the French from regaining a footing in that country . . .'[34] This reflected a nervousness about Egypt, a worry that either a Franco-Russian peace might let Russia control the Danubian provinces in return for a French occupation, or that the French might, with aid from the Mamelukes, simply take over Egypt altogether. The latter possibility was stressed by Misset, the British representative in Alexandria, and also by Collingwood, who further believed that Alexandria in British hands would make an excellent naval base for the eastern Mediterranean as well as yielding commercial benefits.[35] Later the Cabinet conceived a further advantage, Thomas Grenville writing:

I again advert to that topic as still more important from the great dependence which Constantinople is said to place upon Alexandria for supply and provisions, so that in case of war, the capture of Alexandria would not only secure Egypt, but in doing so would to a very great degree distress the city of Constantinople.[36]

Capturing Alexandria was seen as a way of pre-empting any French invasion of Egypt, the fear for India's security lying at the heart of this, despite the obstacles preventing any attack on the subcontinent from that country. Port and shipping facilities on the Red Sea were very limited and the logistical problems of any overland assault via Syria and Persia would have been formidable. The unpracticality of using Egypt for an invasion of India had been pointed out as early as November 1806,[37] but from the Cabinet's viewpoint a French army there would have tied down substantial British troops in containing and/or destroying it. French naval resources might have been insufficient to secure control of the eastern Mediterranean, but nevertheless Collingwood would have found having to blockade ports like Alexandria an extremely unwelcome extra responsibility. Finally the presence of a French army in the Middle East might have prompted discontent among native Indian rulers despite the uncertain nature of direct French participation in any rebellion. Windham for one had already expressed alarm over Napoleon's Indian ambitions and the sending of a French mission to Persia, fearing an overland attack at some point.[38]

Whatever the Cabinet's motivation, the attack on Alexandria could be viewed diplomatically only in the worst possible light, it seeming that once again Britain was leaving her allies in the lurch while pursuing her own ambitions, and in a region, moreover, in which Russia was sensitive to her own interests. Ironically for the ministers, after the swift capture of Alexandria on 16 March 1807, their whole campaign backfired into defeat and humiliation. Prompted by misleading information from Misset, Fraser, the military commander, felt obliged to try and expand the area under British control to ensure Alexandria's food supplies. The attempt met with a bloody rebuff that cost almost 1,400 casualties, Fraser thereafter confining himself to the city, though two additional battalions had to be sent from Sicily to make up his losses.[39]

The Talents' disinclination to face European campaigns was not due merely to disillusion and financial stringency: a major contributing factor was the sudden, apparently heaven-sent, opportunity to expand British imperial power into Spanish America.

Despite the long-felt attraction of this region, prior to 1806 little actual headway had been made towards its conquest despite the plethora of schemes directed at various ministers by what amounted to a South American lobby of those keen to see expansion in the area. Such plans tended to get nowhere while Britain's means were committed to Europe, and anyway there was a sense of caution about the risks involved in such ventures. There were fears that any action might drive Spain further into the arms of France, as well as a nervousness about sparking off a social revolution among the region's already restless inhabitants. Any radical social change could do little for the area's commercial potential and the possible military consequences had already been indicated by the years of vicious warfare on St Domingo following the slave revolt on that island. Pitt was, perhaps, considering possible attacks on the area in the summer of 1805 if the coalition then being formed should fail, but by 1806 there seemed little chance of any ministry opening the Pandora's Box of South American expansion. William Grenville would shortly remark, 'I always felt a great reluctance to embarking on South American projects because I knew it was much easier to get into them than out again.'[40]

All this was to be changed by the acquisitive ambitions of one man: Commodore Sir Home Popham. After the conquest of the Cape, he persuaded the military commander, Major General Baird, to assign him a small group of soldiers and in April 1806 the indefatigable sailor set off to conquer Buenos Aires. This city of some 70,000 inhabitants was duly surprised and captured in June by a British force comprising no more than 1,600 men. Resistance had been negligible and word of the success reached London in September – ministers had heard in July of what Popham was intending – shrewdly accompanied by circulars sent to the business community telling of the profits that would flow from Popham's action: that sent to Birmingham council spoke of the huge new opportunity for trade and of how Buenos Aires was eager for European goods of every description. Popham also sent home £1·1 million in prize money seized from Buenos Aires' public purse, this treasure being hauled through the streets of London in a victory parade complete with crowds, bands and bunting. Publishers printed accounts of the 'New Arcadia' and speculators rushed off cargoes to the Rio de la Plata to try and take advantage of the £2 million per annum that the area would, according to Popham, be worth. Lloyd's

Patriotic Fund reflected national enthusiasm by awarding the sailor a silver vase and *The Times* summed up the general euphoria:

> When we consider the consequences to which it leads from its situation, and its commercial capacities, as well as its political influence, we know not how to express ourselves in terms adequate to our ideas of the national advantages which will be derived from this conquest.

When the breakdown in the peace talks with Napoleon was heard of on 10 October the news was greeted by the cheers of stockbrokers eager not to be deprived of the great new source of wealth.[41]

Such general rapture put the government in a very awkward position. Popham's venture might have been implemented without permission and with the prime objective of gaining prize money for the sailor, but it would have been very difficult for any Cabinet to ignore the opportunities it seemed to offer. Like other ministries before it, the Talents had received their share of plans for South American conquest, but all had been resisted.[42] Presented, though, with a *fait accompli*, ministers felt obliged to try and consolidate the success by sending Major General Auchmuty and 2,000 troops to the Rio de la Plata, simultaneously ordering the errant Popham home to explain his conduct.[43]

From this point, however, the Cabinet changed from having to give grudging support to something it had not sanctioned to being suddenly gripped by a fever of plans for New World conquest. William Grenville initially believed that news of the success might make Napoleon more pliable in the languishing peace talks. Within a few days, however, he was admitting that popular enthusiasm might make any surrender of Buenos Aires, as part of a wider peace settlement, very difficult. Soon, his imagination running riot over the question, he was seeking his brother's opinion on a grandiose scheme for an assault on Central America, this taking the form of two invasion forces, one on the eastern coast and one on the western, the latter picking up troops from India and capturing the Philippines *en route*. Buckingham himself had already put forward a plan to seize Panama while another force, from the Cape of Good Hope, operated off Peru. Even Windham found these notions too fanciful to swallow.[44] Despite this the War Minister was one of the most ardent proponents of South American expansion, writing in July that 'I am more & more of opinion that we ought to take up decidedly this business of S. America.' On 11 September, two days before news arrived of Buneos Aires' fall, he wished that 'part of the force which we are now disposing of, was applied, not to revolutionising, but to the obtaining possession of part of the Spanish settlements in South America'. According to Lord Holland, of those within the Cabinet, William Grenville, Windham, Moira and Sidmouth were enthusiastic about South American ventures. Outside the Cabinet support came from politicians like Buckingham, from the business community and from the Duke of York, who believed that the Rio de la Plata was 'invaluable'.[45]

In October 1806 the government's new strategy started to take shape when Windham appointed his newly promoted protégé, Brigadier General Craufurd, to take command of a force of 4,001 troops.

> The object of your expedition is the capture of the sea ports & fortresses, & the reduction of the province of Chili, to which it is conceived both from the positive information received, & also from a just inference drawn from the sources at Buenos Ayres that your force is probably adequate.

Craufurd was to sail either via Cape Horn or the Cape of Good Hope, the route being undecided at the time, and he was not to extend his operations into Peru, the Cabinet regarding Chile as a base for possible future activity. He was to do nothing to irritate the local inhabitants needlessly and was to make no promises as to policy which might later embarrass the government. Finally he was, by a chain of posts or some other means, to establish communications with Buenos Aires. This latter suggestion has been castigated as ludicrous, but to be fair to Windham, however dubious his geographical knowledge may have been, all his orders rested on a fundamental misunderstanding: the assumption that the inhabitants of Spanish America would welcome the British as liberators. Given locals who were friendly, communications between Chile and Buenos Aires might have been established in some form; as it happened, though, the locals were to prove anything but amenable.[46]

The strategic objective in the autumn of 1806 was consolidation at Buenos Aires by means of troops drawn from Europe and the Cape[47] and gaining control of Chile via Craufurd's expedition. Then, on 25 January 1807, came the terrible news that, before any reinforcements had arrived, the garrison of Buenos Aires had been forced to surrender on 12 August in the face of a popular revolt. The time this news took to reach London is one indicator of the problems inherent in the ministry's strategy, but by then the Cabinet felt unable to face the political repercussions of abandoning the policy and so was compelled to reinforce failure. New instructions were issued on 5 March for Auchmuty and Craufurd's commands to be united under the leadership of Lieutenant General Whitelocke, the new single force numbering, with reinforcements included, some 11,180 soldiers. Thoughts of Chile were dropped and Whitelocke was ordered to secure some point from which the Spanish colonists would find it hard to expel him. Such a position was not to require a large British garrison, certainly one no bigger than his total command. Finally he was told that he had permission to hire local troops to ease the British burden, a freedom indicating that the Cabinet still had no true idea of the hostility felt by the locals towards the British.[48]

According to W. B. Taylor the Talents' South American policy allowed them to opt out of the European war, over which they could not agree.[49] This theory contains elements of truth, but it was nothing new for the ministry. Spanish America offered an area where British interests at their most blatant could be pursued, similar to Sicily, Portugal and Alexandria. Nor could any set of politicians have been expected to face the popular wrath that would have arisen had they tried to withdraw once the wily Popham had spread word of the 'New Arcadia'. Where ministers went seriously wrong was in permitting themselves suddenly to get so wrapped up in enthusiasm for the region's possibilities while simultaneously seeming to forget all its drawbacks. The plethora of schemes for attacks on Chile, the Rio de la Plata, Peru, the northern part of South America and Mexico, with the possibility of a seizure of the Philippines thrown in for good measure, does not suggest a set of men at one with the problems of time and distance. At no moment did the Talents ever seen to grasp that the British in Spanish America were regarded not as liberators but rather as another unwelcome set of outside rulers like the Spanish, and ones, moreover, seen as godless Protestants out for loot. Thus it was that when Auchmuty's force reached the Rio de la Plata and he decided, Buenos Aires having fallen, to seize Montevideo as a coastal strong point, the capture succeeded (February 1807) only after a bloody assault that cost him 350 casualties. Worse was to happen in July when Whitelocke led the combined British force on an attack on Buenos Aires: in savage fighting he suffered 3,000 casualties and was unable to subdue the city, feeling obliged thereafter to evacuate the whole of the Rio de la Plata.[50] Had Whitelocke been more successful the logic behind the whole strategy would still be open to doubt. A substantial force would have been tied down trying to control a sullen population that resented its presence. Furthermore it is questionable whether the commercial benefits would ever have been on the scale anticipated: Spanish America, with much of its population poor and its communications bad, had little to offer as a market and many of its needs were already met by illicit British trading activity.[51]

Embarrassingly, just as the Cabinet became embroiled in South America, so the opportunity to do France serious harm in Europe once again arose. For those ministers more amenable to operations aimed at supporting Prussia and then Russia it meant that pressing their case would reduce resources for Spanish America, a prospect making Continental operations even more disagreeable to those who already regarded such ventures with distaste. Windham referred to 'differences' over South American strategy in February 1807, but correctly anticipated that those opposing the policy would be overcome. Only Thomas Grenville seems to have opposed the strategy consistently; both Howick and Sidmouth, the other noted 'Europeans', both succumbed to the lure of the New World.[52]

The Talents were to be spared the political consequences of some of their military failures by their resignation over the issue of Catholic Emancipation, although their military record in office was to haunt them in opposition and do nothing to make them seem viable candidates for government for the remainder of the period. Without the cement of office to bind them their underlying strategic differences became ever clearer with the passage of time, particularly over the question of the Peninsular War. Of the Talents Cabinet only Sidmouth was to lead his followers back into office, in 1812, and significantly he was a supporter of the war in Spain.

The essence of the Talents' military policy, that Britain's means should be hoarded and then used solely for her own benefit, should not be dismissed out of hand. It was sensible in theory to want to use the nation's resources effectively, but in practice the Cabinet did not do so. To some extent the failure can be pinned on the inadequacies of commanders in the field, but in the last analysis the ministry does appear shortsighted in its approach to the thorny problem of Napoleonic France. While insisting that resources should not be squandered in Europe the Cabinet allowed itself to be sucked into the morass of South America. While displaying support for an ally in the Dardanelles it simultaneously offended that ally by its self-seeking over Alexandria. It encouraged Sweden regarding attacks on northern Germany in spring 1807 but did nothing to back words with troops. The ministry could comprehend strategic targets which encompassed British interests at their most straightforward but failed to understand the need, the essential need, to restrain Napoleon in Europe. As a result it gave little real support to the French emperor's enemies and so, to some extent, helped paved the way for the Franco-Russian alliance via the Treaty of Tilsit, an agreement leaving Britain bereft of any substantial European allies by the summer of 1807. The Talents bluntly declared that those countries which fought France did so for their own interests. At Tilsit the Tsar responded by ditching Britain and following Russian interests in isolation. Supposedly putting Britain first, the Talents failed to recognise that what Britain needed most of all was freedom from Continental threat.

Notes

1 *P.D.*, VII, pp. 307–9, B.M. Add. Mss 58930, Dropmore Papers, ff. 57–8. P.R.O. WO 1/632, pp. 370–3.

2 Aspinall, IV, pp. 403–4. *Historic Manuscripts Commission Reports on the Manuscripts of J. B. Fortescue, Esq., preserved at Dropmore*, 1892–1927, VIII, pp. 217–18 (afterwards referred to as *H.M.C. Dropmore*).

3 For a detailed account of the negotations see Walker. Also Taylor, pp. 74–80.

4 B.M. Add. Mss 58946, Dropmore Papers, ff. 178–81.

5 Mackesy, *War in the Mediterranean*, pp. 130–52. Bunbury, pp. 157–74 and appendix R, pp. 313–14. Fortescue, *British Army*, 5, pp. 330–62.

6 P.R.O. FO 63/50, no. 10. B.M. Add. Mss 58946, Dropmore Papers, ff. 87–v and 90–1v. 58930, f. 184–v.

7 B.M. Add. Mss 58946, Dropmore Papers, ff. 107–8. *P.D.*, X, pp. 537–43. P.R.O. 63/51. Fortescue, *British Army*, 5, p. 366. H. Brougham, *Life and Times of Henry, Lord Brougham*, Edinburgh, 1871, I, pp. 336–9. Brougham mentions orders to kidnap the royal family if they would neither fight nor flee.

8 *H.M.C. Dropmore*, VIII, pp. 270–1, 285, 294, 296, 309 and 313. *P.D.*, X, pp. 546–7.

9 *H.M.C. Dropmore*, VIII, pp. 93 and 97. Durham University Library, the Earl Grey Papers, 2nd Earl, William Grenville to Howick, 23 February 1807, no. 78.

10 *H.M.C. Dropmore*, VIII, pp. 109 and 321–4. The Swedish ambassador to Russia observed at this time that Fox 'is not a man to inspire great confidence' and this seems to have been a widespread view: Carr, p. 50 and n.

11 *H.M.C. Dropmore*, VIII, p. 352. Durham University Library, The Earl Grey Papers, 2nd Earl, William Grenville to Howick, 3 October 1806, no. 55; and same to same, 11 October 1806, no. 57, P.R.O. FO 64/73, ff. 6–8.

12 P.R.O. FO 64/73, ff. 29–31 and 64/74, ff. 2–6.

13 *H.M.C. Dropmore*, VIII, p. 353.

14 P.R.O. FO 65/65, f. 210, and 65/67, ff. 4–5.

15 Sherwig, pp. 179–80. P.R.O. FO 65/68, ff. 24–6.

16 P.R.O. FO 7/83, Howick to Adair, 13 January 1807, no. 1.

17 P.R.O. FO 64–74, ff. 9–13v.

18 *P.D.*, X, pp. 633 and 639–40.

19 *P.D.*, IX, pp. 1037–8, and X, pp. 447–8.

20 *H.M.C. Dropmore*, VIII, p. 401.

21 B.M. Add. Mss 37847, Windham Papers, f. 227. Duke of Buckingham, *Memoirs of the Courts and Cabinets of George III*, London, 1853–55, III, pp. 131–2. Greenwich Maritime Museum, Duckworth Papers, DUC/13, 38 MS 2002, T. Grenville to Vice-Admiral Duckworth, 18 January 1807.

22 C. Grey, *Some Account of the Life and Opinions of Charles, Second Earl Grey*, London, 1861, pp. 135–6. *P.D.*, X, p. 1042.

23 P.R.O. FO 73/38, Howick to Straton, 10 March 1807, no. 2.

24 P.R.O. FO 65/68, ff. 51 and 72–3.

25 Statistics from B.M. Add. Mss 37886, Windham Papers, ff. 145v and 149. P.R.O. WO 1/632, pp. 181–3. B.M. Add. Mss 59290, Dropmore Papers, ff. 139–48; 59286, ff. 48–9 (provisional folio order).

26 Castlereagh gave these figures to Parliament on 13 August: *P.D.*, IX, pp. 1222–3. Transport Department figures in P.R.O. ADM 1/3751 bear him out.

27 *P.D.*, IX, pp. 1037–8; X, pp. 436–7.

28 J. Barrow, *The Life and Correspondence of Admiral Sir William Sydney Smith*, London, 1848, II, pp. 215–16. During the autumn Arbuthnot dithered over whether a squadron should be sent or not, finally deciding, when it was too late to influence the Cabinet's decision, that one would do no good: R. G. Gwilliam, 'The Dardanelles Expedition of 1807', University of Liverpool, M.A. thesis, 1955, pp. 57–62.

29 Gwilliam, pp. 57–9. Aspinall, IV, pp. 488–9. Durham University Library, The Earl Grey Papers, 2nd Earl, Howick to the Admiralty, 21 November 1806.

30 When united with the vessels sent previously by Collingwood, Duckworth's squadron consisted of eight ships of the line, two frigates and two bomb vessels: James, IV, p. 299. For detailed accounts of the expedition's adventures see Gwilliam; Mackesy, *War in the Mediterranean*, pp. 169–80; James, IV, pp. 296–311.

31 Mackesy, *War in the Mediterranean*, pp. 167 and 179–80.

32 Gwilliam, p. 91.
33 Observers at the time noted the lack of troops: B.M. Add. Mss 49482, Gordon Papers, f. 54v; *Castlereagh Correspondence*, VI, pp. 155–7.
34 B.M. Add. Mss 37050, Fox Papers, f. 46v.
35 Mackesy, *War in the Mediterranean*, pp. 184–5. G. L. Newnham Collingwood (ed.), *A Selection from the Public and Private Correspondence of Vice-Admiral Lord Collingwood*, London, 1828, II, pp. 240, 271 and 274–5.
36 B.M. Add. Mss 40096, I, Collingwood Papers, f. 35v. This belief was quite incorrect: Constantinople was able to draw its supplies by land.
37 B.M. Add. Mss 59282, Dropmore Papers, ff. 78–9.
38 Durham University Library, The Earl Grey Papers, 2nd Earl, Windham to Howick, 13 March 1806, no. 6.
39 For detailed accounts of the campaign see Mackesy, *War in the Mediterranean*, pp. 187–94; Bunbury, pp. 187–202; Fortescue, *British Army*, 6, pp. 5–28. Details of Alexandria's food problems in Leeds University Library, Brotherton Collection Box VII, Mulgrave Papers, 19/52. Fraser's original force numbered 5,813: Greenwich Maritime Museum, Duckworth Papers, DUC/13, 38 MS 2136, Transport Abstract (Foretescue, *British Army*, 6, p. 7 n., gives the slightly higher total of 5,914).
40 J. Lynch, 'British policy and Spanish America, 1783–1808', *Journal of Latin American Studies*, I, 1969, pp. 1–7. Kaufmann, pp. 11–15. *H.M.C. Dropmore*, VIII, p. 352.
41 For the capture and the reaction to it: Fortescue, *British Army*, 5, pp. 314–17. G. Pendle, 'Defeat at Buenos Aires, 1806–07', *History Today*, 1952, 2, pp. 400–3. Lynch, pp. 19–20. *Naval Chronicle*, London, 1806, XVI, pp. 373–4. C. Wright and C. F. Fayle, *History of Lloyd's*, London, 1928, p. 229. *The Times*, 13 September 1806. Crouzet, p. 179.
42 Examples of these can be found in Lynch, pp. 15–18, and B.M. Add. Mss 37847, Windham Papers, f. 255v; 37884, ff. 15–17.
43 Fortescue, *British Army*, 5, p. 369 n. Popham was tried by court-martial on his return, but escaped with a reprimand.
44 *H.M.C. Dropmore*, VIII, pp. 333, 352, 386–7 and 418–20. Arthur Wellesley urged the government to abandon any plan to take the Philippines: IX, pp. 481–8.
45 Durham University Library, The Earl Grey Papers, 2nd Earl, Windham to Howick, 13 July 1806, no. 27. *H.M.C. Dropmore*, VIII, p. 321. Lord Holland (ed.), *Memoirs of the Whig Party during my Time*, London, II, 1854, pp. 111–14. B.M. Add. Mss 49472, Gordon Papers, f. 86.
46 B.M. Add. Mss 47884, Windham Papers, ff. 220–7. Butler, CLII, p. 305.
47 Auchmuty finally left with 4,000 men on 9 October and the garrison at the Cape supplied a further two battalions: Butler, CLII, p. 284.
48 B.M. Add. Mss 37886, Windham Papers, ff. 145–51.
49 Taylor, pp. 122–23.
50 Detailed accounts are in Fortescue, *British Army*, 5, pp. 368–429, and Butler, CLIII, pp. 388–93 and 501–6.
51 Kaufmann, pp. 55–6. Lynch, pp. 7–10 and 25–30, points to the

value of the trade without any garrisons on the spot. Capturing Buenos Aires did boost short-term activity, but there were other avenues. In 1799 commerce carried on via Trinidad was worth £1 million; in the first nine months of 1806 bullion imports into Jamaica from Central American dealings came to a value of $1·5 million; and trade could be carried on via Portugal's Brazilian territories.

52 B.M. Add. Mss 41854, Thomas Grenville Papers, f. 353. B.M. Add. Mss 37847, Windham Papers, f. 227. Durham University Library, The Earl Grey Papers, 2nd Earl, Howick to Lauderdale, 1 October 1806. Holland, II, pp. 111–14.

7

The Portland ministry

The advent of a new ministry, one with a strong Pittite element, brought a return to a European strategic orientation and a keenness to support the powers fighting Napoleon in Poland. Early in April 1807 Canning, responding to rumours of Franco-Prussian peace talks, sought to encourage the Tsar towards more energetic measures, the Russian role in any likely peace being seen as crucial. Canning developed this line of thinking by hoping that any future negotiations would include Britain, recognising at the same time that the Europeans would require details of precisely what scale of support Britain would contribute to continued military efforts. In consequence he said that the government was calculating the amount of financial aid that could be provided, bearing in mind that some reserves had to be retained in case of Austrian re-entry. It was also requested that the allies should in future accept more aid in kind, in the form of arms, clothing and the like, to ease the strain on the Treasury. Canning was vaguer respecting direct military help, but he nevertheless insisted that preparations were under way to send troops to the Continent once rumours about a peace had been scotched.[1]

Such assurances reflected the new ministry's approach but did little to show how difficult such military operations were likely to be. In March 1807 there was a disposable force in the UK of 23,586 infantry and 10,026 cavalry. However, of this total, some 5,000 infantry had to be set aside as reinforcements for the East and West Indies, both areas being under threat of disorder. Furthermore an extra 5,000 had to be available either to support the above or for further South American operations. Castlereagh concluded from these figures that only 10,000–12,000 infantry and 8,000–10,000 cavalry could be spared to help the Europeans, and should not be committed until they had won some decisive advantage. Despite such reservations the Cabinet remained determined to try and help its allies, informing the King on 3 April that the troops would be sent either to support them directly, or used in some way so as to distract the French.[2]

Despite such intentions the Cabinet could implement no immediate military operations because of the shortage of transports, the weeks after the ministry came into office seeing Castlereagh desperately trying to acquire tonnage. On 8 April he permitted the Commissioners of Transports to raise the hiring rates and on 13 May told them to provide a weekly report on their progress. This activity was ultimately successful, but took time. In February the Talents had had 68,918 tons of shipping in service, of which only 21,727 tons was either unappropriated or on home service. By June the figure had risen to 105,456 tons on home service and by July to 115,586 tons. It was this accumulation that was to permit forces to be sent to Stralsund and Copenhagen.[3]

Although Mulgrave was urged to send a light squadron to the Baltic to help allied communications, Castlereagh feeling that even a few frigates would be useful if only they were sent quickly, there was little else that could be done while the transports were being assembled. For Castlereagh it was vital to show the allies that 'we were not inattentive to their accommodation', an attitude undoubtedly shared by the rest of the Cabinet. On 28 April the government acknowledged the pressure from the Russians and Swedes for a British force to operate from Stralsund, Hutchinson being told to leave his post with the Prussian court and go to Sweden to co-ordinate plans with Gustavus IV for such an operation; to assist him Brigadier General Clinton was also sent to Sweden as military adviser. On 13 May Canning noted with delight the signature of a Russo-Prussian concert, indicating a continuation of the Polish campaign.[4] Three days later Leveson Gower, back at his ambassadorial post in St Petersburg, was told that Britain was ready to provide Russia and Prussia with assistance to the tune of £2·6 million, though there was no desire for a formal treaty, the diplomat being empowered to hand out the aid as he saw fit. With their shortage of funds and their hope that Austria would soon fight, ministers wanted to limit immediate expenditure as much as possible. However, while providing the finance, Canning also admitted to Leveson Gower that, respecting direct military help, 'it is painful to me not to be enabled to authorise Your Excellency to give more distinct and positive assurances both as to the time and the amount of such a Detachment . . .'. Canning was fully aware of the diplomatic repercussions that could flow from this in the light of the way the Russians had been treated by the Talents.[5]

A further incentive for ministers came at the end of May when it was learned that Sweden and Prussia had agreed to a military convention whereby 10,000–12,000 Prussian troops would be added to a force of 12,000 Swedes in Pomerania. This prompted a British offer of a further £50,000 p.a. for Gustavus IV if he would add another 4,000 men to the total: a treaty formalising this was agreed in June. More important, this nascent allied army prompted the Cabinet early in June to decide to send British troops to Stralsund, it being assumed that they would number 8,000–10,000 and would depart without waiting for Clinton to report. At the time ministers were also thinking of landing another force in the Elbe–Weser region of Germany if the summer campaign went well. On 26 May Castlereagh told his Cabinet colleagues that Britain's home establishment was deficient of 47,464 troops, a weakness exacerbated by 16,000 of those soldiers that were available being organised in fifty-six skeleton battalions. He wondered if, in such circumstances, 13,000 men could be spared for foreign service: ministers evidently felt that the risk was worth it.[6] On 8 June Canning told Leveson Gower of the intended force, now to number 10,000 men, bound for Stralsund, sailing in two divisions under the command of Lieutenant General Cathcart. It was planned to increase the eventual total assembled at the fortress to 27,000, though Canning was nervous that this might not be well received, as such a concentration ruled out any operations in the Elbe–Weser region.[7]

The Cabinet also had hopes of actively employing its Mediterranean forces as well, wanting initially to use the troops in Sicily to assist the Russians via pressure on the Turks. Fox was told on 25 April that the government had no information tending to rule out the employment of those troops at Alexandria or in the Dardanelles, though he was given latitude to act as he saw fit. It was made clear that co-operation with the Russians, if requested by Arbuthnot and/or Duckworth, would be welcomed in London, the Cabinet believing that part of the Sicilian garrison could be withdrawn for such a task. A fortnight later this situation had changed, ministers by then appreciating that the Dardanelles had been strongly fortified and that attacks on the Turks would do little to aid the Russians. Pressure on the Porte would in future be confined to the diplomatic and economic sphere.[8] However, this did not mark the end of the Cabinet's Mediterranean ambitions. Feeling that Naples or some other part of Italy should be attacked by way of a diversion, Castlereagh calculated that, if the Neapolitan troops were included, some 20,000 men could be mustered for this duty. He believed that the Neapolitan court would be enthusiastic, having pressed for such an attack before, and that its troops might make up in numbers what they lacked in quality. He considered that the French in Italy were weak because of the numbers sent to Poland and that, at best, such a campaign would liberate Naples and, at worst, would maul the French before reinforcements could reach them.[9]

Had such an operation been launched, by the summer of 1807 the Cabinet could have claimed that it had 30,000 British and auxiliary troops on the Continent with more to follow. In the Mediterranean, though, its plans were stillborn. Moore, although only the second-in-command in Sicily, was the garrison's military brain and he was implacably opposed to Italian adventures. Having no political sympathies with the new ministers, and despising and mistrusting the Neapolitan court, on 3 July he expressed astonishment at the whole scheme, bearing in mind that 2,000 British troops had already had to be sent to reinforce the garrison at Alexandria and that the Neopolitans had tried and failed to recover the kingdom on their own in May. He believed that, at most, 15,000 troops could be assembled for such a campaign, and that that would mean leaving a mere 2,000 British troops in Messina and Syracuse. Moore also condemned the plan because he claimed to have no knowledge of enemy strengths and dispositions and would have no control over the Neapolitans in any expedition. Yet for the British to attack alone would be folly, their number in any solitary attempt not exceeding 8,000. Exasperated, Moore felt that the ministers had been misled into undue optimism by Drummond, the British representative at the Neapolitan court. The two men had been at loggerheads for some time and the soldier had been nettled in April when Drummond had pressed him to back the pending Neapolitan campaign on the mainland.[10]

Certainly Moore's opinions were unfair to the ministers and, if anything, reflect his own strategic shortcomings. The orders for an expedition to Italy were drafted before word of Fraser's defeats in Egypt and his consequent reinforcing from Sicily had reached London; nor did they know that the Neapolitans had attacked alone in May and been defeated. For his part Moore cannot be excused for what seems complete ignorance of the French positions in Naples and evident failure to appreciate the need for activity. In April he voiced the opinion that Maida the year before had been not so much a victory as a battle which got the British force out of an awkward predicament. His one object seems to have been to avoid Italian operations at all costs.[11]

With Mediterranean lethargy, only the Baltic remained for ministers keen to support their allies, the two divisions for Stralsund sailing on 19 June and 1 July. Yet it was indicative of the sort of problems besetting strategic planners that the first of these departed five days after the shattering Russian defeat at Friedland, and the second six days before the signing of the Treaty of Tilsit. Word of Friedland reached London on 29 June, but no immediate brake was put on British intentions, as it was not clear what the consequences of the defeat would be. Once its scale became apparent, though, ministers were in the uncomfortable position of having British troops potentially isolated in the Baltic were Denmark to become hostile and close the Sound. The Cabinet faced two questions: would Russia continue to fight, and would Denmark now become a French satellite?

Desertion by the Tsar cannot have come as much of a surprise. Disputes over military and financial support had been chronic causes of tension for some time, relations being worsened by the occupation of Alexandria and Russian refusal to renew the Anglo-Russian commercial treaty or to guarantee the rights of British merchants recognised under it.[12] As Russia became less reliable as an ally, so Denmark became more likely as an enemy. The latter had resisted pressure to join the war against France in 1805–06 and had seemed passive before a French violation of her territory at the end of 1806. Furthermore while rejecting offers of an Anglo-Swedish alliance at the end of 1806, the Danes responded to Swedish troop concentrations in Scania by strengthening their coastal defences. Such a measure implied preparation to resist any naval assault, of the sort Britain had launched in 1801, and contrasted very unfavourably with their torpor towards France. There were also fears that the Danes might join some sort of Northern League aimed at Britain, like those of 1780 and 1801, a dread reinforced by the energetic Danish protests against the Orders in Council in January 1807 and the blockade of the Elbe in March, both being steps which threatened the lucrative Danish carrying trade. By 9 June Canning was 'afraid the disposition of Copenhagen is so unfriendly as to want nothing but the assurance of being able to insult us with impunity, to break out into open defiance.' Adding to the tension, *The Times* reported on 22 June that the Danes were preparing their fleet so that it could put to sea at a few hours' notice.[13]

Canning reacted quickly to the perceived threat. On 10 July he submitted a memorandum to the Cabinet pointing out the reported Danish naval activity and enclosed a despatch from the consul in Altona which spoke of French preparations to attack Holstein. Canning concluded that, excepting Gothenburg, the Danes could close all the ports of northern Europe to Britain. He also wondered whether, if they proved unable to defend Holstein, they could defend their fleet. He concluded that Britain's naval presence in the Baltic should be reinforced, with the aim of guarding trade and trying to stop Denmark joining any Napoleonic confederation: a substantial British fleet off her coast would provide Denmark with an excellent excuse for inactivity. Canning's colleagues agreed, Mulgrave writing four days later that twenty to twenty-two ships of the line should be sent to observe the Danish fleet and any enemy activity in the direction of Zealand or Holstein.[14]

The government now moved with considerable speed. On 17 July Castlereagh recommended that a combined land/sea attack be made on the Danish fleet, orders being issued the following day for the stopping of any Danish reinforcement of the island of Zealand. On 21 July Canning observed:

> if it is true, as we hear from all quarters, that Bonaparte has determined upon occupying Holstein, and ultimately forcing the Danes to take part against us, we have not much time to waste in Speculations, but must take measures of vigilance and Precaution without delay.

Within hours of writing this Canning heard news that Napoleon and Alexander I were in the process of forming a maritime league against Britain in which Denmark would play a part.[15] With the collapse of allied resistance in Poland, it seemed all too probable that such a league would be formed. Once again, in a moment of crisis, Britain's strategy would take the form of ruthless self-preservation.

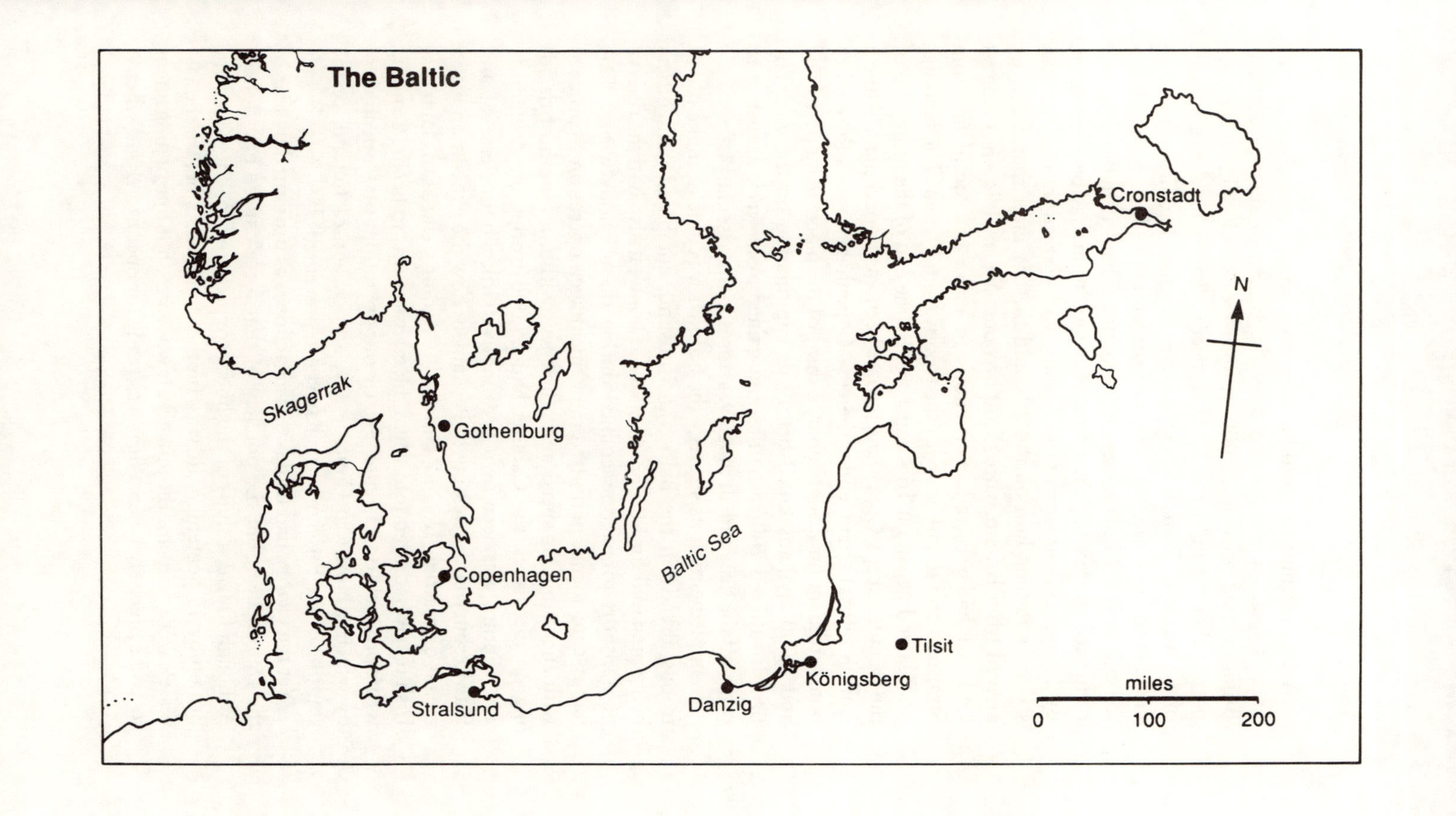
The Baltic
Skagerrak
Gothenburg
Copenhagen
Stralsund
Baltic Sea
Danzig
Königsberg
Tilsit
Cronstadt
N
miles
0
100
200

A final attempt to avoid hostilities was made when the diplomat Francis Jackson was sent to offer the Danes an alliance whereby Britain would provide 15,000 troops or a subsidy, plus naval support, if they would surrender their fleet to Britain for the remainder of the war with France. In Danish eyes the offer had little to recommend it and upon its rejection Jackson authorised the commanders to begin military operations on 14 August. The British build-up had continued apace while these fruitless negotiations had been going on. By 2 August Gambier was off Zealand with sixteen ships of the line, six more joining him on the 8th, and the day after that a convoy arrived from Britain with 19,000 troops. Meanwhile on 3 August Cathcart had received instructions to move his command from Stralsund and to link up with the troops from Britain. The landings on Zealand began on 16 August and by the end of the month all of the island, except Copenhagen, had been easily occupied. After a Danish refusal to surrender the city, Copenhagen was subjected to bombardment on 2 September, a third of the place being destroyed and 2,000 civilians killed before its capitulation on the 7th. The British suffered 200 casualties and gained a six-week armistice to carry off the fleet and all the naval stores in the arsenal.[16]

In implementing its strategy the Cabinet was able to make use of troops already in the Baltic, at Stralsund, combined with others being prepared for European service at home; it also had the reserve of transport tonnage assembled during the previous weeks. This happy coincidence permitted the Copenhagen operation to proceed with such singular speed and efficiency: within a month of deciding on the attack the Cabinet had 25,000 troops on Zealand.[17] The venture was seen as a pre-emptive strike, both Perceval and Hawkesbury later stressing in Parliament how the expedition was a means of guarding Ireland, Hawkesbury going so far as to claim that Irish rebels had been told when the invasion was to occur. Canning wrote privately on 25 September of 'our operations off Copenhagen, by which a Northern Confederacy, an invasion of Ireland, & the shutting of the Russian ports have been prevented'.[18]

Yet the victory had its flaws. The action was prompted by fear of the Danish fleet, but the potency of that force can be questioned. Although fourteen ships of the line were prepared for the voyage to Britain by 19 September, it was another four weeks before the last vessels were ready for the journey. It was a very fine line of judgement to assess precisely when a fleet was ready for operations and when it was not. Gambier later declared that the ships could have been ready for active service in three or four weeks, insisting that their voyage to Britain through bad weather proved their structural soundness. However, Gambier's words, publicly printed, have the whiff of propaganda about them. Of the ships of the line taken at Copenhagen a mere four were to be added to the Navy's battle strength, the scale of repairs required by the others rendering them worthless.[19]

Any failure to anticipate precisely the nature of Denmark's intentions prior to the expedition can in part be ascribed to Canning's poor relations with Rist, the Danish chargé in London, and to his distrust of Garlike, the British ambassador to the Danish court. The latter, Canning believed, was too influenced by the Court's francophile elements and was insufficiently energetic in discovering their true intentions.[20] The simple truth is that in the welter of rumour and fear in the summer of 1807 there could be little British inclination to give the Danes the benefit of any doubt. Whatever the nature of the threat, however, ministers must be given credit for acting decisively once they had perceived a danger. Less understandable was their failure to anticipate the Danish reaction to such a blatant attack. Canning for one expressed the hope early in August that Denmark might join an Anglo-Swedish alliance, and ministers were surprised when they learned on 4 September that the furious Danes had declared war on Britain. This failure made no difference to the attack on Copenhagen, but it caused the Cabinet some uncertainty thereafter and does not reflect well on ministerial thought processes.[21]

One final question should be considered: was the whole operation necessary at all? One author has suggested that it was quite needless, as Denmark, concerned to protect the wealth of her carrying trade, was essentially pro-British. Instead of attacking the Danes Britain should have kept a strong force in the Baltic to rush to their support once they were menaced by Napoleon; this would have gained Britain an ally rather than an implacable enemy.[22] Such theories are unconvincing. All the indications suggest that when it came to the crunch the Danes would have sided with France, the question of their carrying trade merely confusing the issue. The trade rested on Danish neutrality and would have been forfeit whichever side they chose, either via a hostile Royal Navy or via arrest in Napoleon's ports. Nor is it realistic to suggest that a large force could have been maintained in the Baltic pending a cry for help. It would have been a massive drain on British resources and would have been useless anyway had Denmark been attacked in winter – when the Baltic was unsafe and British ships were withdrawn. If the attack gained Britain an enemy, it was one whose teeth had been drawn and who was, thereafter, able to do only occasional harm to British interests in the region.[23]

Once the Cabinet learned that Denmark had declared war various unpleasant possibilities began to take shape. There was now every chance of French troops entering Holstein and, were they to cross to Zealand, threatening an invasion of Sweden. This domino theory went further: if Napoleon secured control of Sweden, and with it Finland, he could then menace Russia's northern border. This in turn would reduce the chances of Russia leaving her new French alliance, an especially disagreeable possibility, as ministers already felt they could discern Franco-Russian tensions, borne out by unofficial Russian feelers aimed at making sure that Britain did not intend to attack Russia or to let Napoleon gain control of Zealand. Initially the Cabinet thought in terms of an extended occupation of the island, despite the armistice terms with the Danes promising its evacuation in six weeks. This would have preserved Swedish security, prevented a Russian fleet being established at Copenhagen in the future, provided a bargaining counter for Hanover, Pomerania and Holstein, and finally would have provided a base from which to menace Russia and discourage Alexander I from taking his new friendship with Napoleon too far.[24] Unfortunately holding Zealand was not feasible. Both the naval and military commanders on the spot had grave moral reservations about breaking the terms of the armistice, but more profoundly any garrison left there would have been at great risk during the winter were the Great Belt to freeze over. Maintaining such a garrison would also have posed severe logistical problems. Such drawbacks obliged the Cabinet to drop the idea. Perceval admitted that his colleagues had given the question a lot of thought, but that to have held Zealand would have required 30,000–40,000 troops plus a blockading squadron, a commitment which would have crippled British strategy in other quarters.[25]

If Zealand could not be held, the next best solution was to station troops directly in Sweden, ministers thinking of some 10,000–15,000 men in Scania. This scheme foundered as well, Gustavus IV, furious at what he saw as desertion when Cathcart's troops were withdrawn from Stralsund (which fell to the French on

10 August), refusing to co-operate. In this fashion no further advantage could be taken of the success at Copenhagen, nor did lingering British hopes of a peace with the Danes come to anything. On 29 October Gambier's fleet and the remainder of Cathcart's troops, 12,000 of whom had already been sent home in the captured ships, returned to Britain.[26]

Tied in with these events was the thorny problem of relations with Russia. Aware of that country's hostility as early as 23 July, ministers were tempted to strike Copenhagen-like at the main Russian naval base at Cronstadt. However, Russia had been an ally and, ideally, might become one again, such a possibility not being rendered more likely by pre-emptive British naval action. Mulgrave for one felt the dilemma keenly. In August he believed that even a demonstration of force would reinforce Russian hostility. By the middle of September, influenced by reports from Russia which spoke of the fury, contempt and bewilderment at the Tsar's French alliance, he had changed his mind, pressing for attacks on the Russian coast that would compel Alexander I to change his policy.[27]

In the short term there were too many obstacles in the way of any assault on Cronstadt, the likely forces being too tied up at Copenhagen for attacks elsewhere, but the problem of Anglo-Russian relations was to remain. Further militating against direct action were Canning's continuing dreams of a great northern alliance of Russia, Britain, Sweden and Denmark, he believing that Alexander I, having surrendered so much at Tilsit, would be powerless without the backing of such a confederacy.[28] Such hopes were finally dashed when Russia, in line with promises given at Tilsit, declared war on Britain in November 1807.

By the end of the year, therefore, Sweden remained the only friendly power in the Baltic, though the unstable Gustavus IV was as much a liability as an asset. His country could contribute little force to the fight against Napoleon, yet needed extensive aid. British hints that it might be better for Gustavus IV to seek some sort of neutrality *vis-à-vis* the warring powers fell on deaf ears, the king having delusions of military grandeur and refusing to abandon the conflict. Compelled, therefore, to go on supporting the Swedes, a renewed subsidy treaty was agreed in February 1808, they being promised some £1·2 million per annum.[29] Making matters more complex still, and Anglo-Russian relations yet more sensitive, was the Russian declaration of war on Sweden early in 1808: seeking compensation for Tilsit, Alexander I had his eyes set on Finland, then part of the Swedish kingdom.

In February 1808 Saumarez, the new naval commander in the Baltic, was told that he was to command a fleet of twelve or thirteen ships of the line, his task being to protect Sweden and destroy the Russian fleet. However, no final decision about the latter objective had yet been taken and further instructions in March did not mention Russia at all. His final orders in April detailed how Sweden was to be preserved from French invasion, but respecting Russia he was merely to investigate the possibility of an attack on Cronstadt.[30] With the Swedish position deteriorating very quickly in Finland, the Cabinet decided to go even further than the provision of ships, money and supplies:[31] in April Moore was ordered to lead a corps of 10,864 rank and file to provide direct military support. Because of the continuing ambivalence about Russia, however, Moore was told that his command was not to be incorporated by, or come under the orders of, the Swedish army; furthermore he was to confine himself primarily to coastal defence duties, so being able to draw supplies from the British fleet and being available for any sudden recall. Although the possibility of operations against Norway or Zealand was not ruled out, Moore was under no circumstances to campaign against the Russians in Finland. Canning seems to have viewed the force as a potential garrison for Gothenburg, its employment freeing Swedish troops for other duties.[32] The expedition reached Gothenburg on 13 May but quickly ran into difficulties. Gustavus IV was unimpressed by Moore's restricted instructions, while Moore for his part felt contempt for the monarch's grandiose ideas and believed that Sweden's means should be concentrated on self-defence. Losing patience, Gustavus IV finally had Moore arrested. Contriving to escape, the British commander responded by bringing his whole force back to Britain, the troops having spent all this time cooped up in transports.[33]

Moore complained that the Cabinet 'had no specific plan' in sending him and that his orders were 'inexplicit and contradictory'. Later on Fortescue thundered that 'the whole behaviour of the Ministers admits of no defence . . .'.[34] However, neither view gives much thought to the Cabinet's predicament, for with Sweden under severe pressure the desire to help an ally was understandable. Castlereagh admitted that it would have been desirable to have had some information about Swedish intentions prior to Moore's departure, but 'the anxious desire His Majesty's [government] feels to afford this Ally, the most prompt support . . . have prevailed over all other Considerations . . .'. Encouraging haste were the assurances of Adlerberg, the Swedish ambassador, as to both the need for help and the welcome it would receive.[35] Unfortunately such assurances were misleading, but if ministers erred it was in trying to help a friendly power quickly, and their speed is understandable, given the pace of events and the tardy appearance of British expeditions in previous campaigns. This hardly warrants Fortescue's strictures, and those of Moore should be treated with caution: detailed orders were a rarity at a time of poor communications and commanders on the spot were expected to exercise their own judgement.

Fortunately the navy's Baltic operations at this time went more smoothly, there being little cause for argument with Gustavus IV when Saumarez was guarding his coasts anyway. No clarification respecting the admiral's attitude towards the Russians was forthcoming in 1808, but that did not stop him from checking a Russian sortie in August and capturing a ship of the line. Nothing was done to alienate the Tsar beyond the requirements of preserving Anglo-Swedish control of the Baltic. By June 1808 Canning was reverting to his former more optimistic attitude respecting Alexander I, believing that Napoleon's treatment of the Spanish royal family could not but offend the Tsar's sensibilities. Hoping for an end to the Russo-Swedish war, or at least for an armistice, the Foreign Secretary wondered if Gustavus IV might not be reconciled to the loss of Finland by being given some colonial compensation. He also still had dreams of a peace with Denmark and a grand Baltic alliance.[36]

Put simply, Britain's Baltic strategy was still falling between two stools. Moore's force was not allowed to fight the Russian army, but Saumarez's ships could fight the Russian navy. Just as confusing was the retention of the ships of Siniavin's Russian squadron, sheltering in the Tagus at the time of the Convention of Cintra, but the release of the vessels' crews to go home to Russia. Once there they could fight the Swedes, a ridiculous situation when it is remembered that Britain and Russia were at war and Britain and Sweden were allies! When he returned from the Baltic at the end of 1808 Saumarez was rebuked for informing the Tsar in September of the situation in Spain and expressing the hope that Iberian developments might induce other powers to fight alongside Britain. He defended himself by pointing to the nature of the 'war' Britain was waging against both Russia and Prussia, both nations trading extensively with Britain and containing many inhabitants who abhorred their relations with France.[37] That Saumarez could be rebuked for trying to implement an approach in September that Canning had been seeking in June speaks volumes for the state of Britain's Baltic strategy at the time.

No formal resolution of this situation seems to have been reached, but during 1809 the idea that Russia should be caused as little offence as possible appears to have been tacitly accepted. With Britain becoming deeply involved elsewhere the resources for an active military policy against Russia were not available anyway. In March 1809 Gustavus IV was driven into exile, his removal allowing the signature of a Russo-Swedish peace in September. These developments lessened the likelihood of any issue appearing that could have prompted Anglo-Russian hostilities. Despite the formal Swedish declaration of war on Britain after the peace with Russia, the main British dread, of a Sweden dominated by Napoleon, did not materialise. It was also made clear that although the 'war' excluded British vessels from Swedish ports, this did not apply to that country's numerous undefended islets and small harbours.[38] In this way the crucial Baltic trade continued and Saumarez remained able to draw at least some of his supplies locally.

The political and military changes marked by the Treaty of Tilsit had a major impact on British strategic thinking with respect to the Mediterranean theatre as well as the Baltic. In June 1807 the Cabinet had already decided in the light of Fraser's defeats to withdraw its forces from Egypt and to rely on diplomatic and economic pressure to keep the Turks out of the French camp. In the wake of Tilsit France occupied Cattaro and Corfu and British commanders became increasingly worried for the safety of Sicily, though the simultaneous collapse of the alliance with Russia at least freed everyone from having to mould policy to Russian needs. The eastern Mediterranean could, in effect, be abandoned and many of the troops in the region brought back to Britain. (See pp. 74–5 for the chaos that was to surround the process.) From 1808 Cabinet interest in the Mediterranean concentrated merely on holding Malta and Sicily and using the troops there for diversionary attacks on eastern Spain. That such a policy would not be followed exclusively would be due to the local commanders.[39]

As the Cabinet withdrew its forces from the Baltic towards the end of 1807 because of the onset of winter, and from the Mediterranean because of its change of strategy, there was another crisis brewing in the shape of Portugal. In July 1807 Napoleon demanded that that country should close its ports to British vessels and the following month insisted on Portugal actually declaring war on Britain, the instructions being backed up by the formation of a French army at Bayonne. By the end of August Castlereagh was hoping that the forces in the Baltic might be quickly freed for service in Portugal, though there was some reassurance in the assessment that it would take the French three months to assemble an army and move it to the Tagus. Like other ministers before him, his concern centred on the fate of the Portuguese fleet and the fear that any resistance to its attempted seizure would be slight. By early September 1807 British ambitions were starting to expand to thoughts of an occupation of Madeira, an island requiring only a small garrison and capable of providing a valuable watering point for British shipping.[40]

The main Portuguese objective remained a healthy desire to preserve the country's neutrality, a war with Britain threatening its colonies and trade, while a war with Napoleon threatened French occupation. While the Portuguese prince regent vacillated between these dilemmas a relentless Napoleon declared war on 20 October and a corps under General Junot marched towards the border. Portugal responded by closing her ports to Britain, a step she had refused in July, and on 5 November Portuguese batteries fired on a British frigate. However, on 22 October de Souza, the Portuguese ambassador in London, signed a convention committing his country to an anglophile policy and a promise that his royal family and fleet would flee to Brazil. With more hostile signs coming from Lisbon the Cabinet resolved to try and implement this agreement by force, ordering Rear-Admiral Smith to the Tagus with nine ships of the line on the 30th. He was to escort the royal family to Brazil, and when his instructions were renewed on 12 November Smith was given the added duty of blockading the Tagus in the face of Portuguese resistance; if this failed to secure a surrender of the fleet he could seize it by force if necessary. Already, on 7 November, Strangford, Britain's ambassador in Lisbon, had been told that Britain would tolerate the closing of Portugal's ports but wanted to occupy Madeira (agreed to in de Souza's convention) and would not agree to any sort of nominal war between the two countries.[41]

Smith reached the Tagus on 16 November and immediately implemented the blockade. With troops already assembled in Lisbon, plus the demands of Siniavin's Russian squadron, which had arrived on the 11th, there were food shortages. Matters worsened when Smith stopped two provision ships from entering the Tagus and threatened to mete out similar treatment to all other ports. The disorders prompted by the shortages, the British pressure, the approach of Junot's troops and, perhaps most important of all, Napoleon's announcement that the House of Braganza had ceased to reign, all prompted the prince regent to action. With nothing to be gained by remaining, the royal family departed for Brazil with the bulk of its fleet, comprising eight ships of the line plus a number of frigates, smaller warships and merchant vessels. Junot entered Lisbon on the 30th to find only one ship of the line, and that not ready for sea, remaining; two others and five smaller vessels were unserviceable. The British success was complete on 24 December when 3,600 troops occupied Madeira.[42]

It is noteworthy that the possibility of extended British military intervention in Portugal was being considered in 1807, just as it had been by the Talents in 1806 and by Pitt after 1797. Villiers, Strangford's successor in Lisbon, was informed on 22 November that Britain was prepared to help put the Portuguese military on a sound footing, but only on the understanding that they appreciated that their troops might have to campaign in Spain: it was felt that Portugal would not be safe until Spain was free of the French as well. There was also talk of British troops being employed in Portugal, but at this stage ministers essentially viewed Portugal merely as a means of helping a potentially rebellious Spain. For the moment such ideas got nowhere, but they interestingly illustrate a psychological willingness to embark on a protracted Iberian campaign and perhaps also a feeling that the French expansion into Spain – there were 52,000 troops in that country by early 1808 – might provoke a revolt.[43]

Despite the successes at Copenhagen and Lisbon, the strategic position at the start of 1808 was a poor one. There were no European allies of substance, and the possibility of invasion was reviving as Napoleon, freed from other distractions, could concentrate his energies upon it. Britain's attempt to secure a foothold in Spanish America had met a bloody rebuff, and, following the incident between HMS *Leopard* and the USS *Chesapeake* in June 1807, when the British ship, searching for naval deserters, fired upon the

American, relations with the United States were exremely strained. Indeed, so bad were they that the Cabinet felt compelled to increase its naval and military strength in North America,[44] levels of force that were maintained until 1812. However, this gloom appeared to lift somewhat early in the year, the French take-over of Spain being checked in March 1808 when Spanish troops at Aranjuez revolted. In the resulting chaos King Charles IV abdicated and Napoleon seized the opportunity to place Joseph Bonaparte on the Spanish throne. By 5 May the former monarch and his son, the Prince of the Asturias, had been bullied into renouncing their royal rights, but by then the seething Spanish hostility towards their arrogant, atheistic French occupiers had exploded into open revolt in Madrid. It was brutally crushed by the French garrison in the capital on 2 May, but the emotions which had prompted it still bubbled away.[45]

These events had not gone unnoticed. On 8 April Lieutenant General Dalrymple, the Governor of Gibraltar, informed the government that there was an uprising in Spain and that it was possible the Spanish royal family might flee into his fortress. Thereafter he kept up a steady flow of intelligence about events in the country and it seems that the Cabinet, already preoccupied with plans for attacking Spain's colonies and some European possessions as well, was uncertain how to regard a Franco-Spanish conflict. Dalrymple later recorded that he sent ten despatches to London between 27 March and 10 May 1808 but received neither an acknowledgement nor any instructions until 25 May. Yet another officer's despatch of 8 April, sent with Dalrymple's, received an answer fifteen days later.[46] In January the Cabinet had issued orders, in response to the seeming collapse of Spain, for the capture of Ceuta as a means of enhancing Gibraltar's security. As late as 17 May these instructions were being expanded to include an assault on the Spanish squadron believed to be in Port Mahon. Suddenly all this changed as Spain turned from enemy into potential ally. On 25 May Castlereagh finally told Dalrymple that, once the force originally intended to attack Port Mahon had reached him, he might employ 10,000 troops to support Spanish resistance in the south. Uppermost in the Cabinet's mind was Cadiz, it being hoped that British troops might be allowed in to secure the chief Spanish naval arsenal as a point on which resistance to the French might be centred. Orders in a similar vein were sent to Rear-Admiral Purvis, commanding the blockading squadron off Cadiz, on 4 June. His chief responsibility was the elimination of the

French vessels that had been sheltering in that port since Trafalgar. Working in harmony with Dalrymple, he was also to try and ensure that Ceuta, Minorca, Majorca and the Spanish squadron at Cartagena did not fall into French hands. Liberal terms were to be offered to induce the governors of those places to co-operate, Purvis also receiving orders to take Spanish officers into his pay with a view to their future employment in Spain or her colonies.[47]

On 1 June the Cabinet informed George III that large forces had been made ready for service, but that it was still undecided whether to employ them in Spain or in Spanish America. (See pp. 98–9 for the ideas previously prompting the notion of an attack on Spain's colonies.) Events decided the matter, for five days later two deputies from the Provincial Assembly of the Asturias, a region in revolt, landed at Falmouth on a mission to seek aid against the French. Their arrival, followed by others from Galicia and the news of the Spanish rising, sparked off a burst of enthusiasm that flared across the political spectrum, an emotion personified in Canning's famous declaration that 'We shall proceed upon the principle, that any nation of Europe that starts up with a determination to oppose [France], whatever may be the existing political relations of that nation with Great Britain, becomes instantly our ally.'[48]

As an immediate sign of goodwill Collingwood was ordered on 6 July to give them all possible assistance, including the release of all Spanish prisoners-of-war on Malta and the transport of Spanish troops to the mainland from Majorca and Minorca. Such a friendly approach, however, was not really matched by the Spaniards themselves. Keen enough to see prisoners released and arms, supplies and money provided, a mixture of suspicion and arrogance prompted a profound reluctance to see British troops in Spain. It was observed from the start that 'the Spaniards seem equally averse to our holding any important garrisons or taking the field with them'.[49] This was to play its part in dictating British strategy. On the last day of June Arthur Wellesley was told that the previous intention to send his command to Mexico had been abandoned in favour of operations in the Peninsula. However:

> As the Deputies from the above provinces [Asturias and Galicia] do not desire the Employment of any Corps of His Majesty's Troops in the quarter of Spain from whence they are immediately delegated, but have rather pressed, as calculated to operate a powerful diversion in their favour, the Importance of directing the efforts of the British troops to the Expulsion of

the Enemy from Portugal that the Insurrection against the French may thereby become general throughout that Kingdom as well as Spain, it is therefore deemed expedient that your attention should be immediately directed to that object.[50]

Such a strategy was not unwelcome, as the French in Portugal were out on a limb and unlikely to receive reinforcements; furthermore, according to a report from Cotton, off the Tagus, Junot's command numbered only some 4,000 men. His destruction would remove the threat of an attack on Galicia and the Asturias from the south and had already been proposed prior to the deputies' arrival. Seizing Portugal would also permit the securing of the remainder of that country's naval means as well as the Russian frigate and eight ships of the line of Siniavin's squadron, a force that had been at the forefront of Canning's mind since the previous September.[51]

One recent writer has misunderstood Wellesley's instructions and believes that he was sent with the intention of campaigning in northern Spain, a belief prompted by the general's visit to Corunna prior to his landing in Portugal. He also criticises his 'characteristically vague' orders, Wellesley being given the options of landing and fighting or waiting for reinforcements from Britain and Gibraltar.[52] Although northern Spain had been considered as an area of possible British operations, by the summer of 1808 there was no doubt in ministers' minds that Portugal was the region to attack. Supplementary orders to Wellesley on 15 July made it quite clear that, although Junot was known by then to be much stronger than had been thought, he remained the target. With this in mind a further 5,045 troops were being sent from Britain plus Moore's corps from Sweden. The Cabinet was anticipating Junot's destruction, followed by British help in meting out similar treatment to Dupont's force in southern Spain. Only if the Spaniards decided to allow a British landing at Cadiz were Portuguese operations to be abandoned.[53] Wellesley's call at Corunna was only by way of a reconnaissance and the misleading habit of some authors of talking of vague orders makes no allowance for the lack of modern means of communication. The general's instructions made the Cabinet's overall strategy quite clear; thereafter, as the man on the spot, it was up to him to decide.

By 8 August Wellesley's command had landed at Mondego Bay and, once joined with the troops from Gibraltar under Major General Spencer, numbered 15,663 men, only 215 of whom were mounted cavalry. On the 21st, after advancing towards Lisbon, Wellesley repulsed a French attack at Vimiero. More and more troops were on their way to Portugal by this time, an abstract of 15 July estimating that there would soon be 30,000 British soldiers in the country. Because of this Wellesley, a junior on the seniority list of lieutenants-general, was replaced by Dalrymple as overall commander and Burrard as second-in-command. Fearful of having to fight Junot through the environs of Lisbon, on 22 August Dalrymple agreed to an armistice, this soon turning into the notorious Convention of Cintra. Under its terms the French would evacuate Portugal but be carried back to France in British vessels together with their baggage, i.e. their loot. The latter stipulation naturally infuriated the Portuguese; nor were Anglo-Spanish relations improved by the fact that, once back in France, Junot's men were free to re-enter Spain. There was much criticism of Cintra in Britain as well, where expectations of a complete military victory had been nurtured. However, for all its disagreeable aspects, the convention still marked a notable strategic victory: the French had been cleared from Portugal and, thanks to an intervention by Cotton, Siniavin's squadron had been secured.[54]

While all this was happening, in London the Cabinet was already planning the next move. On 1 August York pointed out that the Spaniards might soon be in difficulties once Napoleon sent reinforcements across the Pyrenees; they might well demand assistance from Britain, and any army sent to help them should be concentrated at one point for maximum effectiveness. On the 10th Castlereagh was writing that either the French would try to retain Madrid, exposing them to starvation, or they would retire towards Burgos. Believing that the 30,000 British troops in Portugal should be moved into northern Spain, Castlereagh urged his colleagues to come to a decision, talking ten days later of the possibility of expelling the French from the country completely. On 1 September a British force was ordered to advance into northern Spain, it being intended that it would be joined by a further body of 10,000 British troops under Major General Baird plus a Spanish force under the Marquis de la Romana that had been rescued from French control in the Baltic.[55]

Such grandiose hopes did not seem unreasonable at that moment. Writing in the middle of August, Palmerston, soon to become Secretary at War in the next administration, thought that:

Spanish affairs have gone on as well as could have been wished, & as I always expected; this victory of Castanos [at Baylen] must I think be decisive of the war in the Peninsula & cannot fail to influence materially the operations of any contest Buonaparte may engage in with Austria.

Believing that Napoleon had already lost 70,000 men in the Peninsula, Palmerston hoped for stubborn Austrian resistance in a new campaign in central Europe which would encourage Russia to participate as well.[56] In the autumn of 1808 the Cabinet evidently had similar ideas, wishing to follow up the removal of Junot from Portugal and the Spanish destruction of Dupont's corps at Baylen (23 July). After a pause prompted by the furore over Cintra, final orders for Moore to lead a British army into Spain were decided upon on 23 September, a small British force meanwhile remaining behind in Portugal under Lieutenant General Cradock. However, before Moore could concentrate his command at Salamanca, the Spanish armies with whom he was supposed to co-operate had been routed by Napoleon's reinforced armies at Durango (31 October), Espinosa (11 November) and Tudela (23 November). By 4 December the French emperor was in Madrid.[57] Moore responded to these disasters by striking boldly at Marshal Soult's vulnerable corps in northern Spain, a manoeuvre permitting Moore to link up with Baird's division[58] on 20 December. Napoleon riposted with a north-western thrust himself, Moore's army having to undertake a terrible retreat to Corunna in bitter winter weather to avoid encirclement. A French assault on that port was repelled on 16 January 1809, Moore being killed in the action, and the army was evacuated back to Britain: it had lost some 8,000 men and the survivors were filthy, cadaverous and ill.[59]

Alongside these military efforts aimed at a quick Peninsular victory was the provision of financial aid on a similarly lavish scale. By the summer of 1808 the five leading Spanish provincial juntas had been given £1·1 million and there were promises of more once a Supreme Junta had been formed to direct the war centrally. On top of this the Portuguese had been given £60,000 in July and a loan for a further £95,000 was floated in London in November. The letter month saw Chatham reporting that 160,000 markets had been sent to Spain, with a further 30,000–40,000 due to be shipped in December. Some 26,500 stand of arms and 17,000 pikes had been sent to the Portuguese, plus sufficient clothing for 100,000 men. When the Supreme Junta was formed in September 1808 Frere was sent with a further £650,000 in silver and orders to negotiate a commercial treaty covering Spain's colonies, though the Spanish were always to be evasive over this. During 1808 arms and money worth £2·5 million were invested in the Peninsula, and in consequence of the large scale of the actual bullion sent British governments were to experience severe specie shortages thereafter. Before the year was over it was observed that support for Romana's force had to be in the shape of Treasury bills, 'it being impossible', according to Castlereagh, 'to find a sufficiency of silver to meet the many demands at the moment upon our resources'.[60]

Despite the reverses at the end of 1808, it is to the Cabinet's credit that it did not abandon the Iberian strategy. Although much of the opposition's ardour had cooled, Liverpool summed up the government's determination:

> It was difficult to conceive the situation which would better warrant hopes of ultimate success, than that of Spain at this day. The people were unanimous in their resistance to the invader; and it was the only instance since the French revolution in which a whole people had taken up arms in their own defence.[61]

Hopes now, though, centred on the retention of Portugal rather than an immediate and decisive triumph in Spain, a change of emphasis which at least allowed Britain to make full use of all Portuguese resources as was seen most appropriate: it was made quite clear that the Cabinet regarded Portugal as a client state.[62] With the truculent Spaniards at least putting up savage resistance in some parts of their country, particularly in the grim siege of Saragossa (December 1808 – February 1809), and with Austria making preparations to fight once more, it made obvious strategic sense to tie down Napoleon's resources in the Peninsula as far as possible. Having the previous month submitted a memorandum reassuring ministers that Portugal was defensible, in April 1809 Arthur Wellesley returned to that country to assume command of an army numbering 23,455 men. His task was to hold Portugal and he was to avoid campaigning in Spain without prior Cabinet permission, ministers becoming wary of their Spanish allies in the light of their continuing resistance to any idea of a British force in Cadiz. However, Wellesley was to provide troops for that fortress if the Spanish attitude changed, even should such a movement mean abandoning Portugal altogether.[63]

In May Wellesley brilliantly manoeuvred Soult's II Corps from its position at Oporto and then sought permission to march into Spain to attack Victor's I Corps, exposed on the Guadiana, in concert with Cuesta's Spanish Army of Estremadura. Cabinet permission was received for this on 11 June but, short of specie and with his troops exhausted, Wellesley did not advance until the end of the month. Once again a lack of effective Anglo-Spanish co-operation was to prove a major impediment, particularly the Spaniards' failure to provide promised supplies. With Victor by this time reinforced, Wellesley had to fight a desperate defensive battle at Talavera (28 July) and suffered 5,500 casualties in the process. Thereafter the British retreated back into Portugal, narrowly avoiding French encirclement and complete catastrophe. This strategic flop marked the end of Anglo-Spanish military enterprises for some time to come; the lull which then descended on the Portuguese front allowed the training of the local levies to be pushed on, magazines to be established and fortifications improved. These preparations would be crucial in facing the anticipated French assault on Portugal the following year.[64]

Britain's chief military endeavour in 1809 was not, despite all this activity, to be in the Peninsula, but took the shape of the massive assault on Walcheren island in the Scheldt estuary. The motivation behind it was a mixture of the threat posed by Antwerp and a desire to assist, or use, the Austrian campaign in the Danube valley. Rumours about Austria rejoining the conflict took substance in October 1808, when Vienna sought financial aid, requesting an astronomical £2·5 million to cover her mobilisation and a further £5 million for each year she fought. Canning turned down such extravagance in December, coolly pointing out that Britain wanted other powers to fight only if they themselves favoured such a course of action.[65]

There was little obvious British enthusiasm as Austria continued her preparations. Only a junior diplomat, Benjamin Bathurst, was appointed to represent Britain in Vienna and he was not provided with a cypher, suggesting that his despatches were not felt likely to be important. His instructions cautioned him to be wary in his dealings with the Austrians, to take no part in their military decisions and always to remember that they were fighting of their own volition.[66] Such seeming indifference, though, should not be taken at face value. In part it was to deter Austrian financial pleadings, and anyway effective military co-operation was difficult because of the geographical barriers between the two countries. With the Low Countries and Germany closed, sending a minor diplomat was not so much a snub as a recognition of practical difficulties. Once ministers learned, on 22 April 1809, that Austria had actually declared war on the 6th, they appreciated the value of an important military ally who could, if successful, spark off a general rising against Napoleon. In April Austria was sent £250,000 and in July a further £337,000; all told, by the time of Wagram (6 July) Britain had provided £1,185,000, a not ungenerous figure in the light of the support simultaneously given to the Iberian nations.[67] More difficult, as always, was the question of how to provide direct military support.

There were three possible areas of operation for British forces: the Peninsula, the Mediterranean and north-west Europe. Sending extensive reinforcements to the Peninsula, over and above those that were committed anyway, would have been politically difficult after Cintra and Corunna. It also would have meant the removal of the junior Arthur Wellesley in favour of a more senior officer, a step that, whatever its military consequences, would have been awkward politically in the light of Wellesley family influence. More important was the specie shortage, particularly in view of the Spanish and Portuguese reluctance to accept bills in lieu of hard currency. In 1810 Huskisson admitted that 'the demands upon the military chest in the Peninsula . . . were such as to create the greatest apprehension that the chest would be entirely exhausted if the expenditure should be very considerably increased . . .'.[68] As it was, the permission for Wellesley to undertake the Talavera campaign may well have been influenced by a desire to see as much pressure put on Napoleon's Iberian flank as possible. This was the limit of the Cabinet's capacity in that theatre for the moment.

The specie shortage was similarly an obstacle to Mediterranean operations, with the added disadvantage of that theatre's further physical distance. Had, say, 30,000 men been quickly assembled on Sicily for attacks on southern Italy it is doubtful whether they could have achieved more in the face of a likely French withdrawal than was managed in 1805. An assault on northern Italy would have been too dangerous to contemplate. Lieutenant-General Stuart, commander of the Sicilian garrison, was urged in March 1809 to use his troops for diversions in support of the Austrians, but he was nervous for Sicily's safety, particularly in the light of the daring French capture of Capri in October 1808. Other than a brief capture and occupation of the islands of Ischia and Prodica, and a brief sortie across the Straits of Messina, Stuart remained inactive.[69]

That left north-western Europe, and in March 1809 Canning was pressed by 'persons of rank and influence in the Prussian States' to aid rebellions planned in Westphalia and Lower Saxony. Supplying any rebels with arms was feasible, but direct landings in northern Germany, remembering the events of 1805–06, were not a pleasant prospect. The bullion shortage militated against this strategy as well. Any campaign in, say, Hanover would have been on friendly soil and would have meant paying a friendly population for all supplies required. Huskisson believed that the financial problems that would be posed by having 40,000 troops in the Elbe–Weser region would be 'insurmountable'.[70]

All the foregoing helped direct Cabinet thinking to that perennial target, the Scheldt. In March 1809 Canning had wanted to attack Flushing, where, he had heard, there were five enemy ships of the line; any success scored would, he thought, encourage Austria and help eradicate memories of Corunna. Mulgrave also favoured such an assault, observing that it had already been twice discussed in Cabinet and that with Napoleon's armies scattered the chance to strike at the Scheldt was too good to miss. Reducing Napoleon's naval strength was, of course, the primary motive behind all this: any benefit to Austria was secondary. Castlereagh admitted that:

> My notion of the operation was, that it was not to be a protracted operation, that it was neither to lead to a campaign nor to a regular siege, but that it was to take all means of accomplishing its object short of protracted operations . . .

Chatham, who in his role as an army lieutenant-general was to command the expedition, was told that it was not to assume 'any other character than that of a *coup de main*'. Once the enemy naval forces had been destroyed, the troops, excepting a small garrison on Walcheren island, were to come home.[71] The benefit to Austria from this would be minimal. Canning claimed that the destruction of enemy shipping would free British units currently tied down in defensive duties, but that constituted a very vague sort of help.[72] Any success would have virtually no impact on the Danube campaign, and it was only because Napoleon had had to move so many troops eastwards that the expedition seemed feasible: Austria was providing a diversion for Britain, not the other way round.

In its eventual execution the campaign was to be a disaster. Plagued by delays and bad weather, the force did not sail until the end of July, being further harassed through much of August by gales and storms. Its strength finally numbered 39,143 rank and file, some 44,000 men in all, and 235 armed vessels. The rapier thrust at Flushing had turned into a bludgeon aimed at Antwerp. Once landed, a combination of bad weather, inadequate planning and incompetent leadership meant that the expedition made little progress. Not until 15 August was Flushing captured, a delay that allowed the French time to strengthen the forces holding Antwerp and the surrounding country. By the 27th Chatham acknowledged that there was no chance of taking the fortress. Converting the failure to destroy the Scheldt fleet into a catastrophe were the army's primitive medical facilities and the nature of Walcheren itself, a low-lying island notorious for its fevers and rendered more unhealthy still when the French opened the restraining dykes and flooded much of its surface. Insanitary conditions were experienced during the siege of Flushing in particular, and from the end of August the army was gripped by sickness: those laid low numbered 8,000 by 6 September and by the 23rd, out of a remaining garrison of 15,000, there were 9,831 sick. This terrible proportion continued during October and November. By February 1810 4,000 men had died of diseases contracted on Walcheren and 11,000 others were officially listed as sick. Even those who recovered were prone to future bouts of debilitating illness. Wellington grumbled from Portugal in 1811 that the summer rains had had a severe impact on the Walcheren veterans, with over 19,000 men in hospital by October.[73]

Chatham was ordered to bring the bulk of his command home on 2 September, though not until 13 November was the final order given to evacuate the island completely. The delay was in part due to a desire to seal off the Scheldt, but it also reflected the hope that a continued British presence might encourage Austria to renew hostilities, halted by the armistice at Znaim (12 July) following Archduke Charles's defeat at Wagram. Liverpool believed in August that the Franco-Austrian campaign would be resumed and that in its diversionary capacity Walcheren was a 'consolation' following the failure of the expedition's primary objectives.[74]

Despite this the government's strategic thinking still appears confused. Liverpool wrote on 27 October that the Franco-Austrian peace seemed uncertain and that consequently the Cabinet could not decide on the evacuation question. Yet seven days earlier he had written to Wellington that definite news had come of the peace and in the light of this he sought information respecting future operations in Portugal. It is difficult to avoid the conclusion that ministers were loathe to lose their one gain from a failed campaign. On 28 October it was admitted that the Austrian peace made the Cabinet dubious about retaining the island, but naval opinion was still to be sought before any final orders were issued. Finally the painful nettle had to be grasped. With Walcheren difficult to defend during the winter, and with no further action taking place on the Danube, the evacuation orders were issued, the last British troops leaving on 23 December 1809.[75]

Although the Austrians did urge that the island be held, it is hard to find a reasonable justification for retaining it so long. The Austrian appeal was based on the hope of a Dutch revolt, but there was no sign of such an event when the expedition first appeared and it was therefore unlikely with the British bogged down and the Austrians defeated.[76] One may speculate that the primary consideration during the autumn of 1809 was political, as ministers faced the unpalatable consequences of their failure. Nor should it be forgotten that from early September Portland's Cabinet was in its death throes as Canning manoeuvred for supreme power behind the ailing Premier. Once the ministry had finally collapsed there was a hiatus while Perceval struggled to put a new government together. None of this facilitated the process of uncomfortable decision-making.

As a postscript one may question the wisdom of attacking Walcheren at all. Even before it sailed it was known that the expedition was going to a very unhealthy spot. There were rumours that the French garrison there had lost 1,500 men in 1808, and Castlereagh himself had admitted as early as 1805 that troops stationed on the island might find their health impaired. Although the whole expedition was conceived as a *coup de main*, the intention had been to leave a 15,000-strong force behind to hold the place, and this was a large body to expose to potential disease. The immediate responsibility for the spread of sickness among the troops might have been the Medical Board's, rent as it was by internal feuding, but the ultimate blame for operations in such a dangerous area must lie with the Cabinet.[77]

Notes

1 P.R.O. FO 64/74, ff. 33–7 and 39–44.

2 *Castlereagh Correspondence*, VIII, pp. 47–8. Aspinall, IV, p. 552.

3 P.R.O. WO 6/156, pp. 349 and 356–7. ADM 1/3751, abstract of transports, 7 February and 6 June 1807. ADM 1/3752, abstract of transports, 11 July 1807.

4 *Castlereagh Correspondence*, VI, p. 169. P.R.O. FO 65/74, ff. 51–2 and 54.

5 P.R.O. FO 65/69, ff. 38–47 and 48–9v.

6 P.R.O. FO 73/80, Canning to Pierrepoint (ambassador to Sweden), 30 May 1807, no. 2; and same to same, 2 June 1807, no. 4. Sherwig, p. 188. Aspinall, IV, pp. 587–8. *Castlereagh Correspondence*, VIII, pp. 62–3.

7 P.R.O. FO 65/69, ff. 114–16. WO 6/14, pp. 1–2. Aspinall, IV, p. 588. Leeds R.O., Harewood Collection, Canning Papers, 42, Canning to Leveson Gower, 9 June 1807.

8 P.R.O. WO 6/56, pp. 113–15 and 117–18.

9 B.M. Add. Mss 37050, Fox Papers, ff. 160–4.

10 Maurice, II, pp. 162–81. Moore's surly attitude may also have been due partly to his intrigues to replace Fox as the commander on Sicily, a position he finally secured for himself on 10 July.

11 Maurice, II, pp. 165–7. Aspinall, IV, p. 590.

12 A. N. Ryan, 'The Copenhagen Expedition of 1807', University of Liverpool M.A. thesis, 1951, pp. 78–80.

13 A. N. Ryan, 'The causes of the British attack upon Copenhagen in 1807', *English Historical Review*, LXVIII, January 1953, pp. 37–55. *The Naval Miscellany*, V, p. 302.

14 Leeds R.O., Harewood Collection, Canning Papers, 41a, Cabinet minute by Canning, 10 July 1807. Aspinall, IV, p. 604.

15 Ryan, 'Causes of the attack', pp. 50–1. Aspinall, IV, pp. 606–7. Leeds R.O., Harewood Collection, Canning Papers, 42, Canning to Leveson Gower, 21 July 1807. *The Naval Miscellany*, V, p. 307.

16 Ryan, 'Copenhagen Expedition', pp. 134–70. Fortescue, *British Army*, 6, pp. 69–72. Butler, CLII, pp. 619–23. H. Barnes, 'Canning and the Danes, 1807', *History Today*, 15, 1969, p. 538.

17 P.R.O. WO 6/14, pp. 1–2 and 18. Of the battalions allocated to Cathcart on 8 June, eight were with Gambier in July plus a further 2,480 Guards nominated for Continental service in June.

18 *P.D.*, X, pp. 27 and 72. *Paget Papers*, II, p. 363. The satisfaction over Russia's ports was premature.

19 *Castlereagh Correspondence*, VI, pp. 189–90. Gambier's comments were published in the *Naval Chronicle*, London, 1808, XIX, p. 191. For the use of the Danish ships see James, IV, p. 295. Of much greater value than the vessels themselves were the 20,000 tons of naval stores captured at Copenhagen as well.

20 Leeds R.O., Harewood Collection, Canning Papers, 42, Canning to Leveson Gower, 21 July 1807.

21 Leeds R.O., Harewood Collection, Canning Papers, 42, Canning to

Pierrepoint, 4 August 1807. *The Naval Miscellany*, V, p. 300.

22 Barnes, pp. 530–8.

23 A. N. Ryan, 'The defence of British trade with the Baltic, 1808–13', *English Historical Review*, LXXIV, July 1959, pp. 443–6. When poor winds becalmed British convoys at the entrance to the Baltic they were vulnerable to attacks by oar-powered Danish gunboats, the Danes' only remaining naval resource.

24 *Castlereagh Correspondence*, VI, pp. 183–5. Lady Chatterton, *Memorials . . . of Lord Gambier*, London, 1861, II, pp. 41–2.

25 C. T. Atkinson, 'Gleanings from the Cathcart Mss', *Journal of the Society for Army Historical Research*, XXX, 1952, p. 87. Fortescue, *British Army*, 6, p. 77. W. Hinde, *George Canning*, London, 1973, pp. 177–8. *Castlereagh Correspondence*, VI, pp. 186–7. B.M. Add. Mss 49188, Perceval Papers, f. 37–v. *The Naval Miscellany*, V, pp. 324–5.

26 Chatterton, II, pp. 73 and 83. *Castlereagh Correspondence*, VI, pp. 194–5. Carr, pp. 55–6. Aspinall, IV, p. 637.

27 Chatterton, II, p. 20. Leeds R.O., Harewood Collection, Canning Papers, 57, Leveson Gower to Canning, 1 and 17 August 1807; 31, Mulgrave to Canning, 20 September 1807.

28 Leeds R.O., Harewood Collection, Canning Papers, 42, Canning to Pierrepoint, 10 October 1807.

29 P.R.O. FO 73/45, Canning to Thornton (Pierrepoint's successor), 15 January 1808. Carr, p. 58.

30 Ryan, *Saumarez Papers*, pp. 7–9 and 11–13.

31 Military supplies worth £94,000 were sent to Gustavus IV: Sherwig, p. 192.

32 P.R.O. WO 6/42, pp. 11–18. FO 73/45, Canning to Thornton, 20 April 1808, no. 17. B.M. Add. Mss 57539, Moore Papers, Castlereagh to Moore, 1 May 1808, no. 2.

33 For detailed accounts of this force see Maurice, II, pp. 204–31, and Fortescue, *British Army*, 6, pp. 124–36.

34 Maurice, II, pp. 204–5 and 220. Fortescue, *British Army*, 6, p. 137.

35 P.R.O. WO 6/42, pp. 11–13. Durham R.O., Castlereagh Papers, D/Lo/C5, contains a précis of despatches sent by his government to Alderberg and this, one may assume, translated into English for the Cabinet's benefit, was the basis of the belief that Moore would be well received. The Swedes pressed for military support during March 1808.

36 Ryan, *Saumarez Papers*, pp. 41–3. P.R.O. FO 73/45, Canning to Thornton, 10 June 1808.

37 Ryan, *Saumarez Papers*, pp. 52–5 and 66 n.

38 Ryan *Saumarez Papers*, p. xviii. Sir J. Ross, *Memoirs and Correspondence of Admiral Lord Saumarez*, London, 1838, II, p. 173.

39 Aspinall, IV, p. 590. The tortuous process of negotiating with the Turks during the latter part of 1807 is described in *Paget Papers*, II, p. 300 ff.

40 Aspinall, IV, pp. 620–1 and 623.

41 Fortescue, *British Army*, 6, pp. 92–6. P.R.O. ADM 2/1365 pp. 28–30 and 38–42. FO 63/56, ff. 38–48. FO 63/58, ff. 19–27. James, IV, p. 316.

42 James, IV, pp. 317–18. Barrow, II, pp. 365–6. Fortescue, *British Army*, 6, p. 104 and n.

43 P.R.O. FO 63/74, ff. 11–14 and 24–7. Thompson, p. 243.

44 On 1 January 1807 there were eight frigates and eleven sloops in North American waters; twelve months later the squadron there consisted of three ships of the line, seven frigates and seventeen sloops: Leeds University Library, Brotherton Collection Box VII, Mulgrave Papers, 18/30. As for the army, there were 5,043 troops in the region on 1 June 1807; a year later there were 10,071: Fortescue, *County Lieutenancies*, pp. 304–5.

45 G. Lefebvre, *Napoleon*, London, 1969, II, pp. 15–17. Thompson, p. 243. D. Gates, *The Spanish Ulcer*, London, 1986, pp. 9–12.

46 Sir H. Dalrymple, *Memoir written by Sir Hew Dalrymple Bart., of his Proceedings as connected with the Affairs of Spain and the Commencement of the Peninsular War*, London, 1830, pp. 10–11.

47 P.R.O. WO 6/185, pp. 6–13, 17–20, 22–31 and 36–9.

48 Aspinall, V, p. 82. *P.D.*, XI, pp. 890–91.

49 P.R.O. ADM 2/1366, pp. 14–15. Newnham Collingwood, p. 390.

50 P.R.O. WO 6/47, pp. 42–4.

51 Aspinall, V, p. 93. Durham R.O., Castlereagh Papers, D/Lo/C 17–18, Brigadier General Stewart to Castlereagh, ? April 1808. Siniavin's squadron from *Naval Chronicle*, London, 1809, XXII, p. 246, and for Canning's worries about it see Leeds R.O., Harewood Collection, Canning Papers, 42, Canning to Leveson Gower, 29 September 1807; 31, Canning to Chatham, 14 November and 2 December 1807.

52 Davies, pp. 31–3.

53 P.R.O. WO 6/185, pp. 68–71.

54 Gates, pp. 82–92. M. Glover, *Wellington as Military Commander*, London, 1968, pp. 63–5. P.R.O. WO 6/47, pp. 67–9. Dalrymple, pp. 48–51. A detailed account of Cintra can be found in M. Glover, *Britannia Sickens*. Although Dalrymple, Burrard and Wellesley all signed the convention, only the first two were disgraced in the wave of disappointed rage that swept over Britain in its wake: this shabby favouritism was a testament to Wellesley political influence. See R. M. Schneer, 'Arthur Wellesley and the Cintra Convention: a new look at an old puzzle', *Journal of British Studies*, XIV, 1980, pp. 94–119.

55 Northern Ireland R.O., Castlereagh Papers, D3030/2692. *Castlereagh Correspondence*, VI, pp. 399–401 and 403–7. Aspinall, V, pp. 118–19. For the remarkable rescue of Romana's troops: Ryan, *Saumarez Papers*, pp. 31, 36–7 and 39–40; J. Stewart, 'The stolen army', *Army Quarterly*, 66, 1953, pp. 24–31.

56 Bourne, p. 102.

57 Aspinall, V, pp. 127–8. Chandler, pp. 636–42. Gates, pp. 93–105.

58 This had arrived at Corunna on 13 October, but the suspicious Spaniards did not allow a landing to begin until the 26th, this not being completed until 23 November: Davies, pp. 71–2 and 80; B.M. Add. Mss 49482, Gordon Papers, ff. 165 and 167v.

59 Gates, pp. 106–17. Also C. Hibbert, *Corunna*, London, 1961.

60 Sherwig, pp. 198–203. *Castlereagh Correspondence*, VI, p. 452.

61 *P.D.*, XII, p. 22, for Liverpool's speech of 19 January 1809. For opposition gloom see pp. 6–9, 17–21 and 49–52.

62 P.R.O. WO 6/48, pp. 170–9. This included making Beresford commander of the Portuguese army in February 1809.

63 *Castlereagh Correspondence*, VII, pp. 39–41. Aspinall, V, pp. 246–7. *S.D.W.*, VI, pp. 210–13.

64 Gates, pp. 147–52 and 173–85. M. Glover, *Wellington as Military Commander*, pp. 73–80. R. Humble, *Napoleon's Peninsular Marshals*, London, 1973, pp. 104–14. After Talavera Wellesley was made Viscount Wellington, a step reflecting the government's desire to make the most of a highly dubious victory in the wake of Austria's defeat and the stalled Walcheren campaign. The opposition were justifiably furious that a strategic failure should be so highly rewarded.

65 P.R.O. FO 7/89, reply to a request for aid, 24 December 1808.

66 P.R.O. FO 7/88, Canning to B. Bathurst, 27 June 1809.

67 Sherwig, pp. 209 and 212–13.

68 *P.D.*, XV, p. ccccxv.

69 Mackesy, *War in the Mediterranean*, pp. 327–32. Bunbury, pp. 236–52. Newnham Collingwood, pp. 327–9.

70 C. A. Christie, 'The Walcheren Expedition, 1809', University of Dundee Ph.D. thesis, 1975, pp. 47–58. Aspinall, V, pp. 222–3. Leeds R.O., Harewood Collection, Canning Papers, 31, Canning to Chatham, 9 June 1809. *P.D.*, XV, p. ccccxxxii. There were a series of minor revolts in Prussia and Germany in 1809, but they were quickly supressed, and no aid could have been sent, so brief was their flaring, however enthusiastic the Cabinet might have been.

71 Leeds R.O., Harewood Collection, Canning Papers, 33, Canning to Portland, 21 March 1809. B.M. Add. Mss 37287, Wellesley Papers, ff. 160–3. *P.D.*, XV, pp. i–ii and 5xx. *Castlereagh Correspondence*, VI, p. 292.

72 P.R.O. FO 63/74, f. 160.

73 Christie, pp. 144–6, 190–229 and 397–8. Fortescue, *British Army*, 7, pp. 45–6 and 65–82. R. W. Jeffrey (ed.), *Dyott's Diary, 1781–1845*, London, 1907, I, pp. 280–3 and 288. *P.D.*, XV, pp. ii–v, liv and lxii–lxiii. Aspinall, V, p. 303. G. C. Bond, *The Grand Expedition*, Athens, 1975, pp. 72–80. T. H. McGuffie, 'The Walcheren expedition and the "Walcheren fever" ', *English Historical Review*, LXII, April 1947, pp. 191–201. E. K. Crowe, 'The Walcheren expedition and the new Army Medical Board; a reconsideration', *English Historical Review*, LXXXVIII, October 1973, pp. 770–85. Oman, *Wellington's Army*, p. 187.

74 *P.D.*, XV, pp. vii and xx–xxi. *S.D.W.*, VI, p. 332.

75 *P.D.*, XV, pp. xv–vi and xix–xx. B.M. Add. Mss 38243, Liverpool Papers, ff. 223–5v. Aspinall, V, p. 249.

76 *P.D.*, XV, p. xxiii.

77 McGuffie, ' "Walcheren fever" ', p. 195. *Castlereagh Correspondence*, VI, p. 247. Bond, p. 137.

8

The ministries of Perceval and Liverpool

One of the strategic ironies of this period is that, although Europe increasingly preoccupied the thoughts of the war's directors, the years 1808–11 saw Britain attain a peak of colonial conquest at the expense of her European rivals. In the Caribbean the flurry of activity in 1803–05 had been followed by years comparatively free of large-scale operations. With no enemy attack to deal with, other than the constant activities of privateers and warships seeking to prey upon British commerce, ministers felt able to keep their West Indian garrisons at minimum force levels. The only exception was the capture of the Danish islands of St Croix, St Thomas and St Johns in December 1807, seized to prevent them becoming havens for privateers. There were tentative plans to use some islands to launch assaults on Spanish America, but these came to nothing. In consequence of all this the total garrison of Jamaica and the Leeward and Windward Islands in 1808 was 18,055, only a small overall increase on the total of 14,738 pertaining in 1806. Similarly the navy maintained eighty-seven ships of the line, frigates and sloops in the Caribbean in 1806, a figure that fell to eighty-three such vessels in 1808.[1]

Prompting a change, however, was the revolt in Spain. The immediate response was British encouragement for the Spanish colonies to resist any possible take-over, it quickly becoming apparent that the colonies felt a loathing for imperial France that matched that for their mother country. At a stroke a whole series of enemy maritime bases, from islands such as Cuba and Puerto Rico to all the mainland colonies, had been rendered friendly to Britain, removing them both as centres for commerce-raiding and as potential sources of invasion of British islands. The windfall was furthered in August 1809 when the Spaniards, with assistance from British troops, laid siege to and captured the town of St Domingo, the last French outpost on the island of the same name. Suddenly the only hostile places in the whole region were the large French colonies of Guadeloupe and Martinique and their small attendant islands. Were all these now to be captured, something akin to total security for the area would be achieved.[2]

Encouraging such ambitions were reports that the French on these islands were experiencing supply problems, and Beckwith was ordered to investigate as the Cabinet began to consider future operations. In December 1808 he was told to try and take Martinique provided there seemed every chance of rapid success, the general being informed that troops from Nova Scotia would be sent to him to support any assault. These hopes seemed at first to have been dashed when the French were able to reinforce their garrison with 2,000–3,000 soldiers and sailors, plus arms and supplies; *The Times* had already complained how ineffectual the islands' blockade seemed to be, and this appeared to justify the paper's strictures. Nevertheless Beckwith still felt confident, and in February 1809, with 10,000 troops, he attacked and captured Martinique for the loss of 550 casualties.[3]

Keen to follow up this success, in April the government ordered that Guadeloupe be placed under strict blockade in the hope that a surrender might be induced. For the moment more active campaigning was ruled out because the time of year increased the threat of disease, though the Saintes were taken in April to facilitate naval operations off the main island. Once the dangerous summer months had passed, Beckwith was told to attempt Guadeloupe's reduction in the absence of any formal surrender. Once again the general was instructed to avoid any protracted campaign – sickness had already cost him 2,000 men in the January–November 1809 period – and in the event, with the continued use of troops from Nova Scotia, Guadeloupe was taken in February 1810, the small islands of St Eustatius and St Martins also being taken. Resistance was slight, the British suffering only some 300 casualties.[4]

This marked the end of West Indian campaigning, Britain now having seventeen separate garrisons scattered about the various islands but facing no enemy colonies of any sort. Thereafter these garrisons were to be kept to the minimum necessary for internal order, Liverpool stating in April 1810 that the 10,000 troops in the

Leeward and Windward Islands would not be reinforced. The government was confident that there was little danger of French attack and that British naval superiority would enable any lost islands to be recaptured quickly. By early 1812 the naval force in the Caribbean had been reduced to thirty-five ships of the line, frigates and sloops.[5]

Shortly prior to this, the final French possession in Africa had also been reduced with the capture of Fort Louis in the Senegal river. This was never a base on the scale of those in the East and West Indies, but it did provide a haven for attacks on Britain's West African commerce. Buckingham had mooted the idea of using 1,000 troops to take it in 1806, though in the event its capture in July 1809 was managed by a mere 166 soldiers plus some seamen and marines, the whole force operating from Gorée.[6]

With the fall of Guadeloupe the only remaining enemy bases in the world, outside Europe, were the French islands of Mauritius, Bourbon and Rodriguez in the western Indian Ocean and the more numerous Dutch islands in the eastern part of that sea.

The French islands had been a source of persistent concern for years. Keith had prepared to attack them from the Cape in 1796, and from India both Richard and Arthur Wellesley had pointed to the danger they posed. Richard worried about unrest in India which the French might be able to foment from the islands, also expressing concern about their potential for attacks on commerce, a 'piratical power' whose elimination was 'absolutely essential'. Vice-Admiral Pellew also pointed to the commercial danger in 1805, and an unsigned memorandum in Melville's papers speaks of them as a base for attacks on India and a source of privateering.[7] The obvious solution was their capture, but several factors stood in the way. One was the condition of the British forces in India, the troops controlled by the Crown and the East India Company being 9,600 short of their establishment in April 1805. Lack of numbers was accompanied by a lack of reliability among some formations. A sepoy battalion mutinied at Vellore in 1806 and only swift action prevented a spread of the disaffection; then in 1808 European officers mutinied at Madras and the following year there was another revolt, this time at Masulipatam, and there was bloodshed at Seringapatam before the business was ended.[8]

Just as crucial was the attitude of ministers in London, where the chief concern was to maintain a check on Indian expenditure. This would rocket if military expansion was pursued, and just before the resumption of hostilities Castlereagh stated that 'If particular difficulties arise, we must make corresponding exertions; but let us save our means till those difficulties appear, as far as prudence will admit.' This was a hope of a live-and-let-live situation in the Indian Ocean, much to the disgust of Richard Wellesley, who pointed out that attacks on commerce had cost £4 million in 1793–1801. It was therefore with some reluctance that he acknowledged a lack of means for operations outside India and he would not inaugurate such efforts without prior Cabinet consent. This continuing urge to economy blighted any chance of removing the French threat for many years, Governor General Minto writing in November 1807 that 'the smallest relaxation in the economic system which is known to be *indispensable* . . . creates immediate speculation in the money market . . .'. Schemes to remove the French could not develop in such an atmosphere because 'we have under our eye the positive prohibition of the present ministers conveyed in their former administration against such plans'.[9]

Another problem was the widespread belief that the French islands could not be approached because of the reefs that were supposed to surround them[10] and on top of this strategy was further paralysed in the region because of the disastrous division of the naval station in 1805–6. Furthermore, while Pellew and Troubridge squabbled over their command, the civilian organisation of India was little better when it came to strategic decision-making. The Governor General of India had responsibilities both to the Cabinet and to the board of directors of the East India Company, a situation tending in turn to make him overwhelmingly concerned with the well-being of the company's trade to the exclusion of others' commerce. Its trade tended to be carried in its own large, well armed vessels, which were quite capable of defending themselves against all but the most determined forms of attack. Such was not the case, though, with the general Indian Ocean traders. Most of the losses from enemy attacks tended to be suffered by the latter, and this, with the company's trade relatively secure, did not prompt governors-general to act decisively against the French and risk disapproval in London.[11]

Certainly French commerce raiding in the region was carried on with great vigour. During 1807 the port-to-port trade along the Coromandel coast and in the Bay of Bengal was practically annihilated, the Calcutta business houses losing £200,000 in one six-week period and the Indian insurance companies refusing to cover any vessel not under escort. By the end of the following year the Admiralty was asking Pellew pointed questions about these failures and *The Times* sourly noted that twenty-two vessels had been taken by raiders in a four-month period. 'It is lamentable,' the newspaper considered, 'that the only object for which we keep a fleet in India, that of protecting navigation, should be so grossly neglected.' Eight days after this comment, on 22 December 1808, the newspaper recorded that the Calcutta insurance companies had paid out over £2 million in the previous seven to eight years. Suddenly making matters worse, four large French frigates appeared in the Indian Ocean in the early months of 1809, these accounting for five large East Indiamen, one sloop and one Portuguese frigate. On top of these disasters the company lost a further eight vessels that foundered or were wrecked, one of which carried a cargo worth over £1 million. Any lingering complacency over the French islands was shattered.[12]

In both India and London it was decided to act, a conclusion aided by some British successes during 1809, including the seizure of Rodriguez in August and a raid on St Pauls, Bourbon, in September. Neither had encountered much resistance, and this suggested that the islands might be vulnerable. Just as important, an attempted blockade during 1808–09 had allowed the reefs to be charted and the discovery made that the islands could be approached. In May 1810 Yorke voiced the change in government sentiments prompted by the altered circumstances, expressing the view that both Bourbon and Mauritius should be taken, but fearing that it might not be possible until 1811 and the end of the monsoon season. In the interim he wanted preparations for their capture to be pushed on at Madras. By 12 June the Cabinet had definitely decided on the islands' capture in the light of the company's losses, the forces to achieve this being drawn from both India and the Cape. In the meantime the naval blockade was to be maintained.[13]

In India the authorities had come to similar conclusions. On 24 April 1810 Minto stated that the islands must be taken, and the first step came in July when Bourbon was secured for only a small loss. This was followed by a dramatic naval campaign of fluctuating fortunes culminating in an invasion of Mauritius, the island surrendering on 2 December at the cost of only 167 casualties.[14]

The capture of the French islands left only the Dutch East Indies possessions as a source of danger. They had been largely quiescent up to the arrival, in 1807, of the energetic Daendels as governor. His energy and boasting caused some alarm in Calcutta and there were fears that the numerous Arab trading vessels based in the Moluccas might be used to stage attacks on India. In June 1809 a French officer captured on Sumatra spoke of the anticipated arrival of a squadron of seven frigates, and papers in his possession detailed French influence in Burma and mentioned an attack on Bengal. Minto concluded that the danger from the Dutch islands was greater than that from the French. The Cabinet was also aware of the threat, something reinforced when Napoleon annexed Holland in July 1810, a move which promised French-inspired aggression from the Dutch colonies in future. With this in mind, their seizure was ordered, but only so that their military facilities could be destroyed: the islands were not to be garrisoned permanently. To some extent the order had again been anticipated, a minor campaign being waged between February and August 1810 against the lesser islands, their capture making the China trade more secure and a final campaign against Java, to complete the task, more desirable. In April 1811 a force of 11,028 troops sailed against this last objective, a landing being effected in August and the garrison surrendering on 16 September; once again British casualties were light, Java remaining a British outpost in the region until 1815.[15]

Outside Europe all Napoleon's likely bases had now been eliminated, the successes in the Indian Ocean, as in the Caribbean, permitting the Admiralty to reduce the warships committed to it. Just before Java's fall Rear-Admiral Drury had been sent a list of twelve warships that he was the send home, orders of a similar nature being sent to the squadron at the Cape.[16]

The colonial campaigns of 1809–11 were prompted either by enemy weakness or sudden necessity. In no sense should they be interpreted as marking a change in strategic emphasis, for, although it was planned to send troops from Britain to help take Mauritius, a movement that was unnecessary in the event, there were no troop withdrawals from the European theatre. In the West Indies operations were supported by outside forces drawn from North America, a transfer rendered possible by the temporary thawing of relations with the United States. In the Indian Ocean the troops already on station, in India and at the Cape, proved sufficient. The attacks on the French and Dutch islands marked a relaxation of the previous financial stringency only because of the perceived threat to the East India Company's finances from the sudden enemy activity. The relief felt at the news of the capture of Mauritius was reflected in the instruction to fire the Tower guns in celebration.[17]

From the latter part of 1809 the primary field of British military endeavour lay in the Peninsula, Perceval's Cabinet deciding to maintain the effort there despite the disappointments of the previous summer. The south of Spain had not yet been invaded, Wellington was confident of his ability to hold Portugal, and that country was now regarded an important ally in its own right rather than as merely an appendage of Spain. The ministers' main fear was that Wellington's army, Britain's primary land force, would be destroyed, a dread that increased with the mounting French pressure on Portugal during the summer of 1810. Liverpool stressed to Wellington that the country was to be evacuated sooner rather than later if such a step was going to be necessary, the minister being keen to avoid any last-ditch defence of Lisbon.[18]

However, the British position improved with Soult's invasion of southern Spain in the early weeks of 1810. Although this was a serious blow to Spain's ability to pursue the war, and exposed southern Portugal to attack, nevertheless it had the effect of spreading the French armies more thinly over the Peninsula, and, with the sudden new threat to Cadiz, it finally prompted the Supreme Junta to allow British forces into the fortress. This permitted that key city to be more strongly held, Major General Graham commanding 9,500 British and Portuguese soldiers in Cadiz by July, and, as Liverpool was well aware, offered the prospect of further Peninsular operations based on Cadiz should Portugal have to be abandoned.[19] It also offered Britain a strategic insurance policy in the event of eventual Peninsular failure:

> The City of Cadiz is more connected with South America than all the rest of Spain put together, and the establishment of our influence here will greatly facilitate any arrangements we may wish to make hereafter with South America.

The government wanted to see all Spain's means concentrated on fighting the French, but it was aware of the need to keep Spanish America favourably inclined towards Britain whatever the final outcome of the Peninsular War.[20]

In August 1810 Wellington faced a massive invasion of Portugal by a 65,000-strong army led by Massena, this force being opposed by some 50,000 Anglo-Portuguese soldiers. Despite giving the French a bloody nose at Busaco (27 September), Wellington steadily retreated until reaching the fortified lines of Torres Vedras, north of Lisbon, in October. These had, with great foresight on Wellington's part, been constructed the previous autumn and constituted an insuperable barrier. After a protracted and futile siege of the position, Massena was obliged to retreat back into Spain in March 1811, an attempt by him to regain the initiative shortly after being checked at the battle of Fuentes de Oñoro (3–5 May). After this the French abandoned the Portuguese fortress of Almeida, and its possession in Wellington's hands helped secure that country's northern frontier from future invasion. On the Portuguese southern frontier a situation of stalemate ensued, an attempt by Beresford to capture Badajoz being defeated and resulting in the sanguinary battle of Albuera (16 May). For the remainder of 1811 both sides on the Portuguese border were barred from making further progress by the other's fortresses, another attempt by the British to take Badajoz in June being repulsed. In southern Spain Graham won a sharp tactical victory at Barrosa (5 March), but it had little strategic impact and served chiefly to worsen Anglo-Spanish relations, the British claiming that their ally had abandoned them during the battle.[21]

For all this the overall strategic position in the Peninsula was much improved by the end of 1811 from what it had been two years previously. Several tactical successes had been won by the British, Cadiz was securely held, and a large French effort to subdue Portugal had been rebuffed. This reflects credit on the Cabinet for persisting with the Peninsular policy, despite the doubts that one recent writer, G. D. Knight, has cast upon it. Focusing on the figure of Liverpool, the War Minister for these years and a politician closely associated with the strategy, Knight considers that his support of the campaign was 'half-hearted', Liverpool being a man who 'was not going to risk his career on so unlikely a prospect as the Peninsular War'.[22] Were they true, such charges would throw serious doubt upon the determination with which the Cabinet pursued its strategy and the clarity of its thinking. In fact Knight's accusations cannot really be substantiated at all. From 1810 ministers made the Peninsula overwhelmingly the scene of their country's chief military effort[23] and it is astonishing to conclude that Liverpool was anything other than fully committed to it. At one moment he told Wellington that:

'No government could attach more importance to the continuation of it [the Peninsular War] than the present, or be more disposed to direct the whole disposable Effort of the Country to this one object. When I accepted the seals of the War Department, I laid it down on Principle, that if the war was to be continued in Portugal and Spain, we ought not to suffer any part of our efforts to be directed to other objects.[24]

Knight sneers at Liverpool's 'appalling ignorance' and feels that he displayed a 'penchant for small diversionary expeditions'.[25] That the minister was openly nervous in 1810 about the possibility of an evacuation of Portugal is not to be wondered at, but if he was ignorant of military matters he at least did not pretend knowledge or interfere in tactical matters and he frequently sought Wellington's professional opinion before taking a decision. Nor is there any evidence to support the view that Liverpool was keen on other expeditions – quite the contrary: he and his colleagues did everything they could to keep as many troops in the Peninsula as was feasible in the circumstances, not seriously thinking, at least before the end of 1813, of large-scale operations elsewhere. Knight gives little thought to the overall strategic position and is perhaps, in consequence, misled by the thousands of men tied down in various imperial and European garrisons. However convenient the Clausewitz-like theory of concentrating all resources at one point may be, no Cabinet could, in practice, turn a blind eye to the requirements of domestic and imperial defence, or the strategic importance of areas beyond the Peninsula such as Sicily.

Some of the doubt respecting the ministers' attitudes possibly comes from a willingness to accept Wellington's complaints about the way he thought he was being treated at face value. Never one to suffer in silence, he remarked at one point in 1810, 'I acknowledge that it has appeared to me, till very lately, that the Government themselves felt no confidence in the measure which they were adopting in this country.' Most particularly he constantly lamented his army's shortage of money.[26] In one rebuff to Wellington, and to Knight as well, let it be said, Liverpool observed:

I am at a loss to conceive, upon what Grounds you have supposed that the King's Ministers had no Confidence in the Measures adopted for the Defence of Portugal. I should have thought that their language in Parliament must have had the effect of satisfying the World as to their Public Sentiment upon this Subject . . . With respect to their private *Sentiments*, I never knew a question on which there was less difference of opinion in Cabinet, than upon the Subject of Portugal . . .[27]

Indicative of this ministerial determination was the fact that in August 1810, with the crisis looming in Portugal, and only one battalion available for foreign service in Britain and Ireland, it was nevertheless still sent to Wellington. He was also provided with 1,300 replacements, a battalion from Nova Scotia and permission to take up to 1,900 men from Cadiz. By September Liverpool could note that 6,000–7,000 troops had been sent to Portugal to help meet the invasion, this despite the fears of one Cabinet member as to whether an effort on such a scale could be maintained.[28]

From early 1812 Peninsular prospects steadily improved. In January Wellington took Ciudad Rodrigo after a brief siege, this being followed in April by the bloody assault that finally captured Badajoz. Now both the northern and southern routes into Spain were open, the French suffering a further difficulty as thousands of their troops were drawn away for Napoleon's pending Russian campaign. Worsening their situation still more was Marshal Suchet's invasion of Valencia in eastern Spain, which weakened the western French forces and allowed the Anglo-Portuguese army to advance and defeat Marshal Marmont at Salamanca (22 July), the allies entering Madrid shortly after (12 August). This defeat obliged Soult to evacuate Andalusia and concentrate his troops with those of King Joseph in central Spain; now, having failed to take the fortress of Burgos in September and October, it was Wellington who had to undertake a costly retreat back to the Portuguese frontier, abandoning the Spanish capital to the French. Despite this failure, 1812 had witnessed substantial allied progress in Spain; with the securing of the border fortresses and the French evacuation of the southern part of the country the general strategic position strongly favoured Wellington. In November 1812, moreover, Britain's pre-eminent position in the Peninsula was tacitly recognised when the Supreme Junta appointed Wellington commander-in-chief of all allied forces in the region, a step permitting some co-ordination of effort in future campaigns.[29]

The next year saw an Anglo-Portuguese army of 87,999 troops, some 56,000 of them British, advancing once more. On 21 June 1813 Wellington crushed the numerically much weaker French army under King Joseph at Vitoria, though a botched pursuit allowed many of the French to escape in the rout. By November the army was pushing across the Pyrenees, advancing deep into southern France and defeating Soult at Orthez (27 February 1814) and at the costly battle of Toulouse (10 April). The latter occurred after Napoleon's abdication.[30]

The continued emphasis on the Peninsula after 1809 indicated that these years saw no change of strategy respecting the Mediterranean. In November 1809 Liverpool believed that 16,000 rank and file were sufficient to hold Sicily, particularly as the Neapolitan court was being paid £300,000 per annum to improve its own defences and when Stuart, the island's British commander, could draw forces from outlying garrisons to meet any emergency. The previous month Stuart had begun the business of expelling the French from the Ionian Islands, a process completed with the capture of Santa Maura in April 1810, and a measure the Cabinet regarded as secondary but having the effect, if it reduced the Sicilian garrison, of further hindering any possible French expansion in the Balkans. In April 1810 Stuart was told to send four of his regiments to Spain, an instruction he resisted on the grounds of his fears for Sicily. This threat materialised in an invasion attempt that was beaten off in September, but Stuart, resenting what appeared to him as governmental indifference to his situation, resigned his command in protest the following month. His interpretation of his position was essentially correct, for in December orders were issued which assumed that the four regiments previously demanded had been sent to Spain – in fact only one had been dispatched – and instructing the transfer of two more. The strategy was reiterated: the ministers' policy was to abandon the Ionian Islands in any crisis that threatened Sicily, while maintaining garrisons of not much more than 16,000 men on that island and 4,350 on Malta.[31]

Stuart's successor was Lieutenant General Bentinck, who no sooner reached Sicily in July 1811 than he found himself facing a political crisis on the island, compelling him to return to Britain to seek wider authority from the Cabinet. The upshot of Stuart's resignation and Bentinck's perambulations was that in 1811, as in the previous two years, there would be no operations in eastern Spain by forces based on Sicily, despite the fact that ministers had consistently urged them. Ironically this situation would not substantially improve once Bentinck returned to the island to assume command in December 1811. The new commander disliked all notions of serving in eastern Spain, where he would come under Wellington's authority, and had his own grandiose ideas for a campaign in Italy. In 1807 the Cabinet's strategy had been thwarted by Moore's refusal to campaign on the Italian mainland; from 1811 it would be obstructed because Bentinck did not want to do anything else.

As Bentinck himself had to admit, there seemed little disposition among the Italians towards the sort of rising that would have made a campaign there viable. In view of this the Cabinet, which had toyed with the idea of Italian operations, told Bentinck in spring 1812 to stage a diversionary campaign in eastern Spain. He reluctantly sent Lieutenant General Maitland with 7,000 men to implement this instruction in June but remained unenthusiastic, a palpable lack of keenness prompting several despatches from London urging him to persist with the venture. In August Bathurst dismissed a report of Bentinck's that an Italian revolt was imminent, pointedly suggesting instead that continued success in the Peninsula might just prompt such a rising. Mulgrave for one was furious at what he saw as Bentinck's persistent desire to pursue his own strategy rather than that laid down by the Cabinet.[32]

In February 1813 Bentinck seized the island of Ponza, hoping to spark off a revolt in Naples and prevent Murat from sending troops north to reinforce Napoleon. Once again despatches from Bathurst in April and June made it clear that the Cabinet was sticking to its Spanish strategy, and further political turbulence on Sicily in June anyway forced him to abandon Ponza and concentrate his troops on the main island. This situation also prevented him from sending more troops to reinforce the 10,690 men already in eastern Spain by the end of 1812.[33] Nor did the Austrian entry into the war in August 1813 make any difference to the Cabinet's thinking, despite the possibility from then on of military co-operation against the French in northern Italy. Bathurst wrote on 16 September that both Austria and Russia had asked that southern France should be invaded, and achieving this object required all force to be concentrated in Spain. However, Bathurst did relent a little eleven days later, telling Bentinck that he might undertake limited operations to support the Austrians but that these could involve only small numbers of British troops: any units removed from Sicily for such ventures would not be replaced by others from Britain or Spain.[34]

Not until Napoleon's authority was visibly crumbling, at the end of 1813, did the Cabinet start to think of political, rather than purely military, considerations in the way its strategy was formulated. With such thoughts in mind, in December Bentinck was given permission for a possible attack on Genoa, an operation depending upon whether the inhabitants of the city in particular, or of the region in general, should show any sign of wanting to revolt. The interest in Genoa formed part of the Cabinet's desire to see the existence of a strong kingdom of Sardinia as a buffer to future French expansion in Italy. Alongside this possible objective, Bentinck was also told to apply military pressure to Naples if the wavering Murat had still not thrown in his lot with the allies.[35] The upshot of these changes was that in February 1814 Bentinck was able to agree to an Austrian suggestion that he should land troops in northern Italy, Murat having by that time deserted Napoleon. With 15,000 men, 6,000 of whom were British, he was finally able to pursue the campaign he had favoured for so long, achieving the capture of Genoa in April after a few minor skirmishes.[36]

Despite the resistance of local commanders to the notion of diversionary campaigns in eastern Spain, it is hard to avoid the conclusion that in pressing for this the Cabinet's strategy was a sound one. Its determination to see it implemented, moreover, illustrating just how committed to the Peninsula ministers were after 1809. Although the eventual operations pursued in eastern Spain in 1812–13 were of a lethargic nature that produced no startling successes, they did serve to tie down Suchet's forces in that region and prevent him from sending any support to the hard-pressed western armies. At the same time they themselves backed and encouraged the area's regular and irregular Spanish formations. Campaigning in Italy would have situated such forces conveniently close to Sicily, but had little else to recommend it. There was no visible wish on the part of the Italians to support a British landing, there was no coastal strong point available for use in the event of an evacuation being necessary, and for most of the time there was little prospect of support from Austria or Russia. Only when it became a question of the post-war European arrangements did an Italian campaign, aimed at securing a strong Sardinian kingdom on France's south-eastern frontier, appear more attractive. Even then it took place only at a moment when Austrian co-operation was available, when the local French garrisons had been much reduced, and when there seemed a good chance of swiftly securing Genoa as a coastal fortress.

If the Cabinet was determined to keep the Mediterranean as a secondary theatre of operations, the same approach was strongly applied to the unwelcome war with the United States which it faced from June 1812. Anglo-American relations had improved slightly after the fury engendered by the *Chesapeake* incident in 1807, but the fundamental sources of irritation remained – for the United States, the Royal Navy's impressment of its nationals; for the British, resentment at the way the Americans protected naval deserters and used the European war to expand their carrying trade. Caught between two ruthless belligerents, each determined to try and control international trade to its own advantage, the United States vainly tried to free its commerce from outside interference. American measures such as the Embargo Act (1807) and the Non-intercourse Act (1809) tried to remove trading obstacles by, in effect, threatening no trade at all. As such, though, they harmed Britain with her busily expanding cotton mills much more than France, a process culminating in February 1811 with an American demand that Britain should repeal the hated Orders in Council, the series of decrees whereby British governments had tried since 1807 to regulate commerce with Napoleon's empire. The orders had been a bone of contention in Britain for some time already, many people believing that they harmed the British economy but did little damage to France, a view encouraged by the economic crisis of 1811. Under severe opposition attack, Liverpool's ministry finally agreed to their repeal in July 1812; unfortunately the United States, in a mixture of righteous indignation and acquisitive greed aimed at the occupation of Canada, had already declared war the previous month.[37]

As long as Napoleon remained undefeated, the war with the Americans would be a sideshow for the Cabinet, though one that imposed further military demands over and above those already imposed by the years of sour Anglo-American relations. For the navy much greater attention had to be paid to protecting convoys from the large American frigates and fast privateers. Alongside this a blockade of the American coastline had to be implemented both to destroy that country's trade and to hinder its naval operations at source. Early in 1812 there were seventy-seven major warships off the American coast and in the Caribbean: by early 1813 the total had risen to 105 and the government anticipated a further increase to 112 by the end of the year. There were similar demands on the army: in December 1811 there were 7,625 troops in North America, a figure that rose to over 20,000 by the summer of 1813. However, these reinforcements did not, on the whole, come from Europe. Just as the temporary easing of Anglo-American relations permitted troop transfers to the Caribbean in 1808–10, so the capture of all the remaining French islands allowed troops to be sent from the West Indies to North America in 1812–13. Not until Napoleon had fallen from power would forces be sent from Europe on any scale.[38]

Much more crucial than the American war in 1812 was, of course, the renewal of general European hostilities, starting with Napoleon's invasion of Russia in June. This cannot have come as any great surprise to British ministers. They had already the previous August received an approach from the Russians which supported the struggle to liberate the Peninsula, but ministers, though welcoming it, had stressed that Britain wanted other nations to fight Napoleon only if they really desired such a course of action. The Russians were also pointedly told that the Peninsula consumed a large proportion of Britain's resources.[39] There had also been rumours in 1811 that France was going to attack Prussia, the Cabinet being ready to supply that power with arms if necessary and also to leave some small warships in the Baltic during the winter to provide what support they could. In the event such hostilities did not materialise.[40]

The deterioration of Napoleon's relations with the northern powers did, though, prompt the Cabinet to try and restore harmony with Sweden, Thornton being sent to that country in the autumn of 1811 to pursue the elusive hope of Sweden and Denmark joining the allied powers in the event of a Franco-Russian rupture. Initially this approach got nowhere, Bernadotte, the former French marshal who had become Crown Prince of Sweden, being noncommittal,[41] but Sweden was to remain a British diplomatic target. In part this was due to that country's important Baltic position and to the previous good relations between the two. But Sweden also offered the prospect of a comparatively small military power that might be dominated by Britain in a manner similar to Portugal, a nation that could, perhaps, be directed towards the pursuit of British objectives in a way which would never be possible with the more powerful countries. In the event Sweden, under Bernadotte, was to prove slippery and quite unreliable.

With such thoughts in mind the Cabinet responded favourably in March 1812 to Swedish requests for a termination of the formal state of war between the two countries. Britain offered Saumarez's fleet to help protect Sweden, but only limited aid in any war, the Peninsula being cited as the primary theatre of British effort. Ministers hoped that any renewal of warfare in the north would see a Russo-Swedish assault on the French lines of communication, one perhaps aimed at the more restless parts of Germany, but for the moment the Russian reluctance to precipitate any conflict meant that such ideas were nothing more than vague ponderings. Liverpool himself doubted whether Russia would fight in the light of his understanding of Alexander I's character and the continuing Russo-Turkish war – though the latter would be settled in May. The minister comforted himself with the thought that, whatever the outcome of events in the north, they would at least divert Napoleon's troops from Spain.[42] By July 1812 the Cabinet was becoming more impatient with the Russo-Swedish fence-sitting, a Swedish request for a subsidy of £1 million being turned down on the 18th and Bernadotte being threatened with Thorton's removal if he continued to prevaricate over a formal peace treaty.[43]

Not until 24 August was Thornton told that the peace treaties signed with Russia and Sweden had been ratified, by which time the end of summer was approaching and ministers could not anticipate much direct benefit from the northern war, particularly as Bernadotte was remaining cautious and making clear his desire to seize Danish-controlled Norway prior to any campaign on the European mainland. It was December before Thornton could finally confirm that Sweden was actually at war with France once more.[44]

Once it started to become clear that Napoleon had suffered a catastrophe in Russia the Cabinet could begin to consider the possibility of a radical change in European circumstances. In January 1813 Castlereagh observed that there might be a chance of a new grand coalition, the British strategy being clear: 'Whatever scheme of policy can most immediately combine the greatest number of powers and the greatest military force against France . . . is that which we must naturally desire most to promote . . .' Two days after this was penned, the Cabinet decided to provide the first aid for Prussia and also to equip the German Legion, then in Finland, as a 10,000-strong body to serve under Bernadotte. By March pressure on the Crown Prince to abandon thoughts of Norway seemed to have yielded dividends, Bathurst believing that soon Bernadotte would be leading 60,000 Swedish, German and Russian troops against the French.[45]

Several factors indicate that ministers were hoping to strike a decisive blow against Napoleon at this time. Early 1813 saw the first of a series of arms shipments to the allied nations that was to equip thousands of men in the new war. Alongside these came lavish financial aid, 1813 seeing Russia and Prussia being given £2 million in the spring with a further £1 million being set aside for Austria, supplies for the latter valued at £590,000 also being provided. What with support for Sweden and the southern European states as well, Britain's aid to her allies in March–November 1813 came to nearly £11 million, a figure that almost equalled all the subsidies and loans in 1793–1801. If the value of arms and equipment be added in, the final figure for the year comes to almost £13 million. Furthermore this huge sum does not include the aid provided to the smaller countries, such as Denmark, Holland and Hanover, that joined the coalition towards the close of the year.[46]

Once again the financial and material support for Continental allies was to be accompanied by troops as well, for, despite the demands of the Peninsula, the government felt compelled to respond to a Swedish request for British soldiers. In June 1813 a small force of 3,000 infantry was sent to Stralsund, the intention being to use it to garrison the fortress and so release Swedish troops for service in Germany. This did not indicate any abandonment of the Peninsular strategy, the Stralsund force being regarded as only a temporary measure and, while it was sent north, Wellington was provided with 2,000 others. With the allied armies being defeated at Lützen and Bautzen in May, and with the alarming armistice agreed at Plaswitz in June, the Cabinet was by no means sure in the summer of 1813 just how long the new alliance might survive. In such a situation ministers had no intention of compromising the essentials of Britain's own military effort.[47]

That the Cabinet had its doubts about the resilience of the new coalition was clear from its attitude towards the European powers before hostilities had actually resumed. Castlereagh flatly stated in March 1812 that Britain would not make concessions over the future of Hanover. The following year the summer's armistice prompted thoughts about a suspension of subsidy payments and there was a categorical rejection of any notion of repeal of the maritime laws. These suspicions persisted despite the great allied victory of Leipzig (16–19 October 1813), Bathurst worrying that the victorious powers might try to force Britain to surrender some of her conquests in the name of a general peace. These fears prompted Castlereagh himself to go to the allied headquarters early in 1814 in order to preserve British interests, a timely move with the Europeans' subsidies up for renewal. Once on the Continent he helped to steel the coalition's resolve in the face of Napoleon's successes on the battlefields in February 1814, and, following the collapse of peace talks with the French emperor, Castlereagh played a major role in the Treaty of Chaumont. This bound the four leading powers in a twenty-year pact against France, each promising 150,000 troops for the struggle; only when all this was agreed did Castlereagh provide further subsidies.[48]

At the heart of the Cabinet's problem in its dealings with the Europeans was a lack of British troops on the spot in northern Europe. This inevitably weakened the British voice in the allied counsels and was to help bring about the first major shift in strategic emphasis since the Walcheren failure had obliged the concentration in the Peninsula. By late November 1813 the first allied troops were advancing into Holland and, with the French having evacuated Amsterdam, Utrecht and The Hague, on the 20th the Dutch formed a provisional government. The next day Graham, now a lieutenant-general, was told that a deputation had arrived from Holland seeking aid: 20,000 stand of arms plus ammunition, kept ready for just such a contingency since October, were to be sent to the rebels. Alongside this Graham was also to lead a British force to the Netherlands, his task being to assist the Dutch in holding their newly liberated cities and to co-operate with any other allied troops that might appear. He was not to move his command any distance from the coast and, if the opportunity presented itself, was to destroy the fleet at Antwerp.[49] The troops initially sent numbered some 5,500, but they had been 'scraped together' and, excepting 1,600 Guards, comprised mainly second or even third battalions. Eventually, by the end of March 1814, Graham's command would rise to 11,238 rank and file.[50] Nothing better indicates the extent of the Peninsular commitment than the latter weeks of 1813, when the Cabinet had the chance to strike effectively at the Low Countries, the main strategic target, but lacked the experienced troops to do it.

However, from the moment of Graham's dispatch, ministers 'now consider ourselves as much bound to support the cause of Holland as we have the cause of the Peninsula . . .'. Had it been possible at the time the greater part of Wellington's army would have been transferred to the Low Countries, only transport problems, combined with the limited amount of allied support in the area that could be relied upon, prevented such a move. For his part Wellington was strongly opposed to the new campaign, fearing that his own might be starved of resources, but, such was the importance attached to getting the French out of the Low Countries, ministers were prepared to override his objections. For them:

> Our great objective is Antwerp. We cannot make a secure peace if that place be left in the hands of France. When I tell you . . . that Lord Castlereagh is authorised to state that he will not give up any *one of our conquests* unless Antwerp be disposed of as not under the influence of France, you may consider it almost as a sine qua non as far as peace with us is concerned.[51]

As with Bentinck in Italy, the Cabinet was prepared to subordinate purely military considerations – the Peninsular campaign – once it scented victory over Napoleon and the spoils of a possible peace were up for grabs.

In the event it was to seem at first as if the opportunity in the Netherlands had been missed. Not only did adverse winds prevent Graham's force from sailing – it was ready to leave on 24 November but unable actually to sail until 17 December – but British hopes of allied pressure from the east went largely unfulfilled. The latter disappointment was caused by Bernadotte and his continuing determination to compel Denmark to cede Norway to Sweden. A general westward advance after Leipzig would have taken Bernadotte's army into Holland, and Castlereagh urged such a move in December, expressing dismay when, instead, the Crown Prince marched north to attack the Danes. Dismay quickly turned to downright fury at what the Cabinet correctly interpreted as abandonment of the general allied strategy, of attacking Napoleon, in favour of the pursuit of narrow Swedish interests. This provoked a crisis in Anglo-Swedish relations, Castlereagh threatening an end of Bernadotte's subsidy. Not until February 1814 did the devious Crown Prince finally begin to advance southwards from Holstein, continuing British annoyance playing its part in the transfer of two of his corps to the command of the more energetic Blücher.[52]

The eventual British campaign in the Low Countries was to suffer mixed fortunes. Ministerial anticipation of a 'bonfire' of the French fleet in the Scheldt was to be disappointed, Antwerp proving too strong to capture in February and an attempt at destroying the fleet by bombardment being a flop. On 8 March Graham, now joined by the troops formerly sent to Stralsund, attacked the fortress of Bergen-op-Zoom; the attack failed, the British suffering 3,000 casualties. Fortunately the French were too weak to take advantage of their success and when Napoleon abdicated in April Graham's troops were at hand to march into Antwerp. In this respect at least the campaign may be judged a success.[53]

The peace which followed Napoleon's fall lasted almost a year, being abruptly shattered on 1 March 1815 when the former emperor, escaping from Elba with a small military escort, landed in southern France. On the 20th he re-entered Paris in triumph and resumed his throne, the French army, disgusted with the rule of the returned Bourbon monarchy, having flocked back to the Bonapartist cause in droves. On the part of the allied powers, then meeting at Vienna to settle Europe's future political arrangements, there was immediate determination to crush the man whose ambitions threatened them all. So began what was to form a postscript to the Napoleonic period: the Hundred Days. The tactical aspects of the brief campaign which followed, culminating in the battles of Ligny/Quatre Bras and Waterloo (16 and 18 June), have been covered in great depth over the years since, but the strategic elements, as far as Britain was concerned at least, have been neglected. This is unfortunate, as the short 1815 campaign illustrates clearly Britain's strategic priorities at a moment when ministers in London no longer had such a large proportion of their forces committed south of the Pyrenees.

The immediate necessity of reviving the general coalition was assisted by the allied governments' representatives being already assembled in Vienna, they rapidly concocting plans that, by the end of June 1815, would throw some 700,000 troops against France. This was in line with the terms of the Treaty of Chaumont, and as usual Britain was pressed for massive financial subsidies to facilitate the process. The British response was the provision of some £5 million to the assorted powers as well as other payments in response to some special pleading: thus Austria was given an additional £280,000 to help operations in Italy and the always impecunious Russia was provided with an extra £1 million to march her troops westward. Once finance was forthcoming for the hiring of troops from the lesser nations as well, Britain was committed to paying the allies £7 million.[54]

The renewal of warfare also saw immediate British steps to try and guard the Low Countries. It was no accident that Waterloo was fought on the road to Brussels and Holland and that, as in 1793–95, this was Britain's first choice as an area in which to fight. By

21 March 5,500 troops were ready to cross the Channel to Ostend, with a battalion of Guards and six to eight squadrons of cavalry being made ready to follow. Steps were hastily taken to revive the King's German Legion, stores were being accumulated at Ostend and Antwerp, and the defences of Nieuport, Ypres and Tournay were being repaired.[55] Beyond the mere political objective of keeping the Low Countries out of French control, these moves also made military sense. A concentration of forces in Belgium permitted British troops to be combined quickly with their Dutch and Belgian allies, provided a convenient assembly area for the German levies, and allowed co-operation with Blücher's Prussian army, the only other allied army of substance initially available on the French border. Early April saw Mulgrave ordering all work on domestic defences to be suspended so that the engineers concerned could be sent to the Low Countries; he also wanted to send all available field artillery units across the Channel despite a shortage of draught horses. It was also noted at this time that 52,000 stand of arms had been sent, or were on their way to, the Dutch.[56]

Despite all this effort the Cabinet still suffered from the problem of having many of its best troops across the Atlantic in North America, large numbers having been sent there after the first abdication in an attempt to settle the war with the United States: few of them would be recalled in time to fight in the Waterloo campaign. Other units were tied up in garrisons in the Mediterranean and in Ireland, political obstacles preventing a rapid calling up of the Militia and so necessitating more regular troops being retained in the latter country. The net result was that although Wellington was able to command a substantial army of 74,464 rank and file in Belgium, it was a force comprised of troops from Britain, Germany and the Netherlands, many of them of very dubious quality.[57] That this army was able to hold Napoleon's veterans at Waterloo until relieved by the Prussians is one of history's most unlikely military successes, but for the Cabinet it provided a dramatic justification of its strategy.

Outside the Low Countries the ministers' policy consisted of trying to take advantage of Napoleon's political weaknesses with a series of diversions. Attempts were made to revive royalist fervour in the Vendée; no troops were provided but by June the potential rebels had been supplied with 24,000 muskets and other arms.[58] In the Mediterranean Bentinck was told that his command was inadequate to do more than hold Malta, Sicily – with 2,000 men at Messina –

Corfu and Genoa. At the latter recruiting for the Sardinian army was to cease and any men already enrolled were to be transferred to British command: Bentinck was authorised to raise up to 5,000 men provided the cost was not too steep. In May he was also allowed to agree to any Austrian requests for support in operations against Naples, the only proviso being that Genoa was not to be weakened and at least two regiments had to be kept in Sicily. Shortly afterwards, anticipating Murat's removal from Naples, the Cabinet ordered all British troops to be concentrated at Genoa, Sicily no longer being under threat.[59] From Genoa ministers planned to employ their troops on raids on southern France, hoping that the region's royalists, who had been prominent in 1814, might be induced to revolt. In anticipation of such a rising the commander of the Mediterranean fleet, Lord Exmouth (formerly Pellew), had 15,000 muskets ready for their use. The Cabinet hoped that 4,000–5,000 British troops supporting such a rebellion might be able to secure control of one of the coastal fortresses, Toulon or Marseilles being preferred, though it was feared that any undue emphasis on the former might excite allied suspicions. Any such mistrust would doubtless have been strengthened by the ministers' determination to avoid any Austrian requests for troops for an Alpine campaign. In fact the Cabinet wanted 10,000–15,000 Austrian troops to be provided for their coastal strategy, and were prepared to see British units under Austrian command if that would facilitate a policy which, they believed, would seriously tie down Napoleon's forces.[60]

One can speculate about how the overall strategy might have worked in 1815 had not Waterloo and the second abdication finally put an end to the Napoleonic wars. In so far as the campaign did progress, the Cabinet illustrated its strategic priorities at a moment when extensive European action against France was certain and when Britain herself was free from any threat of invasion. In such circumstances it avoided extensive commitments to subsidiary operations, European or colonial, and endeavoured to concentrate its forces. Not this time in the Iberian Peninsula, but in the Low Countries, that area of prime strategic sensitivity.

Notes

1 P.R.O. CO 318/31, Instructions to Lt.-General Bowyer, 5 September and 3 November 1807. *H.M.C. Dropmore*, IX, pp. 485–7. Fortescue,

County Lieutenants, appendix VII, pp. 304–5. Leeds University Library, Brotherton Collection Box VII, Mulgrave Papers, 19/13.

2 *Castlereagh Correspondence*, VI, pp. 374–5 and 395. P.R.O. CO 318/33, Castlereagh to Lt.-General Beckwith (Commander of the Leeward and Windward Islands garrison), 18 August 1808. Fortescue, *British Army*, 7, p. 6.

3 P.R.O. CO 318/35, Beckwith to Castlereagh, 3 January 1809; Vice-Admiral Cochrane (commander of the Leeward and Windward Islands squadron), 5 January 1809; Beckwith to Castlereagh, 28 January 1809. *The Times*, 13 December 1808. Fortescue, *British Army*, 7, pp. 12–16. W. Y. Carman, 'The capture of Martinique, 1809', *Journal of the Society for Army Historical Research*, XX, 1941, pp. 1–4. M. E. S. Laws, 'Martinique, 1809', *Royal Artillery Journal*, LXXX, 1953, pp. 155–60.

4 P.R.O. CO 318/35, Castlereagh to Beckwith, 15 April 1809; same to same, 8 June 1809. 318/37, Castlereagh to Beckwith, 12 August 1809. 318/36, Liverpool to Beckwith, 2 November 1809. Fortescue, *British Army*, 7, pp. 17–25.

5 P.R.O. CO 318/40, Liverpool to Beckwith, 19 April 1810. *Castlereagh Correspondence*, VIII, p. 287.

6 *H.M.C. Dropmore*, VIII, pp. 385 and 435–6. James, V, pp. 204–5.

7 Parkinson, *War in the Eastern Seas*, pp. 87–8. Martin, II, pp. 307 and 754. Scottish R.O., Melville Papers, GD 51/2/274, unsigned memorandum, November 1804.

8 Martin, IV, appendix O, p. 670. Fortescue, *British Army*, 5, pp. 40–7; 7, pp. 579–87.

9 Owen, pp. 581–2 and 584–91. Martin, III, p. 230. Countess of Minto (ed.), *Life and Letters of Gilbert Elliot, First Earl Minto, from 1807 to 1814, while Governor-General of India*, London, 1880, pp. 52–3 (his emphasis).

10 A. A. Aspinall, *The Correspondence of George, Prince of Wales, 1770–1812*, Cambridge, 1963–71, VII, p. 107. A. G. Field, 'The Expedition to Mauritius in 1810 and the Establishment of British Control', University of London M.A. thesis, 1931, p. 64.

11 Parkinson, *War in the Eastern Seas*, pp. 275–95, particularly pp. 279–89.

12 Field, p. 27. H. De Lotbinière, 'Mauritius, 1810', *Mariner's Mirror*, 38, 1952, p. 195. Parkinson, *War in the Eastern Seas*, pp. 365–76. R. J. Cansewall-Jones, *The British Merchant Service*, London, 1898, p. 73. P.R.O. ADM 2/1366, pp. 166–70. *The Times*, 14 and 22 December 1808.

13 Field, pp. 30–3. Parkinson, *War in the Eastern Seas*, p. 366. B.M. Add. Mss 45042, Supplementary Hardwicke Papers, ff. 120–1. Aspinall, *George III*, V, p. 614. P.R.O. ADM 2/1370, p. 95.

14 Field, pp. 36 and 43–87. Parkinson, *War in the Eastern Seas*, pp. 385–407. Lotbinière, pp. 199–208. Fortescue, *British Army*, 7 pp. 597–602.

15 S. G. Rainbow, 'British Expeditions to the Dutch East Indies during the Revolutionary and Napoleonic Wars', University of London M.A. thesis, 1933–34, pp. 179–210 and 221–38. Greenwich Maritime Museum, Yorke Papers, YOR/11, letter 20. B.M. Add. Mss 45043, Supplementary

Hardwick Papers, ff. 43–45. P.R.O. ADM 2/1370, pp. 273–8. Scottish R.O., Melville Papers, GD 51/3/472/18. Fortescue, *British Army*, 7, pp. 609–27.

16 P.R.O. ADM 2/1371, pp. 237–8 and 241–2.

17 Aspinall, *Prince of Wales*, VII, p. 229.

18 B.M. Add. Mss 38243, Liverpool Papers, ff. 223–5 and 232–4; 38244, ff. 98–9; 38245, ff. 27–9. P.R.O. WO 6/50, pp. 42–3.

19 A. N. Delavoye, *Life and Letters of Thomas Graham, Lord Lynedoch*, London, 1868, pp. 302–3 and 397. B.M. Add. Mss 38325, Liverpool Papers, f. 30v.

20 *S.D.W.*, VI, p. 502. Aspinall, *Prince of Wales*, VII, p. 339. To this extent Spanish suspicions about the British interest in Cadiz were justified, but from the British viewpoint the whole question of Spain's relations with her restless colonies was a thorny one.

21 General accounts of the campaigns in 1810–11 can be found in Gates, pp. 219–87; Humble, pp. 122–64; Sir J. Marshall-Cornwall, *Marshal Massena*, Oxford, 1965, pp. 186–250; A. Brett-James, *General Graham, Lord Lynedoch*, London, 1959, pp. 207–27. For a highly detailed account of all the battles and sieges nothing surpasses Oman's *History of the Peninsular War*.

22 Knight, pp. 254–5.

23 For example, in January 1811 the British army numbered 204,650 regulars, of whom 53,570 were in, or on their way to, the Peninsula. Nor does this figure allow for the Cabinet's intention to employ part of the Sicilian garrison in eastern Spain, a use that finally took place in 1812. Outside Britain the Peninsula saw the largest concentration of British troops anywhere in the world: *S.D.W.*, VII, p. 53.

24 B.M. Add. Mss 38325, Liverpool Papers, ff. 45–6.

25 Knight, pp. 96, 109 and 122.

26 Gurwood, VI, p. 347. For examples of Wellington's financial worries see VI, pp. 23 and 121; VIII, p. 198. Also p. 21 above.

27 B.M. Add. Mss 38325, Liverpool Papers, ff. 58–9 (Liverpool's emphasis).

28 B.M. Add. Mss 38325, Liverpool Papers, ff. 53–5. *S.D.W.*, VI, p. 594. Sandon Hall, Harrowby Papers, V, ff. 47–8.

29 Oman, V, pp. 83–5 and appendix XIV, pp. 610–11. Gates, pp. 317–78. Glover, *Wellington as Military Commander*, pp. 100–12. Humble, pp. 165–94.

30 Gates, pp. 383–467. Glover, *Wellington as Military Commander*, pp. 112–20. Humble, pp. 195–204.

31 Mackesy, *War in the Mediterranean*, pp. 357–74. Bunbury, pp. 253–66. Fortescue, *British Army*, 7, pp. 291–2 and 302–3. B.M. Add. Mss 38245, Liverpool Papers, ff. 295–9.

32 *S.D.W.*, VI, pp. 300–1. B.M. Loan 57, 6, f. 623–v.

33 P.R.O. WO 6/57, pp. 161–2 and 271–82. The political upheavals on Sicily that consumed so much of Bentinck's time are described in J. Roselli, *Lord William Bentinck and the British Occupation of Sicily, 1811–14*, Cambridge, 1956, pp. 102–3 and 110–14. Military operations in eastern

Spain are covered in Fortescue, *British Army*, 8, pp. 654–5; 9, pp. 40–67 and 373–81. Also Gates, pp. 397–407. The strength of the British army in eastern Spain in December 1812 is from Nottingham University Library, Portland Papers, PwJd 1973.

34 Nottingham University Library, Portland Papers, PwJd 576. P.R.O. WO 6/57, pp. 273–5.

35 Nottingham University Library, Portland Papers, PwJd 590 and 593. The idea of using a reinforced Sardinia as a bulkwark against France was not new; Mulgrave had mentioned it in 1804 and it had featured in the talks with Russia at that time: P.R.O. 30/58/5, Dacre Adams Papers, letter 122; Sandon Hall, Harrowby Papers, XXXII, f. 77–v.

36 Fortescue, *British Army*, 9, pp. 482–3; 10, pp. 60–4.

37 A detailed review of Anglo-American relations can be found in B. Perkins, *Prologue to War. England and the United States, 1805–12*, Berkeley and Los Angeles, California, 1961, particularly pp. 150–83 and 230–58. Also K. Caffrey, *The Lion and the Union. The Anglo-American War of 1812*, London, 1978, pp. 37–148. Essentially the Orders in Council tried to control neutral trade by forcing vessels to sail via Britain, paying customs duties and buying licences as they did so: for the political battles that they prompted in Britain see Cookson, pp. 215–32.

38 See chapter one for the manning problems caused by the war of 1812. *Castlereagh Correspondence*, VIII, pp. 286–92. B.M. Add. Mss 38326, Liverpool Papers, ff. 160–71. P.R.O. WO 17/1264, 1517, 2241 and 2360. G. E. Watson, p. 874. Fortescue, *British Army*, 8, pp. 451 and 522 n. M. L. Yaple, 'The auxiliaries: foreign and miscellaneous regiments in the British army, 1802–17', *Journal of the Society for Army Historical Research*, L, 1972, pp. 24–5.

39 B.M. Add. Mss 37293, Wellesley Papers, ff. 80–8.

40 Lloyd, *Saumarez Papers*, pp. 188–207. Aspinall, *Prince of Wales*, VIII, p. 137.

41 Bernadotte was one of history's great traitors and Richard Wellesley did not trust him an inch: B.M. Add. Mss 37293, Wellesley Papers, ff. 109–11v.

42 P.R.O. FO 73/71, Castlereagh to Thornton, 13 March 1812, no. 1 (draft); same to same, 14 April 1812. B.M. Add. Mss 38326, Liverpool Papers, ff. 26–7v.

43 P.R.O. FO 73/71, Castlereagh to Thornton, 3 July 1812, no. 3; same to same, 18 July 1812, no. 18.

44 P.R.O. FO 65/78, ff. 37–42. 73/71, Castlereagh to Thornton, 24 August 1812, no. 20; same to same, 10 October 1812, no. 24. *Castlereagh Correspondence*, VIII, pp. 284–6.

45 *Castlereagh Correspondence*, VIII, pp. 301–4. B.M. Loan 57, 6, f. 637–v. Nottingham University Library, Portland Papers, PwJd 551.

46 Sherwig, pp. 309–10.

47 *Castlereagh Correspondence*, VIII, p. 318. *S.D.W.*, VIII, pp. 46–8. P.R.O. FO 73/80, Castlereagh to Thornton, 29 June 1813. Nottingham University Library, Portland Papers, PwJd 576. The troops sent to Stralsund consisted largely of second battalions.

48 Lefebvre, II, pp. 349–50.
49 Renier, pp. 110–15 and 123. Delavoye, pp. 695–6. P.R.O. WO 6/16, pp. 15–17 and 20.
50 *S.D.W.*, VIII, p. 390. P.R.O. WO 17/1773.
51 *S.D.W.*, VIII, pp. 414–15 and 450–1 (Bathurst's emphasis). Gurwood, XI, pp. 384–7.
52 Renier, p. 123. Delavoye, p. 701. P.R.O. FO 73/80, Castlereagh to Thornton, 17 December 1812, no. 76; same to same, 24 December 1813. *Castlereagh Correspondence*, IX, p. 245. Chandler, p. 983.
53 Scottish R.O., Melville Papers, GD 51/2/1084/29. P.R.O. FO 37/72, Graham to Bathurst, 6 February 1814. Fortescue, *British Army*, 10 pp. 1–11 and 33–54. Butler, CLIV, pp. 434–42.
54 J. Christopher Herold, *The Battle of Waterloo*, London, 1967, pp. 43–51. Sherwig, pp. 237–9.
55 P.R.O. WO 6/16, pp. 146–7. WO 6/167, pp. 19–20.
56 *H.M.C. Bathurst*, p. 344. P.R.O. WO 6/167, pp. 25–6.
57 Fortescue, *British Army*, 10, pp. 232–8. U. Pericoli, *1815. The Armies at Waterloo*, London, 1973, p. 109.
58 *H.M.C. Bathurst*, p. 350.
59 P.R.O. WO 6/57, pp. 231–3 and 244–7. *H.M.C. Bathurst*, p. 349.
60 P.R.O. WO 6/57, pp. 255–7, 259 and 262. *H.M.C. Bathurst*, pp. 354–5.

Appendix 1: The chief Cabinet positions with strategic responsibility and their holders, 1803–15

Prime Minister	
Addington	May 1803 – April 1804
Pitt	May 1804 – January 1806
Lord William Grenville	January 1806 – March 1807
Duke of Portland	March 1807 – September 1809
Perceval	October 1809 – May 1812
Earl of Liverpool	June 1812 onwards

Foreign Secretary	
Lord Hawkesbury	May 1803 April 1804
Lord Harrowby	May 1804 – January 1805
Lord Mulgrave	January 1805 – January 1806
Fox	January – September 1806
Viscount Howick	September 1806 – March 1807
Canning	March 1807 – September 1809
Earl Bathurst	October – December 1809
Marquis Wellesley	December 1809 – March 1812
Viscount Castlereagh	March 1812 onwards.

Secretary for War	
Lord Hobart	May 1803 – April 1804
Earl Camden	May 1804 – July 1805
Viscount Castlereagh	July 1805 – January 1806
Windham	January 1806 – March 1807
Viscount Castlereagh	March 1807 – September 1809

Earl of Liverpool	October 1809 – May 1812.
Earl Bathurst	June 1812 onwards

First Lord of the Admiralty

Earl St Vincent	May 1803 – April 1804
Viscount Melville (H. Dundas)	May 1804 – May 1805
Lord Barham	May 1805 – January 1806
Viscount Howick	January – September 1806
Thomas Grenville	September 1806 – March 1807
Lord Mulgrave	March 1807 – April 1810
Yorke	April 1810 – May 1812
Viscount Melville (R. Dundas)	June 1812 onwards

Master General of the Ordnance

Earl of Chatham	May 1803 – January 1806
Earl of Moira	January 1806 – March 1807
Earl of Chatham	March 1807 – April 1810
Lord Mulgrave	April 1810 onwards.

Home Secretary

Duke of Portland	May 1803 – April 1804
Lord Hawkesbury	May 1804 – January 1806
Earl Spencer	January 1806 – March 1807
Lord Hawkesbury (then second Earl of Liverpool)	March 1807 – September 1809
Ryder	October 1809 – June 1812
Viscount Sidmouth (formerly Addington)	June 1812 onwards.

Appendix 2: The strengths and dispositions of the army outside Britain and Ireland, 25 August 1813

In each case the figure is the return for the total number of NCOs, trumpeters, drummers, rank and file for that date.

Anholt, 297
Bahamas, 850
Bengal, 5,440 (1,287 cavalry)
Bermuda, 732
Bombay, 3,216 (985 cavalry)
Cadiz, 1,915
Canada, 12,935
Cape of Good Hope, 4,726 (707 cavalry)
Ceylon, 5,555 (only 1,641 British, the rest Ceylonese)
Gibraltar, 3,135
Heligoland, 366
Honduras, 297
Jamaica, 3,885
Leeward and Windward Islands, 15,248
Madeira, 675
Madras, 9,191 (1,326 cavalry)
Malta, 3,672
Mauritius, 3,888
New South Wales, 1,218
Newfoundland, 708
Nova Scotia, 4,189
Sicily, Mediterranean and Ionian Islands, 15,701 (304 cavalry)
Spain and Portugal, 60,202 (7,260 cavalry)
Stralsund, 3,147
West coast of Africa, i.e. Sierra Leone, Senegal and Gorée, 779

Appendix 3: The disposition of the Royal Navy's warships, 1 January 1807

Cape of Good Hope. One 74, four 64s, one 50, four frigates and two sloops.

Channel Squadron (Keith). Six 74s, five 64s, two 50s, thirteen frigates, thirty-five sloops, one cutter, one schooner and eight bomb vessels.

Channel Squadron (St Vincent). Two 110s, four 98s, one 80, twenty-three 74s, twenty-four frigates, five sloops, one cutter and four schooners.

Convoys and cruisers. One 80, seven 74s, three 64s, one 50, thirteen frigates, thirteen sloops, two cutters and seven schooners.

Cork. Twelve frigates and five sloops.

East Indies. Four 74s, three 64s, one 50, fifteen frigates, five sloops and one cutter.

Jamaica. One 64, fourteen frigates, fifteen sloops, one cutter and seven schooners.

Leeward and Windward Islands. Four 74s, eight frigates, nineteen sloops, one cutter and fifteen schooners.

Mediterranean. One 110, four 98s, one 80, thirteen 74s, two 64s, one 50, seventeen frigates, eighteen sloops, one cutter and one bomb vessel.

Medway. Two 74s, one 64, five frigates, nine sloops and one schooner.

Newfoundland. Two frigates, three sloops and two schooners.

Nova Scotia. One 50, five frigates and five sloops.

Plymouth. One 110, two 98s, three frigates, five sloops, six cutters and four schooners.

Portsmouth and Spithead. Three 98s, three 74s, two 50s, five frigates, ten sloops, one cutter, four schooners and two bomb vessels.

Thames. Two 50s, one frigate and one cutter.

Bibliography

Primary unpublished sources

Buckinghamshire Record Office. Hobart Papers, D/MH/H/War A–C, E–F, W–X.

British Museum. Bunbury Papers, Add. Mss 37051; Collingwood Papers, Add. Mss 40096, volume 1; Dropmore Papers, Add. Mss 58930–48, 59282–90; Fox Papers, Add. Mss 37050; Gordon Papers, Add. Mss 49472–96; Herries Papers, Add. Mss 57393; Huskisson Papers, Add. Mss 38737; Liverpool Papers, Add. Mss 38243–378; Moore Papers, Add. Mss 57539–43; Perceval Papers, Add. Mss 49173–95; Supplementary Hardwicke Papers, Add. Mss 45036–43; Thomas Grenville Papers, Add. Mss 41854; Wellesley Papers, Add. Mss 37274–318; Windham Papers, Add. Mss 37824–935; BM Loan 57, volumes 6, 7, 21 and 108.

Devon Record Office. 152M Sidmouth Papers, C1803–06.

Durham Record Office. Castlereagh Papers, D/Lo/C1–14, 17–19.

Durham University Library. Grey Papers, second Earl.

Greenwich Maritime Museum. Duckworth Papers, DUC/13; Henley, Michael & Son, Papers, HNL/13–14; Journal of Sir Pulteney Malcolm, MAL/104; Victualling Office Papers, ADM/C–D; Yorke Papers, YOR/1–20.

Leeds Record Office. Harewood Collection, Canning Papers, 29–38, 41a, 42–6, 50–3, 57–8, 60–1, 67, 69, 77.

Leeds University Library. Brotherton Collection Box VII, Mulgrave Papers 13, 18–20, 27–8.

National Army Museum. Kennedy Papers, 7807–22; Marsden Papers, 7701–36–24–92.

Northern Ireland Record Office. Castlereagh Papers, D3030/1775, 1857, 1883, 1885, 1902, 1963, 1965, 1971, 2046–7, 2061, 2093, 2252, 2298, 2302, 2313, 2343–4, 2352, 2429, 2557, 2567, 2590,

2593, 2640–1, 2656, 2666, 2692, 2746, 2793, 2809–10, 2945, 3088, 3107, 3137–8, 3145–6, 3169, 3388, 3532, 3897.

Nottingham University Library. Bentinck Papers PwJc 167, 174; PwJd 32, 444–77, 551, 576–600, 1973; Portland Papers, PwF 4117, 7635, 8582–3.

Public Record Office. ADM 1/3743, 3750–2; ADM 2/1360–78; ADM 109–105–8; ADM 110/53; ADM 111/177; ADM 113/24; CO 91/47; CO 137/110; CO 158/7; CO 318/21–3, 25, 27, 31, 33, 35–6, 38, 40; FO 7/67, 83, 88–9; FO 22/44; FO 37/66, 72; FO 63/41–74; FO 64/64, 73–4; FO 65/52–83; FO 73/36–80; FO 933/4; WO 1/96, 164, 186, 208, 282, 284,–5, 305–6, 311–13, 412–22, 595, 605, 629, 632, 717, 728, 741, 795, 802–14, 847, 881–2, 902–4, 946, 1115, 1119; WO 6/13, 14, 16, 33, 38, 42, 47–50, 56–7, 120, 125, 133, 142, 156–7, 167, 185; WO 17: forty different volumes consulted for army strengths in 1809–14; 30/8 Chatham Papers, 102, 119, 121, 152, 240, 243, 250, 252, 257–8 323, 348–50 364, 366; 30/29 Granville Papers, 384, 387; 30/58 Dacre Adams Papers, 5–7, 10.

Sandon Hall. Harrowby Papers, volumes IV–V, IX, XII, XXIX–XXXII, LXXXIII, XCV.

Scottish Record Office. Melville Papers, GD 51 (1), (2), (3).

Primary published sources

Aspinall, A. A. (ed.), *The Later Correspondence of George III*, five volumes, Cambridge, 1962–70.

The Correspondence of George, Prince of Wales, 1770–1812, eight volumes, Cambridge, 1963–71.

Avery, G. (ed.), *The Echoing Green*, London, 1974.

Benjamin, L. S. (ed.), *The Windham Papers*, London, 1913.

Bourne, K. (ed.), *The Letters of the Third Viscount Palmerston to Lawrence and Elizabeth Sulivan, 1804–63*, London, 1979.

British Sessional Papers, Accounts and Papers, volumes VII–XIII, London, 1808–14.

Bromley, J. S. (ed.), *The Manning of the Royal Navy. Selected Public Pamphlets 1693–1873*, London, 1974.

Buckingham, Duke of, *Memoirs of the Courts and Cabinets of George III*, four volumes, London 1853–55.

Chatterton, Lady, *Memorials . . . of Lord Gambier*, London, 1861.

Gomm, Sir W., *Letters and Journals from 1799 to Waterloo*,

London, 1881.
Granville, Countess (ed.), *Private Correspondence of Lord Granville Leveson Gower, 1781 to 1812*, two volumes, London, 1916.
Gurwood, J. (ed.), *The Dispatches of F.M. the Duke of Wellington, 1799–1818*, twelve volumes, London 1834–39.
Harcourt, L. V. (ed.), *The Diaries and Correspondence of the Rt. Hon. George Rose*, two volumes London, 1860.
Historic Manuscripts Commission, *Report on the Manuscripts of Earl Bathhurst preserved at Cirencester Park*, 1923.
— *Reports on the Manuscripts of J. B. Fortescue, Esq., preserved at Dropmore*, ten volumes, 1892–1927.
— *Supplementary Report on the Manuscripts of Robert Graham, Esq., of Fintry*, 1940.
Hogge, G. (ed.), *The Journal and Correspondence of William, Lord Auckland*, four volumes, London, 1861–62.
Horner, L. (ed.), *Memoirs and Correspondence of Francis Horner, M.P.*, two volumes, London, 1843.
Hughes, E. (ed.), *The Private Correspondence of Admiral Lord Collingwood*, London, 1956.
Jackson, Lady (ed.), *The Diaries and Letters of Sir George Jackson, K. C.B., from the Peace of Amiens to the Battle of Talavera*, two volumes, London, 1872.
Jeffrey, R. W. (ed.), *Dyott's Diary, 1781–1845*, two volumes, London, 1907.
Laughton, Sir J. K. (ed.), *The Letters and Papers of Charles, Lord Barham*, three volumes, London, 1907–10.
— *The Naval Miscellany*, volumes I and II, London, 1901 and 1910.
Leslie, J. H. (ed.), 'The Diary of First Lieutenant William Swabey, Royal Artillery, 28 July to 3 October 1807', *Journal of the Royal United Service Institution* volume 61, no. 441, February 1916.
Leyland, J. (ed.), *Papers relating to the Blockade of Brest, 1803–05*, two volumes,London, 1898 and 1901.
Lloyd, C. (ed.), *The Keith Papers*, three volumes, London, 1927, 1950 and 1955.
Londonderry, Marquess of (ed.), *Memoirs and Correspondence of Viscount Castlereagh*, twelve volumes, London, 1848–53.
Markham, C. (ed.), *Selection from the Correspondence of Admiral John Markham during the years 1801–04 and 1806–07*, London, 1904.
Martin, M. (ed.), *The Despatches, Minutes and Correspondence of*

the Marquess Wellesley during his Administration in India, four volumes, London, 1836–37.

— *The Desptaches and correspondence of the Marquess Wellesley, K.G., during his Lordship's Mission to Spain as Ambassador Extraordinary to the Supreme Junta in 1809*, London, 1838.

Maurice, Sir J. F. (ed.), *The Diary of Sir John Moore*, two volumes, London, 1904.

Melville, L. (ed.), *The Wellesley Papers*, two volumes, London, 1914.

Minto, Countess of (ed.), *Life and Letters of Gilbert Elliot, First Earl Minto, from 1807 to 1814, while Governor-General of India*, London, 1880.

Napoleon, *La Correspondence de Napoléon Iier*, volume XI, Paris, 1863.

Naval Chronicle, volumes IX–XXXIV, London, 1803–15.

Newnham Collingwood, G. L. (ed.). *A Selection from the Public and Private Correspondence of Vice-Admiral Lord Collingwood*, two volumes, London, 1828.

Owen, J. S. (ed.), *A Selection from the Despatches, Memoranda, and other Papers relating to India, of the Marquess Wellesley, K. G., during his Government of India*, London, 1877.

Paget, Sir A. (ed.), *The Paget Papers: Diplomatic and other Correspondence, 1794–1807*, two volumes, London, 1896.

Parliamentary Debates. From the Year 1803 to the present Time, thirty-one volumes, London, 1803–15.

Perrin, W. G. (ed.), *The Naval Miscellany*, volume III, London, 1928.

Rodger, N. A. M. (ed.), *The Naval Miscellany*, volume V, London, 1984.

Rosc, J. Holland (cd.), *Selected Despatches relating to the Formation of the Third Coalition against France, 1804–05*, London, 1904.

Russell, Lord (ed.), *Memorials and Correspondence of Charles James Fox*, four volumes, London, 1853–57.

Ryan, A. N. (ed.), *The Saumarez Papers. Selections from the Baltic Correspondence of Vice-Admiral Sir James Saumarez, 1808–12*, London, 1968.

Smith, D. B. (ed.), *Letters of Admiral of the Fleet the Earl St. Vincent whilst First Lord of the Admiralty, 1801–04*, two volumes, London, 1922 and 1926.

Stewart, Sir W. *Cumloden Papers*, 2 volumes, Edinburgh and

London, 1871.
The Times, issues for 1803–11.
Tucker, J. S. (ed.), *Memoirs of Earl St. Vincent*, two volumes, London, 1844.
Wellesley, F. A. (ed.), *The Diary and Correspondence of Henry Wellesley, first Lord Cowley, 1790–1846*, London, 1930.
Wellington, Second Duke of (ed.), *Supplementary Despatches, Correspondence and Memoranda of Field Marshall Arthur Duke of Wellington*, fifteen volumes, London, 1858–72.

Secondary sources (1) Books

Albion, R. G., *Forests and Sea Power*, Cambridge, Mass., 1926.
Anderson, M. S., *The Eastern Question, 1774–1923*, London, 1974.
Anderson, R. G., *Naval Wars in the Baltic, 1522–1850*, London, 1969.
Austin, H. H., *'Old stick-leg'. Extracts from the Diaries of Major T. Austin*, London, 1926.
Baker, N., *Government and the Contractors. The British Treasury and War Supplies, 1775–83*, London, 1971.
Barrow, J., *The Life and Correspondence of Admiral Sir William Sidney Smith*, two volumes, London, 1848.
Barton, D. P., *Bernadotte and Napoleon*, London, 1921.
Bindoff, S. T., *The Scheldt Question to 1839*, London, 1945.
Blanco, R. L., *Wellington's Surgeon-General. Sir James McGrigor*, Durham, N.C., 1974.
Bond, G. C., *The Grand Expedition*, Athens, 1979.
Bourchier, Lady *Life of Codrington*, privately printed, 1873.
Brett-James, A. *General Graham, Lord Lynedoch*, London, 1959.
Brougham, Lord *Life and Times of Henry, Lord Brougham*, three volumes, Edinburgh, 1871.
Bryant, Sir A., *The Years of Victory, 1802–12*, London, 1944.
Buckland, C., *Metternich and the British Government, from 1809 to 1813*, London, 1932.
Buckley, R. N., *Slaves in Red Coats. The British West Indian Regiments, 1795–1815*, New Haven, Conn., 1979.
— (ed.), *The Napoleonic War Journal of Captain Thomas Henry Browne, 1807–16*, London, 1987.
Bunbury, Sir H., *Narratives of some passages in the Great War with France, 1799–1810*, London, 1927.

Burne, A., *The Noble Duke of York*, London, 1950.
Caffrey, K., *The Lion and the Union. The Anglo-American War of 1812*, London, 1978.
Cansewall-Jones, R. J., *The British Merchant Service*, London, 1898.
Cantlie, Sir N., *A History of the Army Medical Department*, volume I, Edinburgh and London, 1974.
Chandler, D., *The Campaigns of Napoleon*, London, 1967.
Cookson, J. E., *The Friends of Peace*, Cambridge, 1982.
Corbett, J., *England in the Seven Years War*, two volumes, London, 1907.
Creswell, J., *Generals and Admirals*, London, 1952.
Crouzet, F., *L'Économie britannique et le blocus continental, 1806–13*, two volumes, Paris, 1958.
Dalrymple, Sir H., *Memoir written by Sir Hew Dalrymple, Bart., of his Proceedings as connected with the Affairs of Spain and the Commencement of the Peninsular War*, London, 1830.
Danson, J. T., *Our next War in the Commercial Aspect; with some Account of the Premiums paid at Lloyd's from 1805 to 1816*, London, 1894.
Davies, D. W. *Sir John Moore's Peninsular Campaign, 1808–09*, The Hague, 1974.
Davis, R., *The Industrial Revolution and British Overseas Trade*, Leicester, 1979.
Derry, J. W., *Castlereagh*, London, 1976.
Delavoye, A. N., *Life and Letters of Sir Thomas Graham, Lord Lynedoch*, London, 1868.
Drescher, S., *Econocide. British Slavery in the Era of Abolition*, Pittsburgh, 1977.
Duffy, C., *The Military Experience in the Age of Reason*, London, 1987.
Duffy, M. *Soldiers, Sugar and Sea Power*, Oxford, 1987.
Elliott, M. *Partners in Revolution. The United Irishmen and France*, New Haven, Conn., and London, 1982.
Elting, J. R., *Swords around a Throne. Napoleon's Grande Armée*, London, 1988.
Emsley, C., *British Society and the French Wars, 1793–1815*, London, 1979.
Esdaile, C. J., *The Spanish Army in the Peninsular War*, Manchester. 1988.

Ferns, H. S., *Britain and Argentina in the Nineteenth Century*, Oxford, 1960.

Fortescue, J. W., *A History of the British Army*, thirteen volumes, London, 1899–1930.

— *The County Lieutenancies and the Army, 1803–14*, London, 1909.

— *Statesman of the Great War, 1793–1815*, London, 1911.

Frischauer, P. *England's Years of Danger. A new History of the World War, 1792–1815*, London, 1938.

Fulford, R., *The Royal Dukes*, London, 1973.

Gates, D., *The Spanish Ulcer*, London, 1986.

Glover, M., *Wellington as Military Commander*, London, 1968.

— *Britannia Sickens*, London, 1970.

— *The Peninsular War, 1807–14. A Concise Military History*, Newton Abbot, 1974.

— *Wellington's Army*, London, 1977.

Glover, R., *Peninsular Preparation. The Reform of the British Army, 1795–1809*, Cambridge, 1963.

— *Britain at Bay. Defence against Bonaparte, 1803–14*, London, 1973.

Gradish, S. F., *The Manning of the British Navy during the Seven Years War*, London, 1980.

Graham, G. S., *Britain in the Indian Ocean. A Study of Maritime Enterprise, 1810–50*, Oxford, 1967.

Graham, G. S., and Humphreys, R. A., *The Navy and South America, 1807–23*, London, 1962.

Gray, D., *Spencer Perceval. The Evangelical Prime Minister, 1762–1812*, Manchester, 1963.

Grey, C., *Some Account of the Life and Opinions of Charles, Second Earl Grey*, London, 1861.

Harvey, A. D., *Britain in the early nineteenth century*, London, 1978.

Haythornthwaite, P. J., *Wellington's Military Machine*, Kent, 1989.

Heckscher, E. F., *The Continental System*, Oxford, 1922.

Henegan, Sir R., *Seven Years Campaigning in the Peninsula and the Netherlands from 1808 to 1815*, two volumes, London, 1846.

Herold, J. Christopher, *The Battle of Waterloo*, London, 1967.

Herries, E., *Memoir of the Public Life of the Right Hon. John Charles Herries*, two volumes, London, 1880.

Hibbert, C., *Corunna*, London, 1961.

Hinde, W., *George Canning*, London, 1973.
Holland, Lord, *Memoirs of the Whig Party during my Time*, two volumes, London, 1852–54.
Hook, T. E., *Life of the Rt. Hon. Sir David Baird*, two volumes, London, 1832.
Horne, A., *Napoleon Master of Europe, 1805–07*, London, 1979.
Howard, M. *The Continental Commitment*, London, 1972.
Howarth, D., *Trafalgar*, London, 1971.
Humble, R., *Napoleon's Peninsular Marshals*, London, 1973.
James, W., *The Naval History of Great Britain*, seven volumes, London, 1837.
Jones, J. R., *Britain and the World, 1689–1815*, London, 1980.
Kaufmann, W. W., *British Policy and the Independence of Latin America, 1804–28*, New Haven, Conn., 1951.
Kincaid, J., *Adventures in the Rifle Brigade and Random Shots from a Rifleman*, London, 1981.
Lavery, B., *Nelson's Navy*, London, 1989.
Lefebvre, G., *Napoleon*, two volumes, London, 1969.
Lewis, M. A. (ed.), *A Narrative of my Professional Adventures, 1790–1839* by W. H. Dillon, two volumes, London, 1953 and 1956.
— *A Social History of the Navy, 1793–1815*, London, 1960.
Liddell Hart, B., *The British Way in Warfare*, London, 1932.
Lloyd, C., *The Health of Seamen*, London, 1965.
— *The British Seaman*, London, 1970.
Lloyd, C., and Coulter, J. L. S., *Medicine and the Navy, 1200–1900*, volume III, London, 1961.
Ludovici, A. (ed.), *On the Road with Wellington* by A. L. F. Schaumann, London, 1924.
Mackesy, P., *The War in the Mediterranean, 1803–10*, London, 1957.
— *The War for America, 1775–83*, London 1964.
— *Statesmen at War. The Strategy of Overthrow, 1798–99*, London, 1974.
— *War without Victory. The Downfall of Pitt, 1799–1802*, Oxford, 1984.
Mahan, A. T., *The Influence of Sea Power upon the French Revolution and Empire*, two volumes, London, 1892.
Marcus, G., *The Age of Nelson*, London, 1971.
Marshall-Cornwall, Sir J., *Marshal Massena*, Oxford, 1965.

— *Napoleon as Military Commander*, London, 1969.
Mitchell, B. R., and Deane, P., *Abstract of British Historical Statistics*, Cambridge, 1962.
Morriss, R., *The Royal Dockyards during the Revolutionary and Napoleonic Wars*, Leicester, 1983.
Oman, Sir C., *History of the Peninsular War,* seven volumes, London, 1902–30.
— *Wellington's Army*, London, 1968.
Oman, C. M. A., *Sir John Moore*, London, 1953.
Pares, R., *War and Trade in the West Indies, 1739–63*, Oxford, 1936.
Parkinson, C. N., *Edward Pellew, Viscount Exmouth, Admiral of the Red*, London, 1934.
— *The Trade Winds. A Study of British Overseas Trade during the French Wars, 1793–1815*, London, 1948.
— *War in the Eastern Seas, 1793–1815*, London, 1954.
Pasley, C. W., *Essay on the Military Policy and Institutions of the British Empire*, London, 1811.
Pearce, R., *Memoirs and Correspondence of Richard, Marquess Wellesley*, three volumes, London, 1846.
Pellew, G., *The Life and Correspondence of the Right Hon. Henry Addington, First Viscount Sidmouth*, three volumes, London 1847.
Pericoli, U., *1815. The armies at Waterloo*, London, 1973.
Perkins, B., *Prologue to War. England and the United States, 1805–12*, Berkeley and Los Angeles, Cal., 1961.
Petre, F. L., *Napoleon's Last Campaign in Germany – 1813*, London, 1974.
Platt, D. C. M., *Latin America and British Trade, 1806–1914*, London, 1972.
Pool, B., *Navy Board Contracts, 1660–1832*, London, 1966.
Pope, D., *Life in Nelson's Navy*, London, 1981.
Reilly, R., *Pitt the Younger*, London, 1978.
Renier, G. J., *Great Britain and the Establishment of the Kingdom of the Netherlands, 1813–15*, London, 1930.
Richmond, Sir H., *Statesmen and Sea Power*, Oxford, 1946.
Roberts, M., *The Whig Party, 1807–12*, London, 1939.
Rogers, H. C. B., *Wellington's Army*, London, 1979.
Rose, J. Holland, *Napoleonic Studies*, London, 1904.
— *William Pitt and the Great War*, London, 1911.

— *Pitt and Napoleon. Essays and Letters*, London, 1912.
Ross, Sir J., *Memoirs and Correspondence of Admiral Lord Saumarez*, two volumes, London, 1838.
Rosselli, J., *Lord William Bentinck and the British Occupation of Sicily, 1811–14*, Cambridge, 1956.
Sack, J. J., *The Grenvillites, 1801–29*, Urbana, Ill., 1979.
Savory, Sir R., *His Britannic Majesty's Army in Germany during the Seven Years War*, Oxford, 1966.
Schom, A., *Trafalgar Countdown to Battle, 1803–05*, London 1990.
Schumpeter, E. B., *English Overseas Trade Statistics, 1697–1808*, Oxford, 1960.
Sherwig, J., *Guineas and Gunpowder. British Foreign Aid in the Wars with France, 1793–1815*, Cambridge, Mass., 1969.
Stanhope, P. H., *Life of the Right Hon. William Pitt*, four volumes, London, 1861–62.
Syrett, D., *Shipping and the American War, 1775–83*, London, 1980.
Thomas, D., *Cochrane*, London, 1980.
Thompson, J. M., *Napoleon Bonaparte. His Rise and Fall*, Oxford, 1969.
Torrens, E. M., *The Marquess Wellesley*, 2 volumes, London, 1880.
Tramond, J., *Manuel d'histoire maritime de la France des origines à 1815*, Paris, 1947.
Ward, Sir A. W., and Gooch, G. P. (eds.), *Cambridge History of British Foreign Policy, 1783–1919*, volume I, Cambridge, 1922.
Ward, S. P. G., *Wellington's Headquarters*, Oxford, 1957.
Warner, O., *The Sea and the Sword. The Baltic, 1630–1946*, London, 1965.
Watson, J. Steven, *The Reign of George III, 1760–1815*, Oxford, 1960.
Webster, Sir C. K., *British Diplomacy, 1813–15*, London, 1921.
Western, J. R., *The English Militia in the Eighteenth Century*, London, 1965.
Whitworth, R., *Field Marshal Lord Ligonier. The British Army, 1702–70*, Oxford, 1958.
Wright, C., and Fayle, C. F., *History of Lloyd's*, London, 1928.
Wrigley, E. A., and Schofield, R. S., *The Population History of England, 1541–1873*, London, 1981.
Wyndham-Quin, W. H., *Sir Charles Tyler, G.C.B., Admiral of the White*, London, 1921.

Yonge, C. D., *Life and Administration of Robert Banks Jenkinson, Second Earl of Liverpool*, three volumes, London, 1868.

Ziegler, P., *Addington. A Life of Henry Addington, First Viscount Sidmouth*, London, 1965.

Secondary sources (2) Unpublished theses

Christie, C. A., 'The Walcheren Expedition, 1809', University of Dundee Ph. D. thesis, 1975.

Dowling, C., 'The Convoy System and the West India Trade, 1803–15', University of Oxford Ph.D. thesis, 1965.

Field, A. G., 'The Expedition to Mauritius in 1810 and the Establishment of British Control', University of London M. A. thesis, 1931.

Gwilliam, R. G., 'The Dardanelles Expedition of 1807', University of Liverpool M.A. thesis, 1955.

Hall, C. D., 'Factors influencing British strategic Planning and Execution during the Napoleonic War, 1803–15', University of Exeter Ph.D. thesis, 1985.

Ham, V. R., 'British War Policy in North West Europe, 1803–10', University of Oxford Ph.D. thesis, 1977.

Hawtin, J. C., 'A Geographical Consideration of the Peninsular War', University of Aberystwyth M.A. thesis, 1967.

Knight, G. D., 'Lord Liverpool and the Peninsular War, 1809–12', University of Flordia Ph.D. thesis, 1976.

Lagnas, I. A., 'The Relations between Britain and the Spanish Colonies, 1808–12', University of London Ph.D. thesis, 1938–39.

Rainbow, S. G., 'English Expeditions to the Dutch East Indies during the Revolutionary and Napoleonic Wars', University of London M. A. thesis, 1933–34.

Ryan, A. N., 'The Copenhagen Expedition of 1807', University of Liverpool M.A. thesis, 1951.

Sanderson, M. W., 'English Naval Strategy and Wartime Trade in the Caribbean, 1793–1802', University of London Ph.D. thesis, 1969.

Severn, J. K., 'Richard Marquess Wellesley and the conduct of Anglo-Spanish Diplomacy, 1809–12', University of Florida Ph.D. thesis, 1975.

Taylor, W. B., 'The Foxite Party and Foreign Politics, 1806–16', University of London Ph.D. thesis, 1974.

Vichness, S. A., 'Marshal of Portugal: The Military Career of William Carr Beresford, 1785–1814', University of Florida Ph.D. thesis, 1971.

Western, J. R., 'The Recruitment of Land Forces in Great Britain, 1793–99', University of Edinburgh Ph.D. thesis, 1953.

Secondary sources (3) Articles

Anderson, M. S., 'The Continental System and Russo-British relations during the Napoleonic wars', *Studies in International History. Essays Presented to W. N. Medlicott*, London, 1967.

Atkinson, C. T., 'Foreign regiments in the British army, 1793–1802', *Journal of the Society for Army Historical Reasearch*, volumes XXI–XXII, 1942–44.

— 'Gleanings from the Cathcart manuscripts', *Journal of the Society for Army Historical Research*, volume XXX, 1952.

Barnes H., 'Canning and the Danes, 1807', *History Today*, volume 15, 1965.

Bird, Sir W. D., 'British land strategy in four great wars', *Army Quarterly*, volumes 30–1, 1930–31.

— 'British strategy in Europe, 1803–14', *Army Quarterly*, volume 40, 1940.

Bond, G. C., 'The siege of Flushing', *Irish Sword*, volume XI, 1973.

— 'The Walcheren fiasco: a diversion turned to failure', *Proceedings of the Annual Meeting of the Western Society for French History*, 1975.

Brett-James, A., 'The Walcheren failure', *History Today*, volumes 13–14, 1963–64.

Buffidon, A., 'The Canada expedition of 1746', *American Historical Review*, 1939–40.

Butler, L., 'Minor expeditions of the British army from 1803 to 1815' *United Services Magazine*, volumes CLI–IV, 1905–06.

Carman, W. Y., 'The capture of Martinique, 1809', *Journal of the Society for Army Historical Research*, volume XX, 1941.

Carr, R., 'Gustavus IV and the British goverment, 1804–09', *English Historical Review*, volume LX, January 1945.

Condon, M., 'Freight rates and the British transport services during the Revolutionary war against France, 1793–1801', *Maritime History*, volume 5, 1977.

Crowe, E. K., 'The Walcheren expedition and the new Army Medical

Board: a reconsideration', *English Historical Review*, volume LXXXVIII, October 1973.

Dallas, H. A., 'Experiences of a British commissariat officer in the Peninsular War', *Army Quarterly*, volumes 13 and 15, 1926–27.

Davies, G., 'The Whigs and the Peninsular War, 1808–14', *Transactions of the Royal Historical Society*, II, 1919.

Fayle, C. E. 'The deflection of strategy by commerce in the eighteenth century' and 'Economic pressure in the war of 1739–48', *Royal United Services Institutional Journal*, volume 68, 1923.

Finley, M. C., 'Prelude to Spain: the Calabrian insurrection, 1806–07', *Military Affairs*, volume 40, 1976.

Glover, R., 'The French fleet, 1807–14: Britain's problem; and Madison's opportunity', *Journal of Modern History*, volume 39, 1967.

Hall, C. D., 'Addington at war: unspectacular but not unsuccessful', *Historical Research*, volume 61, October 1988.

Harvey, A. D., 'The Ministry of all the Talents: the Whigs in office, February 1806 to March 1807', *Historical Journal*, volume XV, no. 4, 1972.

Hudson, F. R. B., 'The English invasion of the river plate, 1806–07', *Army Quarterly*, volume 71, 1956.

Jenkins, H. J., 'The action at Anse la Barque, Guadeloupe, 18 December 1809', *Mariner's Mirror*, volume 61, 1975.

Laws, M. E. S., 'Martinique, 1809', *Royal Artillery Journal*, volume LXXX, 1953.

Lefèvre, A., 'Préoccupations britanniques en 1806: les conséquences de la déroute de la Quatrième Coalition', *Revue d'Histoire Diplomatique*, volume 74, 1960.

Lotbinière, H. de, 'Mauritius, 1810', *Mariner's Mirror*, volume 38, 1952.

Lynch, J., 'British policy and Spanish America, 1783–1808', *Journal of Latin American Studies*, volume I, 1969.

Mackesy, P., 'Collingwood and Ganteaume', *Mariner's Mirror*, volume 41, 1955.

— 'Problems of an amphibious power: Britain against France, 1793–1815', *Naval War College Review*, spring 1978.

Macmillan, D. S., 'Russo-British trade relations under Alexander I', *Canadian–American Slavic Studies*, volume 9, 1973.

McCawley, Renn E., 'England faces invasion: the land forces, 1803–05', *Proceedings of the Consortium on Revolutionary*

Europe, 1750–1850, 1974.

McGuffie, T. H., 'The Walcheren expedition and the "Walcheren fever"', *English Historical Review*, volume LXII, April 1947.

— 'The stone ships expedition against Boulogne, 1804', *English Historical Review*, volume LXIV, October 1949.

— 'Recruiting the ranks of the regular British army during the French wars', *Journal of the Society for Army Historical Reasearch*, volume XXXIV, 1956.

Mullet, C. F., 'British schemes against Spanish America in 1806', *Hispanic American Historical Review*, volume 27, 1947.

Pendle, G., 'Defeat at Buenos Aires, 1806–07', *History Today*, volume 2, 1952.

Rogers, H. C. B., 'Logistics in the Peninsular War', *British Army Review*, volume 62, August 1979.

Rose, J. Holland, 'British West India commerce as a factor in the Napoleonic wars', *Cambridge Historical Journal*, volume III, 1929–31.

Ross, D. G., 'The British invasion of the Rio de la Plata: prelude to independence', *Texas Quarterly*, volume 17, 1974.

Ryan, A. N., 'The British expedition to Copenhagen in 1807', *Historical Research*, volume 25, 1952.

— 'The navy at Copenhagen in 1807', *Mariner's Mirror*, volume 39, 1953.

— 'The causes of the British attack upon Copenhagen in 1807', *English Historical Review*, volume LXVIII, January 1953.

— 'The defence of British trade with the Baltic, 1808–13', *English Historical Review*, LXXIV, July 1959.

— 'Trade with the enemy in the Scandinavian and Baltic ports during the Napoleonic wars: for and against', *Transactions of the Royal Historical Society*, volume XII, 1962.

Schneer, R. M., 'Arthur Wellesley and the Cintra Convention: a new look at an old puzzle', *Journal of British Studies*, volume XIV, 1980.

Silberling, N. J., 'The financial and monetary policy of Great Britain during the Napoleonic wars', *Quarterly Journal of Economics*, volume XXXVIII, 1924.

Stewart, J., 'The stolen army', *Army Quarterly*, volume 66, 1953.

Terraine, J., ' "A question of saddles": Nelson in 1805', *History Today*, volume 24, 1974.

Turner, L. F. C., 'The Cape of Good Hope and the Anglo-French conflict, 1797–1806', *Historical Studies. Australia and New Zealand*, volume 9 (36), 1961.

Walker, F. A., 'The Grenville–Fox "junction" and the problem of peace', *Canadian Journal of History*, volume XII, 1977.

Ward, S. P. G., 'The Quartermaster General's department in the Peninsular War', *Journal of the Society for Army Historical Research*, volume XXIII, 1945.

Watson, G. E., 'The United States and the Peninsular War, 1808–12', *Historical Journal*, volume XIX, 1976.

Western, J. R., 'The Volunteer movement as an anti-revolutionary force, 1793–1801', *English Historical Review*, volume LXXI, October 1956.

Yaple, M. L., 'The auxiliaries: foreign and miscellaneous regiments in the British army, 1802–17', *Journal of the Society for Army Historical Research*, volume L, 1972.

Yarrow, D., 'A journal of the Walcheren expedition, 1809', *Mariner's Mirror*, volume 61, 1975.

Index